Charles 'Nomad' McGuinness

BEING A TRUE ACCOUNT OF THE
AMAZING ADVENTURES OF A DERRYMAN,
PIRATE, IRA MAN, GUN RUNNER, POLAR
EXPLORER, ADVENTURER, MERCENARY,
ROGUE, ESCAPER AND HERO

JOHN McGUFFIN & JOSEPH MULHERON

IRISH RESISTANCE BOOKS

First published in June 2002 by
Irish Resistance Books
4, Craft Village
Derry, BT48 6AR
Tel./ Fax: (028) 71 262 879

http://www.irishresistancebooks.com
info@irishresistancebooks.com

© McGuffin/ IRB
All rights reserved

Front Cover: Charles 'Nomad' McGuinness
Photograph by International News Photos, Inc., 1928

ISBN 0-9539482-1-8

Printed in the Republic of Ireland by ColourBooks, Dublin

All rights reserved. No part of this publication may be reproduced or transmitted in any form or by any means digital, electronic or mechanical, including photocopy, recording, or any information storage or retrieval system, without permission in writing from the publisher. The book is sold subject to the condition that it shall not, by way of trade or otherwise, be lent, re-sold or otherwise circulated without the publisher's prior consent in any form of binding or cover other than that in which it is published and without a similar condition including this condition being imposed on the subsequent purchaser.

DEDICATED TO CHRISTIANE

THANKS TO

Darren – Belfast Central Library, Yvonne Murphy – Linenhall Library, all at Derry Library, Tim McGuinness, Kathleen McGuinness, Micky McGuinness, Fr. Coyle, Frances Mackay of Lifford, the Shiels family of Derry, Jarlath Glynn – Wexford Library Services, Ben Palmer, Roisin Kelly, Patricia Bryce, Ciaran Crossey, Raymond Quinn, Patrick and Shane O'Curry, Fearghal McGarry, Uinseann MacEoin, Dr. Emmet O'Connor, Neil McGowan, Siobhan Mulheron, Joe Quigley, Terry Robson and Joe McAllister.

INTRODUCTION	9
FROM DERRY QUAY HE SAILED AWAY	11
THE DARK CONTINENT	24
THE CRUEL SEA, CHINESE PIRATES AND THAT OLD DEVIL SEX	34
RAIDS, RESCUES AND THE FLYING COLUMN	43
GERMANY CALLING	69
THE RUNNING OF THE GUNS	87
WITH BYRD TO THE POLE	97
THAT ILLEGAL SMILE – RUM RUNNING ON ROCKAWAY BEACH	114
WELCOME TO MURMANSK, TOVARICH!	137
BLOOD AND SAND – THE SPANISH CIVIL WAR	154
NOMAD AND THE GERMAN SPIES	185
IT WAS SAD WHEN THE GOOD SHIP WENT DOWN?	203
APPENDIX I – TREASURE HUNTING AND CAPTAIN THOMPSON	219
APPENDIX II – PIRATES OF THE INDIAN OCEAN	226
AFTERWORD	228
ENVOI	237
BIBLIOGRAPHY	239
INDEX	243

INTRODUCTION

There is a commonly used phrase 'I wasn't born yesterday'. It is used to convey the message that the speaker is not as inexperienced and naïve as the other party might have supposed. When a colonial power asks, indeed urges us, to forget the past and concentrate upon the present they are really trying to act as if we were born yesterday.

We have tried to write an honest biography of **Charles 'Nomad' McGuinness** and have faced more problems than usual.

Firstly, Nomad was born in 1893 and died (allegedly, for his body was never discovered) in 1947. Not too many eye-witnesses around. Further, most information we have on Nomad comes from his own books, which although fascinating, contain exaggerations and down right lies. There are dozens of references to Nomad in different memoirs and histories of the 20s-40s, but mostly they are only scraps of information and often turn out to have been inter-generated – one error being endlessly re-reported for example.

Nonetheless, we have tried, diligently to decipher the palimpsest and present this modest volume to memorialise one of the most amazing sons of Derry.

According to Octavio Paz "The Mexican tells lies because he delights in fantasy". The Irish, too, have been accused of being economical with the truth, but we prefer to think of it rather as a ransacking of the Celtic Unconsciousness.

Nonetheless, as Balzac said:

> "Il y a deux Histoires: l'Histoire officielle, menteuse, qu'on enseigne, l'Histoire *ad usum delphini*; puis, l'Histoire secrète, où sont les véritables causes des événements, une histoire honteuse."

Although it may be said that Time is the Bubonic Plagiarist, we have done our meagre best to decipher legend from fantasy, the braggadocio from the propaganda. We have tried to produce 'une histoire honteuse'.

John McGuffin & Joseph Mulheron – Derry, April 2002

CHAPTER 1
FROM DERRY QUAY HE SAILED AWAY

ANCESTRY

Our protagonist Charles John 'Nomad' McGuinness was born on March 6th, 1893, making him, as he says, a 'Piscean'.

His mother was Margaret Hernan (born in Inishowen on January 30th, 1858). The Hernans were a large and well respected Donegal family who could trace their ancestry at least as far back as Robert Hernan, who lived from 1798 until 1830.

Charles' paternal grandfather, also Charles John, had been born in Donegal but had taken his young family to America in the 1850s and it was in Brooklyn, New York, c. 1855 that Nomad's father, another Charles John, was born an American citizen.

John McGuinness, as he was always called, as a young man set out perhaps to check his family roots, but, for whatever reason he ended back in Donegal where he married Margaret Hernan on February 1st, 1883 in Moville.

One problem that we encountered in recreating the basic McGuinness family was that there are an awful lot of them, and, secondly, and even more confusingly, nearly everyone seems to have had a nickname.

John and Margaret McGuinness lived in Derry. John worked as a skipper on various boats on the Foyle or on runs to Glasgow. Relatives can still recall stories about him giving three tugs on the siren as his boat came up the Foyle to moor so that Margaret could hear and put the kettle on.

They had six children. Jack, who left Derry, married a Cissie Murphy from Tipperary, became a schoolteacher in Halifax, Yorkshire and only made a rare visit back home; Rose, known as 'Daisy' who stayed in Derry and married into the Cunningham family; Bridget Mary, who was of course known as 'Maisie' also stayed in Derry, unlike Charles' older brother Denis Patrick who went to sea early and foundered off Cuba where he is supposedly buried. And then there was Nomad in 1893. A fine sturdy boy. With a startling lack of originality they named him Charles John.

Finally there was the baby of the family, Hugh. He was to be the last of the children because, tragically, Margaret died two weeks after giving birth to him.

John was forty at the time and ill equipped to raise a young family with a baby. And then Mary Ann Coyle came into the picture. She was much younger than John and was never to have children of her own, but she and John got married, two years after Margaret's death. They moved into a series of houses in the Meadowbank area and Mary Ann raised Charles and Hugh. And she nursed John through his last days until he died in April 1926. Nomad had long since left home, Hugh was a teacher in Derry, and Mary Ann was still a rock. She's buried in the City cemetery alongside John. Margaret, the first wife is buried in the Hernan family plot in Shroove, County Donegal.

Nomad makes no mention of any of his siblings, except Hugh. Neither does he mention his mother, apart from spinning a yarn about her being descended from the Spanish family of Hernandos

> "who came to Ireland with the Spanish King's army in 1601, under the picturesque leadership of the gallant Don Aquila. Another member of the Hernandos commanded a ship of the line in the ill-fated Armada. He lost his vessel off the Galway coast when the forces of nature conspired with the British to defeat Phillip III, and the sailors who escaped drowning found shelter in the Irish hills."[1]

Surprisingly, he doesn't mention his step mother Mary Ann at all.

Nor does Nomad mention his father, apart from alluding to the fact that he was "a sea captain and harbour-master" (*see* Afterword re McGuinness' weltanschauung).

But it was his younger brother Hugh, who became a local headmaster, who was his favourite. He was the only one he would write to from around the world, and he had a special soft spot years later for Hugh's children, to whom he wrote at times, encouraging them in their studies and telling them stories.

And then, aged only 15 he ran away to sea.

A Life On The Rolling Main

Caveat:
Here we must again clarify the accuracy of this account of McGuinness' formative teenage years (15-21). For the only source

for young McGuinness' life from 1908 until the outbreak of World War I in 1914 we have to rely on is his 1935 published autobiography *Nomad*, or *Sailor of Fortune* as it was titled in the American edition, which is unashamedly written to amaze and astound the reader and to make some money.

This is not to say that the events he describes did not happen. We have been able to uncover some material which confirms some of McGuinness' stories and we can at least briefly attempt to spread an historical patina on Nomad's swaggering apologia.

Nevertheless, that the young Charles did travel widely is beyond doubt. Brother Hugh received postcards from New York and Venice, Marseilles and Constantinople. Charles' older brother Denis was also a globe-trotter. He may not have communicated with his younger brother, although perhaps contact was difficult, but the faithful Hugh received postcards, obviously the preferred means of communication, from Dublin, Hamburg, South Africa and Argentina amongst others.

Charles John McGuinness was fifteen years of age when he ran off to sea in 1908. His first official job was "as 'cook' though I never boiled a 'spud' in my life" on the 90 ton *Vixen* and "the day the old tub pushed away from the wharf at Londonderry [sic] was the real beginning of my career as a sailor."[2]

McGuinness lasted six months, sailing the winter seas around Great Britain and Ireland.

> "It was a test of mettle; it was a trial by ordeal; it was the elimination of the weak and fearsome; it hardened my muscles, crisped my mind, and stiffened my spine. It was in December 1908 that I left [...] and went back to Derry."[3]

He had also learned about drink.

But early next year (1909) he was back roaming the docks of Liverpool looking for a boat. He may have abandoned the total abstinence of the Pioneer movement, but, according to him he was 'feverishly fingering his Rosary beads' when he went down to Maloney's boarding house to beg a start.

For whatever reason, young McGuinness got his first real start. He signed on the *Cedarbrook*, a four masted bark, leaving Port Talbot for Iquique in Chile.

The conditions were tough, but McGuinness seems to have been in his element. Clambering up the rigging, furling and unfurling the sails and sitting in the fo'c'sle listening, wide-eyed to "yarns of other voyages, ships, shipwrecks, mutinies, and all the manly, tough, red-blooded incidents that make up the life of a square-rigged sailor."[4]

101 days out of Port Talbot, after rounding Cape Horn, McGuinness set foot in South America. He was only 16 years of age and growing up fast. Iquique was hardly a tropical paradise. An arid coast. A scorching hot, lifeless and dull place. But it was still adventure. After unloading the *Cedarbrook* moved South to Antofagusta to take on a load of nitrates destined for New York. Once more round the Horn, flying before the wind. By mid-summer 1909 McGuinness had run away from the *Cedarbrook* and was wandering the streets of New York, an awe-struck young teenager with all of ten dollars in his pocket.

PILGRIM'S PROGRESS

Ten dollars didn't last long. Soon he had signed up on the *Pilgrim*, bound for Australia.

Bully Newman was the master of the *Pilgrim*. A vicious brute. Profane and obscene – which may have offended young McGuinness then but which he obviously got over in the coming years since he was notorious as someone who 'had been known to use the odd obscenity himself'.

The crew were from all nations and spoke many tongues. Bully apparently spent most of the time drinking on his own in his cabin, while the creaking *Pilgrim* continued to take on water and begin to wallow in the high seas.

They survived however, and off Tristan da Cunha McGuinness was assaulted by the second mate Fowler, whom he stabbed and wounded in self defence.

> "Strong westerly gales and a mountainous sea for ever rushing after us, roaring and boiling under our counter. Sometimes it looked as if the whole Indian Ocean had reared up a mighty wall of thundering water that was booming along to engulf the tiny ship fleeing before it. If the men at the wheel had lost their nerve, released their control on the helm for a second, the *Pilgrim* would have broached to, and everything would have been swept overboard.
>
> A few weeks later we sighted Sydney Head. Sydney Harbour never looked so beautiful as in the dawn when we met our tow boat."[5]

The trip had lasted 112 days. It had not been a pleasant one. Nomad jumped ship, leaving "the three month's wages due to me, preferring to be a temporary beachcomber rather than remain on the *Pilgrim* for another day."[6]

Taking the ferry across Rushcutters' Bay he made it to Sydney, from where he worked his way up the coast to Newcastle, sixty miles to the North. He says he worked on an orange plantation for four weeks and then 'the call of the sea brought him back to Newcastle and voluntary slavery', because

> "Four weeks of the rustic life had satiated me, much to my employer's disgust; he had taken a fancy to me and wanted me to stay. But my head was full of masts and yards, the lure of other lands, and the peculiar longing for the sea a sailor has when cooped up inland. The peaceful humdrum of orange groves wearied me; I yearned for loud-voiced mates or bos'ns bellowing their well known orders."[7]

He hung out at mother Hall's, an Irish shebeen owned by an old Irishwoman, and it was there that a boarding house runner arrived one evening to announce that there was a ship sailing "at midnight, bound for 'Frisco; six pounds a month and the best of grub!"

Grabbing his sea bag McGuinness followed the runner. This was too good an offer to turn down. "'Six pounds,' thought I, chuckling. 'My ship has come in.'"

And so, on a rainy night he came out of the fog and climbed aboard his meal ticket to the States only to discover that it was the *Pilgrim* with his old enemy Bully Newman and his mates Corbett and Fowler facing him as he climbed aboard.

The weather had been ideal as they headed for Samoa, skirting Norfolk Island and Tonga but it soon worsened. The *Pilgrim* was loaded with coal – "a fairly buoyant cargo; but she was a clumsy bark, and very wet; shipping seas with every roll. The visibility was poor; for days we could seldom see beyond the bowsprit."

> "One dirty, dark, brick-red morning the glass dropped suddenly – a sure sign of real trouble. We were close-hauled on the starboard tack, carrying three lower topgallant sails, upper and lower topsails, foresail and mainsail, inner jib, fore-topmast stay sail, main and mizen staysails, and spanker.
> We wondered why the old man waited so long in the face of the dropping barometer. He should have shortened sail long ago. […]

Suddenly the mate bawled out: 'All hands on deck. Stand by the gallant clewlines and buntlines. Quick for —— sake!'[sic]

Looking to the windward, we saw a long, white sea rolling towards us, and behind the racing water inky clouds fringed with orange and green. The wind dropped to a dead calm, and the sky, so long murky and dark, was lit up with a terrible and spectral brilliance. It was the most uncanny sight I had ever witnessed, and I felt sure it would be the end of everything once the full force of the hurricane hit the unlucky *Pilgrim*.

Under the terrific pressure of the wind the *Pilgrim* heeled over on her beam ends, with the water running up to, and over, her lee rail. She was making about thirteen knots, scudding along at an angle of thirty degrees, threatening to go clean over at any moment. The mate was hanging on to the mizen fiferail. He motioned to the halyards, and I guessed his meaning. Words were useless in the wind. I hauled out my sheath-knife and slashed the rope; it parted with the crack of a pistol-shot. [...]

[All around masts and sails were splitting.] The masts were garbed like mad ghosts that shrieked in the gale. [...] The screaming of the wind and the slatting of sails and cordage made a deafening inferno of sound. [...] Down came the fore t'gallant mast, [...] weighing a couple of tons. [...]

Masts, yards and gear were now thrashing overboard like demons that had descended from the skies [...]. It was death to approach this whirling, tangled confusion."[8]

By 'some freak of luck' they weathered the hurricane, but they presented a sorry sight when the storm had calmed.

Nearly all the crew had injuries, from broken bones to serious cuts and the *Pilgrim* herself presented a sad spectacle. She would obviously never reach the golden gates of San Francisco. They were somewhere near the Malden or Jarvis islands, about 1,000 miles north of Tahiti.

A glance at the atlas will show that this was a particularly bad position to be in. Right in the middle of the Pacific. The only alternatives were to try and head south for Tahiti or north towards Hawaii. To make matters worse, the boat was under three feet of water which was rising in the hold. The pumps were of no use since the coal had blocked the bilges. The skipper gave the order. 'Stand by to abandon ship.'

And so McGuinness found himself and eleven other men in an 18 foot lifeboat adrift in the wide Pacific. They watched as the *Pilgrim* finally sank beneath the waves. They lost sight of the second lifeboat, skippered by the first mate.

Luckily the lifeboats were intact and provisioned with fresh water and food but, as Nomad was to put it:

> "Twelve men (with very little in common save their allegiance to the sea) from five nations do not make exactly 'good companions'. We had no shelter from the sun, save in the shadow of the boat's sail, and at midday this was of little avail when the sun was nearly overhead."[9]

Sleeping was difficult, or, as McGuinness rather poetically put it:

> "Our parched and hacked lips were impervious to the mock-relief of Morpheus."

> "By night we hung a lantern on the solitary mast of the boat, in the vain hope that some lynx-eyed native, somewhere, might see it. This, accidentally, became the means of providing us with extra rations. Flying-fish spotting the light flew at it, and we were often rudely awakened by receiving a slap in the face, as one of these fell into the boat ricochetting off the sail."[10]

They tried fishing, "but all we caught in seventeen days were four fish that looked like bonita, but were tough and scaly". Suffering from exposure, thirst and under-nourishment, their skins covered with boils and blisters, they finally limped into Papeete, Tahiti, 18 days later. There was no sign of the other boat, which never showed up and whose sailors met a watery grave in Balboa's 'peaceful' ocean.

Bully Newman and his cronies made their way to the States. McGuinness, fired by the works of Robert Louis Stevenson decided to stay on in the Marquesas islands to try his hand at pearl fishing.

> **"Errors, like straws, upon the surface flow;**
> **He who would search for pearls must dive below."**
> (Dryden, Prologue All for Love)

McGuinness was a well read man for his time. He taught himself to write – there is no evidence that any of his books were ghost-written – and he has the occasionally excellent turn of phrase. What is strangely missing is any attempt at political analysis from this opinionated and well travelled adventurer. In his two books – including one specifically about his stay in Soviet Russia under the Stalinist regime, he uses the word 'communism' fewer than a dozen times, and socialism and fascism not at all. In his 'articles' in the *Independent* 'anarchists' get a couple of mentions but are described as 'freemasons', which betrays either an incredible ignorance or a desperate desire to get paid by the Blueshirt owners of the *Independent*.

There are some comments on 'the under dog' with whom McGuinness says he empathises. The Irish rebels. The Irish peasantry of Donegal – 'far more honest than the Dublin jackeens'. Some black slaves in Africa. But the nearest he gets to speaking out against Imperialism – and this is at the height of the Empire – is when he is in the South Seas, clearly his favourite place on all his travels (*see* Afterword – weltanschauung). Below is an extract from his pearl fishing reminiscences.

PEARL-FISHING IN THE SOUTH SEAS

By Charles John McGuinness

My year at pearl-fishing through the Society group and Marquesas was a most pleasurable interlude. Robert Louis Stevenson had filled my imagination with fascinating pictures of the South Sea Islands and the life of beauty and languor in these pin-points of Paradise. I was now seventeen, and too restless for a lazy existence in the tropics. Since then, however, I have promised myself that some day I will go back there to stay [*see* Afterword].

The landfall of a Pacific island has a lure for the eye. First, a row of palms growing out of a blue sea, lined with a fine, thin streak of snowy white where the sea breaks on the coral reef surrounding the island, or else a verdure-clad cone in all the shades of wonderful blues and purples, changing, as approached, to a rich verdant green delicately underlined with the same faint white pencil mark. So the picture takes on new aspects of colour and shadow. There is nothing so alluring to youth as the silhouette of a tall palm against the purple; a faint tinkle of music and soft undulations of natives singing.

It is regrettable that civilization is rapidly spoiling the South Sea Islanders. They are more adept in absorbing the white man's vices than his virtues. Perhaps we have better teachers in the beachcombers and traders than in the missionaries. Even the religious visitors bring them only the veneer of Christianity, and leave them our conceits and hypocrisies. I except the Orders which specialize in medical missions and sanitation. The white traders' venereal diseases have afflicted thousands of these children of nature, and they haven't the white man's resistance or knowledge to combat the ravages of a social plague.

Some romancers of the South Seas have pictured all the women as being highly seductive in face and figure. In reality a few might qualify as dusky chorines, but they are not encountered with any frequency. If Venuses are few, however, most of the women are at least comely, with contagious smiles revealing perfect dental equipment. They are always singing or humming, and their hard, shapely bodies sway to the slow rhythm of their own music. Their reign of beauty is, of course, brief, but, like all tropic blossoms, their flowering is radiant. From a continental viewpoint, the most beautiful of them is the half-caste, who inherits the charm of the native and the wiles of the white woman. These women are nearly all the daughters of French traders, and many of them receive a convent training in Paris. Through much intermarriage with Chinese, the Tahitans will soon disappear as a distinct race. Chinese half-castes are singularly fascinating, with their almond eyes and *svelte* bodies.

It is a challenge to the white race that the marauding trader and the missionary should do the native equal harm by the vices and by the virtues they bring him. And, to add insult to injury, the missionary teaches him a false modesty, making him wear clothes, herding him and his family indoors in a home-life utterly foreign to his ancestors, and softening him for the thrust of any disease that the boats may carry from port to port. A generation ago half of Fiji died from an epidemic of measles brought by a man of the cloth.

Most missionaries from Europe have marched in the van of the trader and soldier. It has been an unhealthy triumvirate, and it brought only degradation to the brown races of the South Seas. Samoa, for instance, is a pitiable example of white interference. New Zealand took the island on mandate and the natives detest their sovereignty. They sometimes respected the German who ruled them, but it takes a gunboat in the harbour to instil the fear of Britain in their peaceful hearts. Most of the New Zealanders I have met are ashamed of the occupation, and pray to be relieved of the odium that it brings.

It was midsummer in Papeete when I joined the lugger *Annette*, which had just been fitted out for a pearling cruise in the Marquesas. The captain was a Frenchman who spoke splendid English, and had served many years in the British merchant marine. He was a sociable man who got loyalty and support without effort at discipline. A word from him in a kindly fashion was better than a bull whip from the skipper of the *Pilgrim*.

> For many months we cruised through the Marquesas and part of the Society Group. I became fascinated by the skill and daring of our staff of pearl-divers, and made a few attempts myself at this difficult art. I am a fair swimmer, but I was no match for the boys, who dropped into fifty or seventy feet of water to gather shells in the pearling beds. Most of our boys were from Puka-Puka, an island famous for its divers. They plunged into the water without diving-helmets or suits, and appeared minutes later, often as quickly as their precious catch, which we pulled to the surface in baskets. Occasionally one is attacked by an octopus, shark, or ray, and loses an arm or leg, but the shark's white belly is a fine target for a sheath-knife, and the odds are sometimes in favour of the diver.
>
> The divers spoke a French jargon, and served as interpreters in our frequent excursions to the island ports and villages. Since then I have become a sort of polyglot, and through a knowledge of the idiom of French, German, and Italian have crossed many borders without difficulty. The skipper knew all the island dialects, which was not a difficult feat of memory, for the dictionaries of each tribe could be written on a child's slate. Their words were limited to the necessities of life and the trappings of death."[11]

McGuinness, or perhaps his publisher, decides then that some coy sex is required (the book was published in 1934 and reprinted in 1935) and the reader is introduced to the 'chief's prettiest daughter' (who else) who goes by the rather improbable name of Lola. This is on Nukuhiva Island in the Hakapo village, "where the balmy evenings were spent in dancing, feasting, and drinking".

As the lugger rode though the sapphire sea and entered the lagoon the natives rushed forward to treat the white men as gods.

Ending up with the fair Lola, McGuinness gallantly gave her

> "some choice trinket from our stock in trade – a pair of brass bangles, or anklets studded with coloured glass, and these were her delight. When she danced at the banquet in my honour, these trinkets were, apart from the flowers in her hair, the only clothes she wore, and they became her nicely."[12]

Perhaps it is as well that very few copies of *Nomad* or *Sailor of Fortune* reached Derry, or Nomad's rare trips home might have been even rarer.

Three day banquets. Each male guest would have the woman of his choice. Garlands of hibiscus flowers. Huge gourds of palm wine. Hors-d'œuvres of live goldfish. Roasted pig, yams and breadfruit. Singing. Dancing. "A velvety South Sea night, laden with the perfume of tropical blooms, the perpetual drone of the surf breaking upon the coral reef, flickering torches throwing dancing shadows, flashing white teeth, and the graceful, lithe figures of boys and girls moving to and fro." And a lot of drunken dirty Caucasian sailors?

A swim in the lagoon in the morning. Lunch and siesta in the hammocks, ministered to by the ever attentive Lola, murmuring "Charles, Charles, *je vous aime*." (No 'tutoyer'?)

> "But the day for sailing would come. We would go on board loaded with island generosity, sorrowfully heave anchor, and, escorted by swimmers and canoes, slowly sail out through the opening in the reef. [...] We would tearfully embrace; a long passionate kiss, with promises of undying love. [...]
>
> It was such a scene as I have just depicted that rang down the curtain on my first real love-affair."[13]

Did this really happen? Is it just a fantasy? If it was so good why did he leave – he wasn't on military service and could quit ship at any time? We will never know, but it adds another small piece to the enigma that was Charles McGuinness. And, to be fair, even though he is writing over twenty years later, at the time Charlie was only 17 going on 18, and the South Seas must have presented heady times to the young man from Derry.

PRE-WAR RAMBLINGS

The next three years seems to have been spent in an aimless peregrination, always seeking new experiences and surroundings. He made 'many successful cruises' with the *Annette*, collecting the black pearls but "the tranquillity of life began to irritate me, [...] I decided to get out of this poppy land."

He parted amicably from the crew and their 'decent' French skipper in German Samoa and made his way back to Newcastle in Australia. He had an aunt and an uncle there – part of the Hernan clan, but he makes no mention of them. He then details a bizarre trip on the *Brookshire* (not it's real name apparently) which featured a drunken skipper who had lost his sealed orders. Eventually they found out that they were supposed to sail for Java. The firemen on the crew mutinied and pelted the skipper and chief engineer, who was also drunk, with rotten fruit. This degenerated into a mini-riot with everyone throwing anything they could find from coal to cabbages at each other. The 'mutiny' fizzled out and after a three week stay in rain sodden Java they visited Christmas Island. Racist violence broke out between the Whites and the Chinese sailors, and McGuinness describes seeing a 'fellow Irishman' cutting the head of a Chinaman and then shovelling his body overboard. The Irishman, whom he merely calls 'Paddy' was "a peculiar character. He gave most of his pay to beggars and children, and would sob violently at a sentimental song of home and mother. In the World War he probably won the VC."[14]

The entire crew was, hardly surprisingly, dismissed and, back in Australia Nomad tried his hand in the Coolgardie goldfields for a few months before, in 1912, making his first trip back home to Ireland, via Falmouth on the *Port Jackson*.

From 1912 until 1913 he claims to have fitted an enormous amount of travel in. First on tramp steamers through the Levantine ports of the Mediterranean, the Black Sea, South and West Africa, the West Indies, Central America, Mexico, Brazil, China, Japan, and Siberia. This itinerary seems, to say the least, to be 'over ambitious', for he next claims to have ended up panhandling and riding the rails with a hobo partner called Ryan in Canada. Then it was sailing on a lake steamer from Toronto to Montreal.

> "Here I joined the Canadian Militia for a brief while. [...] Do not confuse it with the 'movie' conception of the Canadian Royal Mounted. [...] I got a pair of pants eighteen inches too long, a tunic that wouldn't fit a midget, and a cap that fell over my ears. It was an *opéra bouffe* army that should win any war by doubling up the enemy with laughter."[15]

Most of his fellow 'volunteers' were starving strikers or hobos. The venture collapsed but McGuinness claims he got an honourable discharge and shipped out to Cape Town with a cargo of livestock – troublesome Missouri mules.

1914 sees him back in Europe. In Venice he gets drunk on Grappa with a buddy, Hubert Green, and ends up in a fight with the carabinieri who they beat up and threw into a canal. Securely bound and "with ten or more criminals we were escorted into a huge gondola" and to the dreaded St. Marco's prison – "a cruel dungeon".

The British Consulate produced 'an alienist' who cheerfully testified that being Irishmen "the poisonous drink had affected their minds to incite a murderous impulse."[16] Case dismissed and he and Hubert made for Constantinople, but got delayed in Sulina in Romania. Another fight, this time with Norwegian sailors and another few nights in jail. It was summer of 1914. The great war loomed. They set off up the Danube to Galatz and Ibraila.

Notes.

1. McGuinness, Charles John: *Nomad*. Methuen, London 1934, p. 1.
2. ibid., p. 2-3.
3. ibid., pp. 4-5.
4. ibid., p. 7.
5. ibid., pp. 20-21.
6. ibid., p. 21.
7. ibid., p. 23.
8. ibid., pp. 27-28.
9. ibid., p. 31.
10. ibid., p. 32.
11. ibid., pp. 34-37.
12. ibid., p. 37.
13. ibid., pp. 40-41.
14. ibid., p. 49.
15. ibid., p. 53.
16. ibid., p. 56.

Chapter 2
The Dark Continent

June 28, 1914. Sarajevo. Gavrilo Pricip lights the fuse which kills the minor Archduke Ferdinand and sets off 'the war to end all wars'. As Ferdinand is being 'promoted to glory' as some of the papers of the time described it, Nomad was steaming up the Danube to Galati and Braila in Romania.

> "War was inevitable. We hurried home via Hamburg. On August 2nd I arrived back in Ireland. Two days later England declared war."[1]

McGuinness alleges that in the Guildhall Square in Derry he "harangued a crowd urging immediate action. 'England's difficulty is Ireland's opportunity!' The young men were with me in sympathy, but there were no active leaders." So, all of three days later McGuinness tried to join the British Navy.

> "I presume that my action was a typical sample of Irish inconsistency. [...] I thought the war would be over by Christmas and I was mighty anxious to see some real action before it finished. As were millions of others at that time, I was sadly lacking in military foresight."[2]

The early days could hardly be described as exciting for such an adventurous and experienced mariner. Delivering coal to the Grand Fleet in Scapa Flow. Then down to Swansea and finally Chatham Naval barracks. There Nomad volunteered for service on the *Sirius* and shortly was steaming out of Sherness for 'an unknown destination'.

And what was he thinking in those first days of the great conflagration?

> "I didn't really care which side I was on, British or German; all I wanted was the thrill of a naval battle. I did, however, have a slight grudge against the Germans; I considered their declaration of war unethical. As an Irishman, I considered England our own private grievance and political diversion. The Kaiser had no right

to poach on our preserves. At least he should have entered into some kind of agreement with our Irish leaders."[3]

LITTLE CATHOLIC BELGIUM

Within a few days Nomad was at work with the *Sirius*' gun crew, lying a few miles off Middlekerke and bombing away with their six pounders and twelve pounders, blowing the hell out of 'little Catholic Belgium', who so many Irishmen had joined up to save under the advice of John Redmond.

> "Every time we fired the *Sirius* heeled over with the recoil as if a monster from the deep had lain heavy hand on her."

Nomad at least got to experience the 'thrill of a naval battle'.

> "We had registered two direct hits; [...] A German battery was entrenched behind the houses, and soon they were dropping shells all around us. We steamed off out of range, then returned, zigzagging as before. It was unpleasant work with the deafening roar of the guns at close quarters and the smell of burning cordite from the cartridge cases. Then the incessant rolling of the ship made it difficult for us to maintain our footing. A rack of six-inch projectiles broke loose, and these heavy, slippery cylinders were rolling from side to side, threatening to break our legs or explode and blow us all to pieces. [...]
> At night we had visitations from aircraft, planes and dirigibles. They tried to blow us out of the water by dropping aerial bombs from low altitudes. We retaliated with our anti-aircraft gun, but on the pitching vessel it was a waste of time."[4]

The *Sirius* was based in Dunkirk (Dunkerque) through October-November 1914 and they saw the horrors of the retreat from Mons.

McGuinness narrowly missed getting torpedoed – the sister ship the *Hermes* took the hit, and the *Sirius* continued bombarding Middlekerke, Zeebrugge, Nieuport and Ostend as part of Admiral Bacon's Dover Patrol.

Perhaps typifying the efficiency of the British Army in those parlous times McGuinness and his crewmates were next issued with heavy winter equipment and then all sent off to the sweltering tropics, cruising off West Africa down 'the torrid coast' of the German Cameroons.

THE CAMEROONS CAMPAIGN

The Allied history of West Africa in World War I sums up the 'Cameroons campaign' as follows:

Conclusion: Allied victory after a nineteen month campaign.
Allied Gains/Losses: Cameroons conquered. British lost 4,600 casualties, 1,668 of who were killed, most died of diseases. The French lost 2,567 dead.
Axis Gains/Losses: Unknown. (In fact the Germans lost fewer than 100 men plus, of course, a lot more 'native bearers'.)

One would, in all fairness have to say that if this is a 'victory' it was a remarkably Pyrrhic one.

In 1914, the Cameroons were as big as France and Germany combined and in the possession of Germany, albeit with a sparse population of about 500,000 including about 2,000 Europeans. To defend this vast colony the Germans fielded a colonial force, a *Schutztruppe*, of 200 German officers and NCOs and 1,550 African soldiers. In addition there was a police force of 40 Europeans and 1,255 Africans. These forces were only designed for internal peacekeeping, not fighting a war.

As in Togoland, the Senior British Officer in West Africa was in England when the war started. By the 22nd August, 1914 the French agreed to place land and sea forces as the disposal of the officer, Brigadier General Charles Dobell for the attack on the Cameroons. Dobell sailed for Lagos, Africa on 30th August. The British force in West Africa was not large, but were three times the size of any force the Germans could muster in the area. In 1914 the West African Frontier Force numbered 242 British regular officers, 118 British NCOs, and 7,733 African Soldiers. A grand total of 8,093 men which did not even match a World War I division. None of the British led African troops was trained as well as the *Schutztruppe*, and none had experience in working in anything bigger than Company level.

Three quick victories/skirmishes put the Germans in a position from which they could threaten Calabar, the main port in Nigeria at the time. The British Colonel Carter was blamed for the defeats, sacked and sent home. He was replaced by the assistant commandant of the Nigeria Regiment, Lieutenant Colonel Frederick Cunliffe. Allied morale sank. Another attack was launched against Kusseri, the chief German post on the Cameroon's frontier in the Lake Chad region. Near the mouth of the Muni River, they launched a seaborne assault with 600 tirailleurs and, after stiff fighting on land and sea, sank two German ships and on 21st September successfully established a beachhead.

Eventually, when more and more British and French forces, including naval supplies, arrived the Allies were able to capture Douala. Douala was not the capital of the Cameroons, but a port and therefore a valued strategic asset for the German controlled Cameroons. Little had been done to defend the port, the authorities had only placed a battery at Yoss Point, and nine old ships were sunk in the channel at Rugged Point, six of which were ineptly placed on the shoals clear of the channel. Only one of the merchant ships which had taken shelter in the harbour when the war started was armed.

Douala itself was a European settlement with several fringe African villages. The town had about a hundred European residencies and the African villages housed about 30,000 Africans, two railway lines led into the well planned modern settlement.

Nomad only spent three months in the Cameroons and did not enjoy it one bit. He describes how he and his team had to act as glorified porters, tracking military equipment up river in the sweltering jungle 'but never getting close enough to the Germans to fire a shot'. "The country is rich in big game, and many unexplored areas are the haunts of pygmy elephant and gorilla. The country is rich in ivory, ebony, mahogany and all tropical products."

Although only there three months before the *Sirius* sailed south "content to leaving the soldiering end of the campaign to the Army",[5] McGuinness pointed out that the campaign was basically futile. The Germans, numbering no more than 1,000 resorted to guerrilla warfare and basically rang rings round the British and French who, in addition, lost thousands of men to disease.

By March 1915, the Allies had two major forces successfully established in the Cameroons. They blundered around the jungle, argued with their French allies and suffered totally unnecessary casualties for a large amount of territory which had little or no strategic value.

The Cameroons were divided between France and Britain on 4th March 1916, and, despite all England's endeavours, the French took the Lion's share.

South Africa

Thus, the Cameroons campaign had ended before the Easter Rebellion broke out, but this is the reason that Nomad gave for deserting in Simonstown in South Africa after hearing the news, obviously out of date and vague, from Dublin. "I determined to leave the ship. I had heard about De Wet's thrust against the British in South Africa and decided to join him. I left the *Sirius* at Simonstown, and hurried to Bloemfontein in the Orange Free State."[6] This seems, to say the least, disingenuous.

Christiaan (Rudolf) De Wet (1854-1922) had long been defeated. Nonetheless, McGuinness apparently signed up with the South African Engineers for service in German East Africa and then the South African Expeditionary Force under Generals Jan Smuts and Van Deventer.[7] Nomad enlisted under the name of Hennessey.[8]

There was somewhat chaotic training at a small camp Potchefstroom outside Johannesburg under the infamous Sergeant-Major O'Shea who scared half the volunteers off. Nomad seemed not to have had too much of an opinion of his fellow soldiers.

> "The Irish drank and fought amongst themselves. The cousin Jacks played cards and went to the camp mission. The Scotch [sic] drank furtively and took long walks. The English did nothing much in particular. The Dutchmen held Kaffee Klatches and studied their paybooks. The Jews bought up old clothing, ran gambling schools, loaned money, and in general put the army on a firm financial footing – for themselves!"[9]

By July 1916 they were en route to Kilindini, the port of Mombasa via Durban. En route McGuinness claims he got into a row with a drunken Yorkshire soldier called Bradshaw, who attacked him. Nomad felled him and Bradshaw accidentally died. Nomad was court martialled but acquitted because the court martial officer had himself been assaulted by the belligerent Bradshaw. After that Nomad became the troop's pugilistic champion and fought a prize fight against 'an ebony opponent, only a generation out of the bush and as tough as mule meat'. (McGuinness frequently referred to other races by nomenclature now regarded as decidedly 'non-pc'.)

Prior to the arrival of Smuts' men – and prior to McGuinness' arrival – Von Lettow and Captain Looff, the commander in the south, had actually had quite a pleasant war. Until the defeat at Morogoro the German officers had canned foods from home, paté, sausages, pickles, champagne and wines laid down in German cellars before the war. The brewery at Dar es Salaam had turned out an excellent German beer until a British cruiser blasted it with shells and destroyed the fermentation casks. When they captured the town on September 4th (1916) Nomad deplored the destruction of the brewery and mourned the town's inability to provide 'a decent drink'.

But Colonel Paul von Lettow was resilient. Many, including Edwin Hoyt and McGuinness, although they never met, described the German as "the greatest guerrilla fighter ever who could give Che Guevara cards and still win".[10]

Von Lettow took to the bush and led the Allies 'a merry dance'. Nomad claims that the Germans became expert at living off the land, manufacturing salt, drugs, alcohol and even paying for commandeered cattle with money. Nomad relates 'sporadic skirmishes' with the Germans around the foothills of mount Kilimanjaro "but German bullets were not a tenth as deadly as the plague-bearing insects". There were jigger fleas, matakini flies, scorpions and centipedes. One by one the men came down and were put out of action by malaria, dysentery, blackwater fevers and other plagues. McGuinness, in censored postcards to Hugh, bitterly complained about the deadly mosquitoes.

The war in East Africa cost 50,000 lives through gunfire and many times that figure through disease.

> "The black carriers died in myriads through inhuman treatment. The poor savages were drafted into the white man's bloody game, and their lives were held as cheap as insects.
>
> Fighting in a jungle is fighting in the dark. The Germans had better knowledge of the terrain than the Allies, and we suffered incessantly from ambush and sortie. I was captured with another Irishman by name of Farrelley in a surprise attack between the Kiseaga and Ruaha rivers."[11]

But the Germans were on the move and although resourceful in foraging didn't need hungry Irish mouths to feed. Farrelley and McGuinness 'escaped' and trekked 150 miles through the insect and fever ridden jungle, encountering elephants, leopards, giraffes, apes, hippos and rhinos and finally rejoined their comrades at Korogwe.

The Allied forces would venture out into the bush seeking the Germans but rarely shot or captured any and in fact suffered daily casualties. Nomad's close friend, "a splendid South African named Forbes" was shot next to him. Nomad dragged him back into the trench but it was too late. "'Save yourself Hennessey,' he croaked and died a few moments later."

And then there was the infamous 'bee attack'. McGuinness relates 'a brilliant plan' by a German engineer.

> "One day a convoy of our mules and wagons loaded with foodstuffs, clothing and sundry munitions was making slow progress along the trail in the dense bush between Tanga and Korogwe. The Askaris moved ahead [...]. The transport was guarded by Boers from the Cape [...].
>
> Along the trail a German engineer conceived a brilliant plan of harassing the enemy with bees. The German Askaris, some of whom were trained beekeepers, gathered hundreds of swarms and attached the bees to convenient trees along the trail. Not only bees were drafted into service, but also their more vicious cousins, the yellow jackets, wasps, hornets and every African insect equipped with a 'bayonet'.
>
> The nests were connected with wires, strung in sequence and running back to a central location in the bush. Here the German engineer waited beside his switches and a dry cell battery system [...]. The Germans had felled some trees across the trail [...] [and as] the cavalcade piled up behind [...] the blacks [were ordered] to cut through the barricade. Then came the signal and the master switch sent its electric agitation into the nests and swarms. Without warning millions of bees, wasps and hornets swept down on their huge prey.
>
> [...] Mules, oxen, and horses stampeded and dashed into the jungle to die in agony. The jungle echoed with the screams of animals and men. [...] Scarcely a living thing escaped. The blacks and whites perished in a death of excruciating torture. Their faces were unidentifiable. [...] Victory had come to the Germans without firing a shot. There may have been a few survivors, but when our troops came up there were no survivors to tell the tale. I got the complete details in the German camp after my capture with Farrelley."[12]

Hennessey, Farrelley and then Conroy. The three Irish musketeers. Getting drunk, disobeying orders, eating and drinking strange food and drink (like urine) with the natives. Safaris. Bridge building and fighting, more with their own fellow troops than the elusive Germans. Particular hostility was shown to the 'little Catholic Belgians' for whom the war was allegedly being fought. McGuinness alleges that

"It was common knowledge that many of the Belgian Askaris were cannibals – sometimes with the permission of their superior officers. [...] I can relate one barbarous episode, which is fastened on the Belgian Askaris beyond hope of denial. I was in the hospital in Dar-es-Salaam recovering from a severe attack of malaria when a dozen or more East Indian matrons and maidens were brought in for treatment. [...] The Belgian human jackals had swept down on the village and carried off the women to satisfy their great passion of tasting human flesh!

There was no love lost between the Belgian whites and the British South Africans, who shared my nonchalance towards the story of the Uhlans in Flanders when we knew all about the brutalities of Leopold's men in the Congo to have any sympathy for Belgians, whoever they were."[13]

Perhaps, with just a twinge of envy, he ends his African tales by adding:

"I have often watched a detachment of Belgians on the march, followed by their officers in home-made palanquins. These dandies would be resting with a bibi, or concubine, while the black litter-bearers struggled along with the precious cargo. Cohabiting with the native women is an open practice in the Belgian Congo – an unsavoury alliance for white officers, as these dusky courtesans share their favours without distinction of colour."[14]

Nomad objects to miscegenation?

Nomad then digresses on his dislike for big game hunting and the rich white trophy hunters, yet he goes on to describe with relish all the bizarre animals which he and his two Irish comrades ate.

Coming back in an open boat from Zanzibar, where they'd crossed over to smuggle back some liquor to camp they were stuck in 'the water-logged tub' and 'almost burnt to death'.

Farrelley was not the best pleased.

"Here I am dying in a God damned boat, after ducking bullets in fourteen battles, and it's all your fault, you little Derry lobster."[15]
The Irishman had golf ball sized blisters and "without the five bottles of whiskey we had to consume we'd have perished for sure."

They made it back and delivered the drink but by the time they got out of the hospital their 'comrades' had drunk it all. "Apart from the five bottles of whiskey we drank on the way back and which saved our lives we got nothing," Nomad complained.

Eventually 'Hennessey' and Farrelley arrived back in Durban, Natal with a crowd of casualties – 'the wounded, diseased and the insane.'

Nomad had tired of Africa. Farrelley, the soldier, opted to stay, but Nomad the sailor wanted the first ship out of there.

Notes.

1. McGuinness, *Nomad*, op. cit., pp. 57-58.
2. ibid., pp. 57-58.
3. ibid., p. 60. McGuinness no doubt is attempting to be slightly facetious to try and explain his somewhat unorthodox behaviour but even he should have recognised that in fact it was England who declared war on Germany and not vice-versa.
4. ibid., p. 62.
5. ibid., p. 64.
6. We are grateful to Micky McGuinness for providing his uncle's British Naval Record, which shows that he served from December 1914 until jumping ship in Mai 1916. The naval records also confirm that he had tattoos of a crucifix, crossed hands, crossed flags, as well as a ship on his right forearm.

7. The Allied Front in East Africa facing the Germans also consisted of the Indian Expeditionary Force, the East African Forces, Rhodesian regiments under General Northey, Belgian troops drafted in from the Congo and Portuguese troops from Portuguese East Africa.
8. He explains it thus: "I enlisted under the name of Hennessey, which is the southern Irish form of the Gaelic name MacAonghusa. McGuinness, O'Shaugnessy all come from this clan name." ibid., p. 67.
9. ibid., p. 68.
10. Hoyt, Edwin P.: *Guerrilla – Colonel Von Lettow-Vorbeck and Germany's East Africa Empire.* MacMillan, London 1981. Hoyt writes "in my opinion von Lettow was the most successful guerrilla leader in world history, and his record has never even been approached by any others, in terms of impact on his enemies, in terms of survival in the field with no sources of supply for months on end, in terms of managing a racially mixed fighting force with enormous skill, in terms of sheer courage and heroism, and finally in terms of superb generalship that kept his enemies almost constantly guessing." (p. 206) Nomad concurred: "he is one of the greatest soldiers of the World War. With a few men he held off 300,000 troops with 137 generals, and right up to the date of the Armistice was undefeated. For four years he outguessed his enemies, using every artifice of man and nature to plague his pursuers, and yet played the war game strictly according to the rules." (McGuinness, *Nomad*, op. cit., p. 74).
With a force of 5,000 men 'most of them natives' von Lettow-Vorbeck defied the British until the end of the war, was never beaten, cost the British 250,000 troops and an incredible £70 Million. *See* also Newman, Bernard: *German Spy.* London 1936, pp. 7-8.
McGuinness is scathing about the French Foreign Legion who "as is well known, is recruited from wasters, convicts, and every variety of ne'er-do-well" (McGuinness, *Nomad*, op .cit., p. 73).
11. McGuinness, *Nomad*, op. cit., p. 75.
12. ibid., p. 80.
13. ibid., pp. 82-83.
14. ibid., p. 83.
15. ibid., p. 90.

Chapter 3
The Cruel Sea, Chinese Pirates and That Old Devil Sex

Shipwrecked

The 18 months back pay he received when he left the hospital did not last Nomad long in the bars and whorehouses of Durban. In early November 1917, he accepted a job as mate on a tug boat, the Portuguese *Magellan* bound for Kilwa in East Africa. They cleared Durban with a huge barge in tow loaded with 300 tons of coal.

Nomad expressed concern about the condition of the boat and whether or not it could make the 2,000 mile trip through the Mozambique channel and the Indian Ocean. When he reached Lourenço Marques (now Maputo) in Delagoa Bay "I was tempted to leave the ship at the Portuguese harbour, but lacked a coward's courage to abandon a foolhardy venture".[1]

Not far out of Delagoa Bay and the weather worsened. The monsoon season was almost upon them and, against all maritime common sense, hundreds of tons of coal had been stored on the deck as well as in the barge. But it was a military contract and 'marine precaution counted as naught'.

> "Suddenly a Himalayan peak of white-plumed water came racing along, and, with a thunderous roar, folded over us. The doomed boat heeled over on her beam ends until her mast and funnel were almost parallel with the sea. The huge wave engulfed the engine-room and, as the fires were swiftly extinguished clouds of steam hissed up the grating. [...]
>
> 'Jump for your lives!' I bellowed against the wind. [...] Desperately we swam away from the hull on order to avoid the vortex when the tug should founder."[2]

Two engineers and the cook went down, never to be seen again. McGuinness and another sailor tried to reach the barge but it was swept out into the mystic. They struggled back and found a few survivors clinging to the life boat, which had shot up from the depths 'like a projectile, her air tanks adding velocity.'

They managed to get the life boat upright but had to stand in it up to their waists in water. There were six survivors. At first the water was relatively warm but as night came down the cold began to get intense and the men were only wearing singlets and shorts.

A South African Dutchman went 'loco' and jumped overboard. Each time they pulled him back by the rope attached to him he went overboard again. 'The look in his eyes showed he was stark staring mad'. 'A little Cockney lad' was the next to go. He unfastened his rope and disappeared from the boat, floating alongside with his life belt.

McGuinness and the other survivors had to watch helpless as they were savaged by tiger sharks, which fed on whale offal in Delagoa Bay. Several boats passed them during the night but they weren't spotted and their cries went unanswered.

Of the 13 man crew three had gone down with the ship, four had been blown away on the barge, two had gone overside and there were four of them left.

The next day they were off Inyacka Island and the boat began to sink. The captain and the second engineer were on their last legs when the good ship *Liberador*, which had been sent out to look for them finally spied them, picked them up and returned them to Lourenço Marques. But it was too late for the skipper and engineer. They died on the dock. 'Hennessey' and another crewman called Connelley were the only two survivors. The luck of the Irish?

> "Under maritime law as it was then pay ceased immediately a vessel foundered. I received £3 for my experience, and the loss of all personal property and papers. This loss, perhaps, was a blessing in disguise, for it gave me a plausible reason why I could not produce documents to support my statement of war service, which, in truth, would have proved embarrassing, despite the fact that I had joined up in August 1914 and served in the Navy, Army, and Naval Auxiliaries."[3]

The British Consul however gave him the fare to Durban. Connelley was left behind in the hospital where he died shortly afterwards. Nomad is the sole survivor of the *Magellan*.

But, within a week he signed on again. This time on 'a decent square-rigger', the *Medway* under skipper Captain Williams, 'a pleasant man'. McGuinness was third mate. The cargo was, yet again, coal, this time bound half way round the world to Iquique in Chile, the nitrate port of call on the Pacific coast of Chile. The *Medway* also carried 20 British cadets whom Nomad says he taught the rudimentaries of 'fisticuffs' and how 'to catch albatross'.[4]

As someone who had literary pretensions and was steeped in the lore of the sea and its superstitions it seems strange that this 'Ancient Mariner' would invoke the curse of the albatross, but he details how to capture the 'magnificent bird' with a simple metal trap.

> "The feathers and down of these creatures are exceedingly soft and beautiful. I have made coats from their pelts, and carved cigar- and cigarette-holders from their wings and leg bones. The feet, too, are made into tobacco-pouches and one can always distinguish a real Cape Horn sailor by his pouch and souvenirs."[5]

Modern day readers may well approve of his sentiments on sharks:

> "Originally, I suppose, the ugly brutes were created for some definite purpose, but the squeal of the Boer sailor haunts me, and whenever the opportunity occurs I have no compunction whatever in hooking and chopping up one of them and casting him to those cannibal brothers and sisters of his who dog the wake of the ship."[6]

Few ecologists these days would however, we suspect, approve of him harpooning porpoises.

> "The porpoise is an exhibitionist – a graceful one too. She glories in racing the ship. I have watched them circle a vessel a dozen times before, as a grand finale, diving under the keel. It is a pity, perhaps, to harpoon these frolicking pigs of the sea; but ocean pork is such a delectable relief from the barrelled salted variety."[7]

At Iquique they unloaded the coal and loaded up with saltpetre for the return trip to Capetown. Iquique was 'as boring as usual' but Nomad and another Irishman, Paddy Burke, did manage to get 'locked up in the hoosgow' after they had beaten up some insolent locals and then attacked the local police in a 'Chinese beer garden'. The kindly Captain Williams bailed them out and paid for new police uniforms.

By the beginning of 1918, after a 'record 54 day trip back, a mark that may never be beaten by a sailing ship' Nomad was back in South Africa. He says he liked the *Medway* and its crew. He made more trips as a coalman to Colombo, Penang, Singapore and Hong Kong.

There, unfortunately the *Medway* was laid up in the Taiku dockyard to be sold. The English crew shipped back to London but Nomad decided to stay in Hong Kong to attend the Navigation School to 'get my mate's ticket'. (He had apparently been sailing for years without having bothered to obtain one.)

THE PIRATES OF THE CHINA SEAS

Most of the sketchy references to McGuinness include hints or rumours that he had 'been a pirate' in the China Sea and the Indian Ocean. That he had captained war junks and was associated with women pirates as well as ruthless male marauders. The American newspapers in particular exaggerated McGuinness' 'yarns' and embellished them shamelessly. Of course there always had been pirates in the China seas. There were when Nomad was there and they're still there in the year 2002. There were also some famous women Chinese pirates, but the sad truth is that Nomad, although piratical by nature, did not actually capture a pirate junk or battle with 'slant-eyed sea demons'.

To be fair, he never claimed in his books to have done so – but he did little to dispel the stories which arose over the years regarding the sailor of fortune.

> "The trade of buccaneering, in one form or another, is actually in the blood of the South China coast people. These hills, these rocky islands and waters, have for centuries been their territory, by right or might. When the plucky Portuguese arrived in the fifteenth century they immediately declared war on the brigands, and Macao was handed over to them by the Son of Heaven as a token of appreciation for what they did to suppress the activities of the marauders. The Chinese authorities, Imperial or Republican, have never been strong enough to cope with the situation, and the Portuguese of Macao, or the Hong-Kong British of today, cannot very well start any punitive expeditions of their own on foreign territory."[8]

Aleko Lilius wrote this in 1930 and it was published in New York. Many people read it and perhaps even Nomad.[9]

At least his account of his trip with 'Whisky Brown' and a 'gang of Chinee cut-throats' provides a 'ripping yarn'. For what it's worth, here is an abbreviated version.

"Leaving the dockyard late one evening, I was accosted by a character known to every white and yellow in the coast trade, a skipper by the name of 'Whisky Brown'. No one knew his real name. [...]

'McGuinness,' he ordered abruptly, 'come and have a drink.'"

After 'tiffin time' in the King Edward and numerous glasses of Canadian Club whiskey, Nomad was propositioned. Brown had agreed

"to navigate a freak junk down the coast to Singapore, and take with him a horde of yellow cut-throats as crew. Would I go along as mate?
Of course I would."

The bizarre vessel turned out to be a graft of two huge teakwood junks that had 'run the coast since the days of Captain Cook'. She turned out to be an excellent craft.

"Our pirate crew was indeed the pick of the Gulf of Bias, a notorious stronghold for sea bandits. Piracy, by the way, is a sort of Robin Hood business in China, and members of the bands infesting the Gulf of Bias were specially noted for their skill as seamen. Hence their services were in fair demand, for at times it is good politics to hire a pirate crew. The chance of robbery on the high seas is lessened thereby, while a particularly vicious bunch of fighters proves advantageous should another 'non-union' pirate band try conclusions. Besides 'Whisky Brown' enjoyed a high rating among them; any ship he commanded was practically immune from attack. And moreover – a strange thing, but, I learned, a true one – a 'Chink' pirate's word is his bond. A white streak shall I say, among the yellow!

[...] 'Number One Chink' insisted that a holiday must be declared on my behalf to appease the gods. [Rice was poured overboard, the bow was drenched with samsu, joss sticks were burned, one string fiddles whanged and flutes piped shrilly.]

And then, late in the day, 'Number One Chink' declared that the auguries were favourable [...]. The following morning, after an evening spent with fan-tan and opium pipe, the joss sign, something like a Union label on a hat or a suit of clothes, was painted on the side of the ship as a piratical symbol to warn off competition." [...]

"She [the ship] carried sufficient cutlery, guns, and ammunition to start a revolution. Every chink was armed with a sword about three feet long, and carried a long-barrelled pistol strangely reminiscent of Chinese Gordon's campaign or the Taeping uprising. My own arsenal consisted of two modern Lee-Enfield rifles and twin Colt revolvers with plenty of ammunition."[10]

Although highly suspicious of the trip, Nomad had to admit that it was uneventful. Fourteen days to Singapore where the boat was paid for. Nomad got his £45 and never got to fire his 'arsenal'. It was back to Hong Kong.

There were of course famous women pirates. One of the most famous in the 19th century had been Cheng I Sao who was also known as Ching Yih Saou, or Ching Shih.[11] In the early 19th century, taking over after the death of her husband she commanded a huge fleet of rapacious freebooters. At the height of the Confederation, which she ruled with an iron fist their fleet was larger than many countries navies. Two hundred ocean going junks, each armed with 20-30 cannons and able to carry up to 400 pirates. There were between 600-800 coastal vessels armed with up to 25 guns and carrying 200 men. In addition there were hundreds of raiding junks from which to plunder the coastal and island villages. Pillage, kidnap and extortion, it was all grist to the mill. She retired as wealthy dowager and her son became a Chinese general.

In his book, Lilius describes another pirate leader who was about when Nomad was in the China seas, but he clearly models her on Cheng I Sao, and, as we discuss below in footnote 9, others may have plagiarised Lilius.

And now, Romance raises its blushing head.

Nomad somewhat slyly titillates his more libidinous readers by describing his romantic adventure with a beautiful maiden. As he recalls it for us, he became friendly with an unlikely Chinese businessman called 'O'Mara' who was 'proud of his Celtic heritage'.

> "His father, I learnt, was the son of a wild goose of Erin who, three generations ago set out for Saigon and there married a Chinese mandarin's daughter whose mother was French. O'Mara himself had married a Portuguese half-cast from Macao and had a residence in Saigon and another at Canton."

It was at the family home in Canton where Nomad met and fell for

> "the Chinaman's two daughters, vivacious girls with faces as fragile as porcelain. Tutors had been imported from France in

order to supply finesse in continental manners, and the O'Mara girls undoubtedly were splendid linguists despite their cloistered lives. I was astounded by their knowledge of world affairs, and the cosmopolitan charm of their speech, equally fluent in French, English, or the native Cantonese.

O'Mara had given me a job as chief officer on one of his four vessels, the *Nem Wah*, but as she was under repair [...] I spent an unforgettable fortnight in the company of Inez and her sister Isobel. Inez's eyes, with the slightly Oriental angle, were adorable. She inherited beauty from each strain of Celt, French, and Portuguese. [...] She was fascinated with the subject of Ireland. She had read several descriptive books of the country. Most of her information was of a superlative character, so I preserved the illusion, even tinting the rainbow. I told her of ancestral halls of Erin, her moss-covered ruins, her round towers, and her great heroes like Finn and Cuchulain. The girl would probably never see Ireland, so why should I spoil everything by telling her of the one-room shebeens that sometimes shelter man and beast, the poverty and the misery of the poor, and the feuds of North and South?

Inez and her relations were Catholics, and had the benefit of a private chapel and personal confessor. I imagined my presence was not acceptable to the venerable padre [...][and] believe he was more than anxious to see me aboard ship with a one-way ticket, and disturbed Inez with his dark prophecies.

But it happened all the same. We fell head over heels in love, and for long hours wandered through the Eden-like gardens surrounding the house, building castles for the future. To me it was only a dream. Every moment I expected a pinch to wake me. She was too beautiful to be real, the romance too good to be true.

'Charles,' she whispered one evening under an amber moon, when the perfumed gardens filled my heart with a drug, 'if you marry me you can be a Captain in my father's fleet, and eventually become a great merchant like him.'

'But what what would your father think of the plan?'

'He thinks that would be a splendid plan. He likes you, and when we are married he says we can visit Ireland for our honeymoon.'

I made no answer to that. The suggestion was disturbing. I preferred that she should cherish the Erin of her dreams, much as I love my own land and the beauties of its rivers, lakes and mountains.

Two weeks later I went to my ship, the *Nem Wah* and left Inez still in the ecstasy of first love."[12]

Perhaps not very chivalrous, but purple prose.

Alas, however, it seems remarkably similar to numerous 'Chinese pirate romances' which had been appearing since the 1920s. Compare it to this piece by Aleko Lilius, who travelled there and, for example was very taken by his 'pirate woman'.

> "What a woman she was! Rather slender and short, her hair jet black, with jade pins gleaming in the knot at the neck, her earrings and bracelets of the same precious apple-green stone. She was exquisitely dressed in a white satin robe fastened with green jade buttons, and green silk slippers. She wore a few plain gold rings on her left hand; her right hand was unadorned. Her face and dark eyes were intelligent – not too Chinese, although purely Mongolian, of course – and rather hard. She was probably not yet forty.
>
> Every move she made and every word she spoke told plainly that she expected to be obeyed, and as I had occasion to learn later, she was obeyed." [She went on to ask me about Finland and would she like it there.][13]

But back to a perhaps not totally heart broken McGuinness. He did see Inez briefly when he returned after six months at sea but 'it ended badly, with her breaking down and prostrate with grief. Parting was the most difficult task of my existence.' Nomad went on a bender, quit the *Nem Wah* and then shipped out, as usual hauling coal to and from Shimonoseki in Japan to Keelung, to Formosa, Nagasaki and Yokohama – 'but always the tearful face of Inez haunted me like a spectre.' He claims he spent a brief period in Vancouver lumberjacking, 'but it was a dull, routine existence – hard work and bad whisky.' He returned to the Orient.

In Manila he heard rumblings about an Irish rebellion and decided to return home – via San Francisco. There he signed on the 'Yankee bark' *Annie M. Reed* bound for England and owned by none other than 'Frisco's Mayor 'Sunny Jim' Rolph (one of the most corrupt politicians even by California standards. He, of course, subsequently became Governor of California).

Nomad finally reached England after 103 days, having had his first trip through the Panama Canal – previously he had always gone round Cape Horn. But he was back. That was all that counted.

Notes.

1. McGuinness, *Nomad*, op. cit., p. 97.
2. ibid., p. 98.
3. ibid., p. 103.
4. ibid., p. 104.
5. ibid., p. 106.
6. ibid., pp. 104-105.
7. ibid., pp. 106-107.
8. Lilius, Aleko Eugene: *I sailed with Chinese Pirates*. J.W. Arrowsmith, London 1930, p. 57.
9. The book proved popular and reading his account of the female pirate Lai Choi San must give any reader of Sir Arthur Ransome pause for thought. Did Ransome know Lilius's book, or know of the legendary Chinese pirate who appears in it, and if so was the eponymous Missee Lee in Ransome's best seller, in part, modelled on Lai Choi San? (To be fair, Ransome, who had married Trotsky's sister Evgenia had actually been to China in 1925).
    Whatever Lilius's influence may have been on Ransome, his account was evidently a hit with Milton Caniff, the author of *Terry and the Pirates*, a popular comic strip of the 1930's, who used a glamourised version of Lai Choi San, The Dragon Lady as one of his main villains.
    Lilius's son Eric Lilius, says his father tried, unsuccessfully, to sue the publishers of the comic strip for breach of copyright. (For more brief information on pirates of the Indian Ocean where Nomad spent several years, *see* Appendix II).
10. McGuinness, *Nomad*, op. cit., pp. 109-111.
11. *see* Cordingly, David: *Under the Black Flag*. Little, Brown and Co., London 1995.
12. McGuinness, *Nomad*, op. cit., pp. 113-115.
13. Lilius, op. cit., p. 38.

Chapter 4
Raids, Rescues and The Flying Column
Derry & Donegal 1920-22

Things were hot that July of 1920 when the sailor of fortune returned to his native city. The RIC were enforcing a curfew. Sectarian fighting was endemic with heavily armed Protestant Loyalists engaged in nightly sniping at their Catholic neighbours. The Catholics fought back of course, but they were frequently outgunned. The Loyalists were allowed to have weapons, Catholics were not. Additionally, there was open collusion between the British Army, particularly the Dorsetshire Regiment and the Loyalists whom they supplied with an assortment of weaponry. Older IRA men like Patrick Hegarty, Johnnie Fox[1] and Donal McDermott had been arrested and the unit was in disarray. Younger men were needed.[2] Nomad soon became the leader of a small group of IRA men – Dom Doherty, Johnnie 'Lip' Kennedy, Tommy McGlinchey, Pat Moore, and George McCallion and a very young Neil Gillespie, but they were seriously outnumbered and short of trained men and weapons.

Ironically, in his two memoirs Nomad only mentions his father, a ship's captain who skippered the coal boat the *Carricklee* twice. This despite the fact that even before Nomad had arrived back in Derry one of the main suppliers of small arms to the Republicans in the Maiden City was a Norwegian Oscar Norby[3] who sailed with Nomad's father on the *Carricklee*. Nomad chose to indicate that his father knew nothing of this and that he had personally recruited Oscar Norby after his return in 1920.

In Belfast sectarian pogroms against the Catholic ghettos were the order of the day. Catholics were intimidated out of their jobs, burnt out of their homes or slaughtered, like the ill-fated McMahon family, by police death squads and Loyalist paramilitaries and UVF men.[4]

In Derry City, where Catholics outnumbered Loyalists, their position was initially less dangerous, but, because of Unionist gerrymandering, Catholics had no say in the running of the city.

Consequently, unemployment was endemic in the Catholic slum areas of the Bogside and Brandywell, Catholics could not legally bear arms and were virtually excluded from their own city.

In July of 1920 when McGuinness returned, the city was like a town on the Western Front. Businesses were closed and shops boarded up to prevent looting and sniping. Bodies of those shot dead by snipers or by the British 'peace-keeping' soldiers who regularly machine-gunned the streets during curfew hours, often lay in the streets for days with relatives being too afraid to dash out and drag the corpses back into the little terraced houses. Serious trouble had finally reached Derry on June 18th, 1920. On that night members of the Dorset Regiment handed out rifles to 'some 20 Orangemen' who began firing down Fountain Street and Albert Street into Bishop Street and Long Tower Street, the Nationalist quarter.[5]

A man called John McVeigh was killed. So was John Farren and a man called Mallet who was due to travel to the USA the next week. Led by an ex-Army sergeant, the Orangemen continued to pour fire all round. A Mr Price who was staying at the Diamond Hotel was the next to die, followed by a Mr McLaughlin.

The shooting continued for 3 hours, with the RIC having abandoned the town centre to the Orange mobs while the British soldiers stood by. On that night five Catholic Nationalists were killed and 24 injured.

On the next Monday the Orange mobs were out again, this time sniping from Walker's monument, Carlisle Road, John Street and the Protestant Cathedral, the Orange Hall and the Masonic Hall in Magazine Street.

Paddy Shiels, who later that week was to be appointed Derry O/C, rounded up 12 volunteers. Armed with three rifles and nine pistols they marched up Waterloo Street and cleared the Orangemen from the Diamond where they had taken up positions. An Orange sniper on Walker's Monument was 'taken out'. But while the Orangemen had the upper hand no troops were sent to protect the populace until the IRA had assumed a temporary dominance when the Queen's Regiment were sent up from Belfast in response to Unionist calls for martial law.

IRA explosives at the time were mostly home made, using resin, oatmeal, sugar and potassium chlorate. By now bombs had been prepared and there were plans to blow up the bridge over the Foyle, thus cutting the West Bank of Derry off from the Loyalist Waterside, but on June 24th, 1920, a curfew was imposed on Derry for the first time ever. Only British soldiers and the RIC were allowed on the streets after 10.30 p.m. The bridge got a reprieve, which it has enjoyed to this day.

The populace responded to the curfew. Each night local youths tied strong thin black rope across streets where they knew the soldiers would patrol. Broken glass and barbed wire was used to slow down the armoured cars and the lids of the manholes and sewers were taken up. The troops were reduced to foot patrols in the dark and were frequently attacked.

But the curfew did little to cool the sectarian fighting around the Protestant Fountain quarter.

Jim McDermott in his excellent book *Northern Divisions* gives the following report on the 'dark days in Derry from April to June in 1920':

> "As a result of the success of Derry nationalists in the 1920 local elections the tension in the city spilled over into riots. The RUC used considerable force to quell these riots and both RIC and British troops bayonet charged and fired into the Catholic crowds. The IRA returned fire, killing the local head of the Special Branch. In retaliation the UVF fired from Derry's Walls into the Bogside, and UVF patrols set up road blocks on the only bridge across the River Foyle. The RIC did not try to stop them, although the British troops intervened after a few days and restored order. These disturbances were not nearly so serious as the outbreak of violence in Derry in June 1920. Between the 16th and 23rd June, eight Catholics and four Protestants were killed in savage street fighting. Jack McNally described the IRA as engaging with the British troops during this period.
>
>> "The Derry City Unit of the IRA fought back to protect the Catholics and their properties and they were attacked by the RIC. Peadar O'Donnell, who was in charge of the Republican forces in Donegal, brought his men into Derry [City] and a fierce battle raged between them and the RIC and British Army units, which had been drafted into Derry."
>
> In fact the battle raged far more between the resurgent UVF and IRA, with the British Army and RIC largely keeping out of the way. A Belfast solicitor, J.P. O'Kane, asserted this pogrom was started deliberately. 'In June, 1920 two emissaries of the Ulster combination left the Kildare Street Club in Dawson Street to start the pogrom in Derry. One of, them, a military officer, was identified on the streets of Derry fighting beside the pogromists.'

The violence in Derry might have been spontaneous but it was very intense. On June 19 loyalists took positions on Derry's walls and fired into the Catholic districts. Four Catholics and a Protestant were killed. Over the next few days UVF patrols took over the city centre and the Foyle bridge. The Belfast Telegraph recorded that: 'The nationalist party did not seem to be as well provided with arms as their opponents but maintained a rigorous defence.' The IRA dug in on the grounds of St. Columbs College and were joined by local ex-servicemen from the area. The conflict was bitter and sectarian. Two Protestants were killed. A workman named Dobbin was shot and his body dumped in the Foyle, but far more significant from a Unionist viewpoint was the killing of Howard Mackay, the son of the Governor of the Apprentice Boys."[6]

Bishop Street had become the cockpit of the fighting. Protestants from the Fountain area poured relentless fusillades of shots across at their Catholic neighbours. McGuinness soon appointed himself in charge of a few Republican vigilantes and took over a nearby abandoned house to, in his words, "protect the Nationalist community".

In his book the sailor of fortune laconically and, some might say, callously describes a particular incident in this internecine conflict:

"A Catholic labourer, with whom I was acquainted, tried to cross the street during a lull. Immediately he was picked off by an Orange sniper. His body lay in the middle of the roadway, a stream of blood running from the hole in his chest.

Generally speaking women-folk were spared from the fire, although some suffered injuries trying to defend their men from murder.

One old hag, who lived close by, repeatedly walked out of her house screaming vile and blasphemous epithets at the Pope and Catholics in general. We paid no attention to her at first – until she hobbled over to the body of the murdered workman. But, dipping handkerchiefs into the pool of blood which surrounded him, she shrieked with ghoulish glee. Three times, she returned for more blood, kicking and abusing the corpse and reviling the Pope. At last, we trained our rifles on her, warning her off; but she misjudged her immunity and, cursing the mothers who bore us, insisted that we were the brood of whores and bitches.

'Let's draw lots and shoot her. That isn't a woman – it's a devil!' I said to my companions.

We drew and the task fell to me. As a warning to her I fired several random shots. My companions did likewise. Then, during a lull, she once more strode into the thoroughfare carrying white strips which, apparently, she was distributing amongst her neighbours as souvenirs of papist blood.

Just as she bent down to dip her rags in the red pool, I fired – so did the others, forgetting the lottery in their anger. The hag spun round and fell beside the body she was desecrating.

Under a white flag, her friends ventured forth and pulled the corpse out of the street. When the siege ended, however, the walls of the city were plastered with filthy epithets concerning Catholics. Some of these were printed in the blood of the victims."[7]

It is true that Nomad often exaggerated but contemporary accounts of the sectarian riots in Derry at this time seem to confirm this gruesome tale.

Shortly after the June riots the British Army formally took over in Derry. Tanks and armoured cars rumbled through the streets and the Army and police openly sided with the Loyalists, handing out yet more guns and ammunition. Two full British regiments occupied the little streets of the ghettos of the City of the Oaks. Word came up from Dublin from Michael Collins himself. Flying Columns were to be set up in the hills of Tyrconnell.

The First Flying Column in Donegal was led by Peadar O'Donnell and consisted of O'Donnell and 13 volunteers.[8]

Nomad was appointed the O/C of the Second Donegal Flying Column. The Column went on a series of route marches to South-West Donegal.

Guns and munitions were scarce for the Republicans so Nomad and the other Volunteers, including the faithful Dominic Doherty, Johnny 'Lip' Kennedy, Tommy McGlinchy, Pat Moore, Ginger Callan and Hughie Martin, set about a series of 'expropriations'. British banks in Glenties, Ardara and Mount Charles were raided for funds. Weapons were captured from ambushed British Tommies and the hated Black and Tans. At night the Column would camp in the remote Poisoned Glen up by Bunbeg or in the hills around Fintown. Frequently, they were protected by the dispossessed Irish peasantry who eked out a bare existence in the hills by manufacturing poitín (moonshine whiskey).

The Column's tactics were similar to those utilised in the South West by freedom fighters like Tom Barry and Dan Breen. An ambush on a British patrol and then an escape through the bogs where the British, without local knowledge, dare not follow. Hit and run, the traditional tactics of a small guerrilla force. Though outgunned and outmanned, they were able to inflict serious casualties on the British troops who were more at home in the streets of Birmingham or Manchester than the beautiful hills of Donegal.

It was while operating around Glenties, Ardara, Mount Charles, Rossbeg, Fintown and the Poisoned Glen that Nomad took time to try and formulate his political thinking, always rather flexible and vague at the best of times.

Twelve years later in *Soldier of Fortune* he vouchsafed that:

> "The Irish soldier, gambling against long odds, is an idealist. The Irish politician is an opportunist, lacking the scruples of the warrior. I have little respect for the Irish politician at home, in America, or elsewhere. The souls of Pearse, McDonough, Plunkett, Mellowes, Connelly [sic], and McBride will never rest in peace until the goal of the poet and soldier is achieved.
>
> Poor Mick Collins! He was my friend and a brainy fighter who made a fool out of the men in Dublin Castle but he was out of his depths when he pitted his strength against the whirlpools of political trickery."[9]

Nomad went on to castigate the 'purple-coated dignitaries' of the Catholic church who excommunicated the IRA freedom fighters, but this must be contrasted with his usual *volte face* years later after the Spanish Civil War (*see* Chapter 10).

With regard to military matters, Nomad also claimed that his 'South African experiences proved valuable'. Describing an episode in the hills near the Poisoned Glen when the British Army were trying to round up the Column he describes the following action:

> "I estimated the distance [of the approaching British soldiers] at a thousand yards, and accordingly ordered the gun-sights fixed at that range. The boys were equipped with Lee-Enfields and Mausers, but I was afraid that an itching finger might press a trigger before the proper moment. Our retreat was well covered on the other side of the hill, and, moreover, no pursuers could catch us before we gained a haven in the glens. [...]
>
> Not until the rear sections [of the British] were abreast, however, did I give the order to fire. Then twenty rifles barked together, and, through my glasses I registered twelve hits. Not bad marksmanship for the Irish Army!"[10]

The engagement lasted four hours until, running out of ammunition, the Column retreated in good order through the bog to avoid getting surrounded.

Such raids and rural fighting continued in Donegal throughout 1920 and McGuinness and his men were 'out on the moss' for most of it. But then, in February 1921 word came to Nomad that he was wanted in Derry. A senior IRA Brigadier, Frank Carty, was in Derry jail under sentence of death.

Rescue of Frank Carty – February 21, 1921

Frank Carty had had a distinguished career in the armed struggle. He had been the Vice-Brigadier for the IRA in Sligo. Captured in April 1920, he had been lodged in Sligo jail. IRA Brigadier Pilkington had decided that Carty must be freed and had mobilised the entire battalion to effect a jail break. On June 13, IRA men, led by Pilkington himself, had scaled the 32 foot high weather-beaten stone walls of the prison, captured the guards and extracted the keys to the cells from a sleepy Governor Reid. The party had then sledgehammered their way out through the main gate and made good their escape under the noses of the British stationed a mere two hundred yards away at the military barracks. The operation had been a great success, but Carty's freedom was to be short-lived. He had commanded the local Flying Column successfully for five months until in November of 1920 his luck again ran out. He was surrounded by a group of Black and Tans in a house in Moylough, Tubbercurry, and captured after a fierce gunbattle in which he suffered a serious wrist injury.

Taken in chains north to the maximum security prison in Derry, he languished there in the prison hospital throughout the winter. He was charged with shooting two RIC men and faced the death penalty. Unlike Sligo, Derry jail was a medieval type fortress built on the side of a steep hill by the old city walls. No one had ever escaped from it since it was built in 1824. According to Mícheál MacUileagóid in his otherwise excellent book *From Fetters to Freedom*[11] the IRA were not strong in Derry in those days and there were no official plans to try and rescue Carty. That is, until Michael Collins contacted 'his old comrade Nomad McGuinness who rescued Carty singlehanded'. In fact it is extremely doubtful that Collins had ever met McGuinness previously, let alone been an old comrade. McGuinness' comrade and, when it came to the gun running, sponsor, was Liam Mellows, according to Desmond Greaves (*see* Chapters 5 & 6). McGuinness admits in his account that he had 'some local help' but modestly accepts that without him Carty would never have escaped.

Leaving the column in Donegal, McGuinness made his way back into his native city.

What follows is his account of the Carty escape, which has been taken up and repeated in shorthand by several sources. In essence, much of it appears to be true. There is little or no doubt that McGuinness was the 'main man' when it came to the escape, but others deserve credit too.

Although the fortress was regarded as escape proof, there were still ways to get messages and contraband in and out of the prison. Using an old contact, who ran the small tobacconist's shop in Bishop Street, opposite the main gate of the jail, he smuggled in a message to Carty by bribing a warder. First a message and then a hacksaw. Then the ubiquitous black soap, with which to deaden the sound of sawing and, mixed with cobwebs, to disguise the breaks in the bars. Carty was told to play up his injuries and get sent to the prison hospital block at the back of the jail yard abutting Harding Street.

The first attempt was to be made just before dawn on the morning of Saturday, February 12, 1921. In his book, Nomad describes the abortive attempt as follows.

> "The coil of rope, fastened with a steel hook to grip the top of the wall, was in readiness – also the silk ladder to bridge the gap between cell window and wall. [...]
>
> At four o'clock, I ascended the roof of an outhouse directly under the [forty foot] wall nearest to Carty's hospital cell. I coiled the rope carefully, taking care not to offer an exposed silhouette to any vigilant eye. The streets were lined with sandbag barricades and [British Army] machine-gun emplacements. Any moving shadow became an immediate target.
>
> Satisfied that all was clear, I heaved the rope. The hook missed the wall coping by a foot, and clattered down with a horrible din, echoes rumbling throughout the yards. Prepared for the worst, I cocked my gun and waited – one minute, five minutes, ten minutes. But nothing happened! Again I coiled the rope, measuring the distance carefully. This time my efforts were successful and the hook gripped the top of the parapet.
>
> Up the rope I scrambled, the silk ladder coiled around my waist. Then came a further misfortune. I had scarcely climbed ten

feet when a piece of old coping stone broke loose under my weight and the heavy stone tumbled down, missing me by a fraction of a foot."[12]

Again McGuinness waited, gun at the ready, prepared to shoot it out. But with dawn approaching, dispiritedly, he had to call it off. The Protestant section of town was no place for him to be found in when the sun came up. He retired to his 'safe house', but he did not give up. Long after McGuinness had retired, Frank Carty paced his hospital cell, ready for the signal to push the sawn-through bars aside. Only when dawn reddened the sky did he return dejectedly to his bed. The word was that he was to be court-martialled next Tuesday. It was a sure death sentence.

At lunch that Sunday, however, another message came in from Nomad. It was accompanied by a ball of fisherman's twine. And so it was that at 4.30 a.m., on the 15th of February 1921, the day he was to be taken before the British court-martial, Frank Carty again stared out through his prison bars, tensely awaiting the signal.

Outside McGuinness was laboriously clambering over the yard walls of the Protestant terrace houses in Harding Street. As the Guildhall clock chimed the half hour Carty heard Nomad's low whistle. Tying the end of the twine to the bars he lobbed the bundle up and over the wall. Two quick tugs – the 'all clear' signal – quickly reassured Carty and he tugged back. Below, Nomad was attaching the thin rope ladder to the twine and Carty was trying to haul it up and over the wall. Once more disaster struck, the ladder snagged on the coping. Wasting precious minutes, McGuinness freed the line and then tried again. Again the ladder snagged, this time catching on the serrated edge of the top of the wall.

But Nomad would not give up. Uncoiling the rope from around his waist, he attached it to the twine with a note for Carty. Shortly after the rope was firmly attached to the bars of his cell with Nomad pulling on it from outside the wall. Next came the difficult task for the giant Carty to ease his bulk through the small space that opened after he pushed aside the sawn-through bars. His injured wrist hindered him and for a time it appeared that he would be stuck half-in and half-out of the barred hospital window.

'Come on,' muttered McGuinness, straining on the rope to keep it taut enough for Carty to haul himself across the fifteen foot gap that separated the hospital window from the prison wall. Not daring to look down at the forty foot drop beneath him, Carty painfully crawled along the sagging rope. With desperate energy, he managed to haul himself up the last few feet and gain the top of the wall.

Seconds later, he had scrambled down the remains of the rope ladder and was clasping McGuinness's hand as they stood in the tiny backyard of Moore's house in Harding Street. Praying that they would not hear the booming of the cannon which would signal that the break had been discovered, they crept through the sleeping Orange alleys, made their way across Abercorn Street and headed for the Catholic ghetto. As they left, McGuinness' men sprinkled cayenne pepper behind them to put off the bloodhounds which he feared might pick up their scent.

Thrilling stuff, no doubt, but, alas, McGuinness is gilding the lily a bit here, and other authors have taken him at his word and repeated the story as 'fact'.

In reality the escape was organised from the start by the Derry IRA O/C Patrick Shiels. On January 30th, just after Carty's capture and incarceration, the Derry O/C ordered McGuinness, Dom Doherty and B. Doherty to report to 4 Chamberlain Street. There they found Shiels and four senior IRA officers, including Joe McKelvey from Belfast and Dick Barrett from Cork (both of whom were subsequently to be murdered by the Free State government while in custody on December 8, 1922). Shiels had originated the plan to rescue Carty and instructed Nomad and his comrades.[13]

It was Shiels who smuggled in the hacksaw blades and a ball of strong cord. The duplicate keys were obtained for a house in Harding Street which abutted the prison hospital building and was owned by the Heeney family who were on holiday at the time.

On the night of the failed attempt McGuinness and Dom Doherty and two other volunteers had met at John and Lizzie McLaughlin's[14] little house in Harding Street. They had with them some strong rope and oak rungs. As related by Nomad, the attempt had to be aborted when the hook failed to catch after numerous efforts. They had to come back four days later.

Shortly before the curfew hour they arrived at Heeney's in Harding Street, only to discover that they had forgotten the duplicate key. McGuinness had to smash the window, Dom Doherty squeezed in and let the rest of them in. They spent the next four hours crawling from one small Unionist back yard in Harding Street to another groping in the dark for the weighted cord which Carty was supposed to throw from the window where the bars had been cut. At last Doherty found it. The rope ladder was attached, and, as the four of them strained to hold the line taut, the fifteen stone Frank Carty, albeit wounded, crawled laboriously across the divide, forty foot above the grounds of the small prison cemetery.

When Carty landed down in the back yard beside them they embraced, in tears, made their way back over the backyard walls and holed up in Heeney's until curfew was over in the morning. Then they took Carty up Abercorn Road, across Bishop Street and Barrack Street and into Long Tower Street where other volunteers took him to his billet. The following night he was shipped out to Scotland on Nomad's father's coal boat, the *Carricklee*.[15]

Bill Kelly, who, years later, interviewed Carty, by then a successful officer in the Free State Army, about his 'saviour' recorded these contemporary opinions of McGuinness:

> "Charlie was a swashbuckler to the manner born. Slightly over medium height and sturdily built, he walked with a swagger, and, on shore, he invariably wore a black trench coat and a black trilby hat. It seemed as though it was his intention to display himself, to trail his coat, as it were, and provoke the RIC and Black-and-Tans into some action against him. A dangerous way to go about in these dangerous times. There was something about Charlie's dark features which, though pleasant looking, warned that he was not a man to be trifled with. In fact, he didn't know the meaning of fear."[16]

And so, two nights later, as the authorities continued to ransack Nationalist homes in Derry, the *Carricklee* sailed out the Foyle. As it did so, a row boat pulled out under cover of darkness and a rope ladder was thrown over the side. Up scrambled Frank Somers, aka Frank Carty. The elusive Mr. Hennessey rowed back to the shore alone. The next day the stowaway was being welcomed by the Republicans of Glasgow, where he was soon to begin lecturing and training the local contingent of the IRA. And Nomad was back on the streets of his native Derry.

THE SHOOTING OF SERGEANT HIGGINS

"Was the assassin respectably dressed?" asked the Derry City coroner John Tracey. "Very respectably," replied James Clarke who had been standing next to the late Sergeant Higgins (48) when, as District Inspector Chubb so picturesquely put it, he "was launched into eternity in the twinkling of an eye." This seemed to perplex the good coroner. It would apparently have made more sense to him if the IRA volunteer who had executed the Royal Irish Constable had been attired as befitted the lumpenproletariat. But then, Nomad McGuinness was always noted for his sartorial taste. According to Neil Gillespie the shooter was Nomad McGuinness.[17]

It was April 4, 1921, barely five weeks since the rescue of Carty and it had been a busy Friday evening for Nomad McGuinness who had approached the Sergeant outside St. Eugene's Cathedral and 'launched him into eternity' with three headshots from his Peter the Painter. The Catholic crowd who stood on the corner of Creggan Street had made no attempt to interfere. Although Sergeant Higgins was a Catholic – as indeed were some 80% of the RIC in 1920 – the average Catholic/Nationalist had little sympathy for the RIC who were, with justification, regarded as 'Quislings' who were repressing their own people at the bidding of their British masters.

McGuinness had pocketed his gun, strolled round the corner and disappeared into one of the little houses in William Street whose door had been left conveniently ajar. When he emerged a few moments later, he was wearing a priest's soutane. Sauntering down the street with two bombs in his pockets, he prepared for the night's next events. It was 8.30 p.m., and he was headed for the City electrical station, the billet of the King's Own Yorkshire Light Infantry. Before he could get there, the evening took a bizarre turn. A young RIC constable came running up and grabbed him by the arm as he turned the corner a few blocks from the scene of the shooting. As Nomad was about to go for his trusty painter, the breathless constable blurted out "you've got to come quick, Father, the Sergeant's been shot. He's got to get the last rites."

Given that he'd just pumped three bullets into Sergeant Higgins' brain – part of which was now strewn on the pavement – Nomad probably felt that any further 'assistance' that he might give would be at best cosmetic. Apart from anything else, Nomad was at that time a professed pagan and pagans didn't go in much for the Last Rites of the Holy and Apostolic Church, but, *noblesse oblige*. As the cops pushed the gawking crowd of bystanders back, the ersatz priest knelt over the dead Sergeant.

McGuinness blessed himself, the dead Sergeant and then the crowd. "I'm sorry, I have to go, another mission of mercy." Checking that the grenades were safely stowed in the inside pockets of his cassock, he slipped away as a stretcher was arriving for the ex-RIC man.

Fifteen minutes later, having met with his small team of volunteers, he was outside the British Army base. Grenades were hurled over the wall, seriously wounding privates Albert Todd and Cecil Cairns along with Constable McLaughlin. As Nomad faded into the night and the Crown forces came running out of the base, firing wildly, McGuinness's men opened up, cutting down another soldier and critically wounding Constable Michael Kenny. As the smoke cleared, it was obvious to the Nationalist cognoscenti of the Maiden City that 'Mr. Hennessey' was back in town. But not for long. McGuinness headed back to Donegal to take over the Column again, organising raids and ambushes and night attacks on British Army barracks at Lettermacaward, Ardara, and as far away as Pettigo. It was business as usual for the sailor of fortune. And then a message from Dublin. Frank Carty had again managed to get himself arrested during a police raid in the East End of Glasgow. The message was terse and to the point.

> "I want you to investigate this problem, and if there is any way of effecting a rescue, I want you to try, and am confident of your ability to succeed.
> Regards,
> (Signed) MICHAEL COLLINS"[18]

The next night the trusty *Carricklee* had another stowaway who sat drinking Swedish Schnapps with Oscar Norby. Below decks were six armed men, all part of McGuinness's team. The new plan which Nomad had concocted for the release of Carty was more to his nautical liking, involving as it did, nothing less than piracy on the high seas.

Contacts had informed McGuinness of the identity of the vessel which would be used to transport Carty back to Ireland. Confident of some assistance from a couple of Republican sympathisers amongst the crew members, he planned for he and his men to board the vessel. He had, as he put it, "sufficient medical dope to paralyse the whole British Army". The steward was to slip this in the sentries' tea, and, once afloat, McGuinness's men would seize the skipper and hi-jack the ship which Captain McGuinness would then sail to Inishowen Head on the Derry-Donegal border.

But it was not to be. When McGuinness appeared at Sinn Fein HQ in Glasgow and tried to put his plan to the Glaswegian IRA Commander, an eccentric priest named Father McRory, the plan was, as he put it, "scotched". There were many Republicans in Glasgow who were irked by their inability to strike a blow for Irish freedom.

Father McRory was one of them, and he was steeped in Irish history. Three of his particular heroes were Allen, Larkin and O'Brien, the Manchester Martyrs who had been hanged on November 23, 1867, after the rescue of two Fenian prisoners, Tom Kelly and Captain Tim Deasy.

Some thirty men had surrounded the prison van taking the Fenian prisoners to jail, smashing the van and, in the process, shooting dead a Sergeant Brett.[19] The prisoners had escaped but three men had been captured and executed, to take their places in the Republican pantheon "high upon a gallows tree". What Irishmen in England had done over a half century before could be repeated in staunchly Republican Glasgow, argued the priestly Commander.

Wisely fearing disaster, McGuinness and his men packed up and left the city that night. The next day, on the afternoon of the 4th of May, the prison van carrying Somers-Carty left the courthouse from the Drygate entrance to the jail when a group of armed men attacked the van from all sides. Shooting broke out and Inspector Johnson was shot through the heart. But a stray shot jammed the Black Maria's lock and the attempt failed. Carty remained a prisoner. In two minutes, the gun battle was over and the attackers had dispersed. McGuinness was later to claim that "his plan would have worked, but that those idiots in Glasgow were incompetent".[20]

In Derry Shiels had been appointed Divisional Intelligence Officer, and Charlie Mawhinney was the new Derry O/C.

Arrests in Glasgow had turned up the name of the elusive 'Hennessey' along with his beloved black trilby hat. Nomad was later to recount that after the treaty at least six people were arrested, including a cousin of his and his IRA aide-de-camp Owen Callan. All had been accused of being the notorious 'Hennessey'. But for the time being, Derry wasn't safe and it was back to the bogs of Donegal. Within a month, he and his men had raided and attacked the British barracks at Glenties.

Writing of his time in the Donegal hills, McGuinness was to display his 'working class principles'. Quoting Dean Swift, he wrote approvingly: "Ireland has a nobility, but you'll find it in the hovels..." McGuinness then went on to contrast the Gaelic speaking people of the Donegal mountains with the urban folk of the cities:

"Personally, I am not an admirer of the citizen of the garrisoned Dublin, Limerick, Cork or Wexford. There is a marked cleavage in their mien and mutual opinions. A mountain man is a proud fellow, possessing spine and spirit; a fighter who never flinches under heavy fire. I like the mountain lads, too – quick, taciturn and ever dependable. Their women are dark-eyed and dark-haired, more reticent than the blue-eyed, fair girls of the milder counties. They are lithe, strong and solid, the equal of their men in tilling the stingy soil and caring for the pigs and cows.

Living conditions are poor, but they make the best of a tough existence. The sacrifices of the mountain women during the war were heroic. When we were on the run, seeking asylum from the military, they surrendered their beds to tired Republican soldiers and shivered through the long night in the barn, if they were fortunate enough to have a cow or a donkey.

Often they dashed miles through dangerous bog and over lonesome mountain trails, seeking medical aid for the wounded, or carrying important dispatches to commandants. Frequently they were part of the volunteer network of espionage which made the Sinn Fein intelligence so effective in frustrating British surprise attacks."

"Patriotism and economics are inseparably companions. […] Patriotism is strongly influenced by the colour of ink on the ledgers."[21]

That was how McGuinness put it and this was his justification for the relentless series of raids on British owned banks. The wealthy soon learned that their ill-gotten gains would not be safe in an Irish owned bank. "Money made in Ireland, must stay in Ireland," that was the rationale at least.

But Nomad's luck was shortly to run out. In June of 1921, he and five of his men hit the bank in Ardara. The raid was a success, but, on their way back to their dugouts near Rossbeg, they were ambushed by a large party of Black and Tans. In the ensuing gunfight, McGuinness and his second in command Ginger Callan held off the Tans and enabled the other four members of the column to make their getaway but soon the position of the two men was dire. Chased across the bog by wildly firing Tans, they made for the sand dunes where they hoped to find some cover.

Just before they reached the beach, Nomad was hit on the hip. An inch higher and it would have gone through his left lung, the doctor was later to say. Callan dragged him into the dunes where Nomad bade him goodbye, handing over the dispatches and the money taken from the bank raid, with instructions to get them to Hughie Martin, the adjutant. (Interestingly, Brady says that it was Martin who was with Nomad and who he urged to leave and not Ginger Callan. Nomad however should be the best evidence on this.)

Cradling his carbine, McGuinness prepared to sell his life dearly. He held the pursuing Tans off for half an hour while Callan got away but then another bullet tore through his hand, putting him out of action. It should be noted, that in this action Nomad's courage has never been questioned. His men later attested to his bravery which enabled them to get away. He may have had many faults, but no one could accuse Nomad of being a coward. (And hope to live.)

Cautiously the Tans approached the sand-pit. McGuinness lay there, barely consciously and bleeding "like a stuck pig". Several of the RIC men were for shooting Nomad on the spot, but a soldier intervened and he was dragged back to the dugout, which the soldiers blew up by tossing Mills bombs into the shelter. Next the injured Derryman was given the "third degree" by his interrogators according to the local papers. McGuinness says that although he said nothing all the time he was seething. It was obvious, to him at least, that someone had informed. He also believed that the informer was 'a yellowback called Kelly who was an atheist who lived locally with a distinguished local doctor'.

After three days in Glenties police station with little or no medical treatment, McGuinness was transported by lorry to Donegal barracks. It was there that he learned, through the Sinn Fein intelligence network, the identity of the man who had betrayed the column. "A certain Mr. Kelly," as Nomad was to put it. At once word was sent to Hughie Martin, the new O/C of the column. Kelly was to be arrested, tried and executed.[22] But McGuinness was on the move again, first to the notorious Castle of Drumboe (soon to be the scene of an infamous murder of four Republicans, Daly, Larkin, Enright and O'Sullivan by the new 'Free State' government – March 14, 1923) and then to the British army barracks at Ebrington on the Waterside of Derry. There he was accused of the murder of six soldiers during the shoot-out in the dunes.[23] Luckily for him his alias 'Hennessey' still confused the authorities.

Ebrington barracks was then a vast military institution, consisting of a prison with some thirty Republicans housed there, long rows of army barracks, magazines, a hospital and stables. On one side stretched the parade grounds where the British soldiers drilled daily. McGuinness was housed in a large steel shed which abutted the prison. One wall was comprised of the steel plates bolted to the ground. Even if he managed to get out of the iron shed, there were guards all around and three high walls to be crossed before he could get out.

The first step, naturally, for Nomad, was to get escape material smuggled in. "A very dear girlfriend in Derry" arrived shortly on a visit. She was careful to present the warder with a clandestine bottle of whiskey and a bottle of wine. In return, she was able to present "dear Charlie" with a long oblong cake for his birthday. After all, sure wasn't it probably his last. After his wound had healed he'd be off to the firing squad. It was a case of the old cliché actually being true. Within the cake were concealed three hacksaw blades, a wood-saw blade and a steel jemmy. (Nomad may have been a ladies' man, but rather than a 'very dear girlfriend' smuggling the contraband in, it was brought by two *Cumann mBan* stalwarts, Ms. McGuinness (no relation) and Ms. Doherty.)

Nomad, still suffering from his wounds, enlisted the assistance of another prisoner, Paddy Reilly, whom he had known from his days in the Flying Column. Painstakingly, they took it in turns to saw away at the steel plates where they joined the wooden plates which bolted them to the ground. With a sentry patrolling outside day and night, the least scraping sound would have been overheard. Accordingly, each night, the sentries were serenaded by Nomad's fellow prisoners with a 'Republican musicale' consisting of militant nationalist and Republican songs, while McGuinness and Reilly scraped cautiously away, each night taking care to fill in the cracks with soap and cover them with dust. By the night of July 2, 1921, all was ready and word was smuggled out for a covering party to be outside the perimeter walls at midnight the next evening.

By 11.30 p.m., all was set. The guard who was due to go off duty at midnight had been "fortified" with whiskey "from an admirer", and as he exchanged drunken thoughts with his relief, the two IRA men, aided and abetted by the other prisoners, peeled back one sheet of steel which had been severed from the ground and burrowed underneath, scraping the loose earth behind them. Within a minute they were out and crept to an open wash-place which had a one foot deep alcove in which they could secrete themselves until after the relief guard had made his first round.

The first wall was a daunting 18 feet in height and had broken glass and barbed wire on top of it. Nomad had made his escape rope from a torn strip of blanket and had a noose fashioned at the top of it. Atop of Reilly's shoulders Nomad hooked the noose on one of the iron bars which supported the barbed wire and began to climb. Again, a prison bar failed him and he came tumbling down. He and Reilly crawled back to the parlous safety of the wash place as the guard made his rounds. As soon as he had passed, the two men were back at the wall. This time an iron bar held and, cat-like, the ex-mariner scrambled aloft, in the process cutting himself badly on the barbed wire.

Hurriedly, he threw the rope down to Reilly. The heavier man tried three times, desperately to make it up the rope. Once he made the top but got caught in the wire and could not clear the spikes. Finally, he gave up. 'Go it alone, Charlie, and good luck', as he slid down and abandoned the attempt. 'Good-bye, mucker,' whispered Nomad. "If you hear shooting you'll know I didn't make it."[24]

On his own once more, McGuinness lost no time in crawling along the wall until he came to a tall tree which abutted the far side. Using this he made his way onto the roof of one of the military garages. He could see two guards nearby by the light of their cigarettes and, spotting a skylight open, he slipped inside and onto the top of an armoured car.

Waiting for the sentries to move on he took stock of his position. He had a long way to go yet and the grounds were crawling with sentries. Slipping out of the garage door and creeping along in the shadows, Nomad encountered a second wall. This proved easier to surmount; and, crawling along the top of it, he found himself on the stables' roof. There while waiting for another sentry to pass he tried to staunch some of the blood which poured from the freshly opened wounds on his hands and hip. There was no turning back.

Sliding down a drain pipe, he set about the long arduous crawl across the parade ground. McGuinness was later to recount that "how long it took me to wriggle across the open ground, I do not know, but I died a hundred times on that long journey." At last he reached the perimeter wall. It was fourteen feet high and had no crevices, cracks or iron bars to offer assistance. As he lay in the grass and contemplated failure, his hand touched a long greasy pole which had been left near the base of the wall. To most people, it would have proved of little help, but to a man who was used to climbing the topgallants in a gale on a vessel rounding Cape Horn, it proved no great obstacle, wounds or no wounds. Leaning the slippery pole against the wall at a forty-five degree angle, Charlie shimmied up it and over the wall.

As he landed on the hard earth in his bare feet – he had lost his shoes at one of the first walls – the full enormity of his task sank in. He heard the Guildhall clock chiming four a.m. It had taken him four hours to escape the prison. Any IRA volunteers who might have been there to assist him had long since left. With the curfew it was exceedingly dangerous to be out at night. Worse still, he wasn't even in his native Derry City. Ebrington barracks was situated across the River Foyle, surrounded by hostile loyalist country. The only bridge across the river was heavily patrolled.

Still losing blood, he crawled down to the riverside and hid underneath a string of railway wagons. As dawn was preparing to break, he edged himself into the bitterly cold water and swam towards a small rowboat, anchored some hundred yards from the shore. Once in the rowboat, he cautiously paddled across the Foyle, arriving at a wharf where several steamers were moored. Abandoning the boat, he quickly made for a small dockside hotel, owned by one of his relatives. But before he could make it, he heard the echoes of hoof-beats. It was an RIC patrol. Hiding in a doorway as they passed, McGuinness weighed his chances and decided to return to the dockside.

Boarding a steamer, he went in search of fresh clothing, bandages and water. In his words, he was a "desperate spectacle, with bare, bleeding feet and half-naked body." Fully prepared to attempt to overpower the first person he encountered, Charlie's luck finally turned. Breaking into a cabin he discovered a long lost uncle whom he hadn't seen since childhood. Blood proved thicker than water.

Later that morning he was safely ensconced in one of the safest billets in Derry – right in the heart of the Unionist Fountain district. Nomad had a friend who lived there, a man who no one but Charlie knew was a Republican sympathiser. It was there that Frank Carty had been hidden the previous year. Now McGuinness himself was in hiding until the hue and cry died down. Four days later, as the authorities continued to ransack the City and surrounding villages and as the prisoners in Ebrington were being put in handcuffs and leg-irons, 'Father' McGuinness, clad in priestly vestments, was in a horse drawn carriage and heading for the hills of Donegal. He was, he claimed, "itching to get back to his column and step up the action." Once more, fate intervened.

What Nomad refers to as "an unwelcome armistice"[25] was called. Pending further negotiations the Column was to be stood down. Once more Collins wrote to McGuinness. "Come to Dublin at once. Full details on your arrival at Army Headquarters." Leaving Hughie Martin in charge,[26] and armed, as always, with his revolver, Nomad took the train South. He was about, did he but know it, to embark on some of the most hazardous missions of his adventurous life, missions which would inscribe his name in the Republican annals. The sailor of fortune was about to go in for gun-running on a grand scale.

Notes.

1. Nomad and many other Derry men did time during the 'recrudescence of sanguinary disorders' in the North-West of Ireland in what is still euphemistically referred to as 'The Troubles', but few Derry men were incarcerated in more penal institutions than Johnnie Fox. He was interned in Frongoch, Ballykinlar, Newbridge, Derry Jail, Victoria military barracks in Belfast, Richmond military barracks in Dublin, Lewes Jail and finally Wormwood Scrubs.
2. One such was Charles Mawhinney, of 33 Westland, Derry City. A Protestant IRA man who taught engineering at Magee College and Derry Technical College. Before being interned he was the C/O of the Derry IRA unit who convened a Sperrin Mountain training camp. Arrested in the 'swoop' on the Erin Hall, while interned on the Argenta he became the ship's O/C. He was transferred to Derry jail and subsequently promised a position with the Department of Agriculture if he agreed to leave for the Free State and renounce the IRA. He refused, and, despite being in bad health saw internment through until being released on December 15, 1924. He subsequently married the famous Republican nurse Linda Kearns.
3. *See* Liam A. Brady's series of articles in the *Derry Journal*, May-June 1953.
4. Owen McMahon, a well-known Belfast City publican and Nationalist along with three of his sons and a young barman he employed were all brutally murdered in the McMahon's Kinnaird Terrace house off the Antrim Road on the night of March 24, 1922. Needless to say, no one was ever arrested for their murders. This was because their killers were a police murder gang led by the infamous District Inspector J.W. Nixon. Nixon went on to become a Unionist Member of Parliament in Stormont. In 1934 when McGuinness published his first book *Nomad*, he mentioned the McMahon murders, stating (p. 118):

> "The wiping out of the McMahon family of Belfast, father and seven sons who were in no way affiliated with the I.R.A., will for ever remain as a stain on the well-spattered escutcheons of Ulster. One man who has since been elevated to parliamentary honours was charged with the order of execution of the McMahons and is luckier than he knows to be alive to-day..."

(Nomad was alluding to a plan by Michael Collins to have the 'Butcher' of the McMahons executed which fell through because Collins died at Beal na Bleath before it could be put into operation.)

Nixon immediately sued the London publishers Methuen & Co., asserting that this was a clear reference to himself. McGuinness by this time (1935) was in Russia and unreachable and so the spineless Methuen paid the blood-stained Nixon £1,250. Nixon continued in the Stormont parliament for many years despite orthodox Unionist disquiet because he knew where 'too many bodies were buried.' His last 'prodigy' in his declining years, was a young 'firebrand evangelist' named Ian Paisley. More information on Nixon, the McMahon murders and the pogroms in Belfast is available in McKenna, G.B. (Thomas Donaldson ed.): *Facts & Figures. The Belfast Pogroms 1920-22.* Donaldson Archives, Belfast 1997. *See* also McDermott, Jim: *Northern Divisions*. Beyond the Pale, Belfast 2001.

Nixon has gone down in the Belfast Republican folklore as the leader of the murder gang during the Belfast pogroms, and he was a sectarian killer, but he was only the No. 2 in the 'Cromwell Clubs', a front for the RIC/RUC murder gang. The leader was District Inspector Richard Dale Winnett Harrison from Kilkenny. In 1920 he was an officer in charge of the detective office in Belfast, from where he ran the murder gangs. Harrison and Nixon were to have a falling out, when Nixon wanted to continue as a popular Unionist rabble-rouser and Harrison was opting for retirement and respectability - he was appointed City commissioner. Harrison lived until the age of 99 not dying until 22 April 1982 at his house on the Upper Malone Road.

5. Liam Brady, *Derry Journal*, 13.05.1953. The Derry defenders included Alfie and Pat McCallion, Seamus McCann, William Cullen and Frank Shiels.
6. McDermott, op. cit., pp. 29-30.
7. McGuinness, *Nomad*, op. cit., pp. 119-120. The 'blasphemous old hag' was Margaret Mills of Bishop Street, shot June 23rd 1920. To be fair, her family, years later vehemently denied this, her grandson, who wasn't alive when his granny died, claiming that she was loved by 'Catholics and Protestants alike'.
8. Liam Brady, *Derry Journal*, 24.05.1953.
9. McGuinness, *Nomad*, op. cit., p. 121.

10. ibid., p. 124.
11. MacUileagóid, Mícheál: *From Fetters To Freedom. The Inside Story of Irish Jailbreaks*. Sásta, Belfast 1996, pp. 81-83.
12. McGuinness, *Nomad*, op. cit., pp. 129-130.
13. Copy of Derry IRA letter, Paddy Shiels to the Dublin Government 1924. In the author's possession.
14. Lizzie McLaughlin was a teacher and one of six women teachers who were dismissed for being in the *Cumann na mBan* and refusing to take an oath of loyalty to the Crown. She subsequently married a Colonel McNally of the Irish Army.
15. Liam Brady, *Derry Journal*, 22.05.1953.
16. Kelly, Bill (ed.): *Sworn to be Free. The complete Book of IRA Jailbreaks 1918-1921*. Anvil Books, Tralee 1971, p. 122
17. Neil Gillespie in: Uinseann MacEoin: *Survivors*. Argenta Press, Dublin 1980, p. 162.
18. McGuinness, *Nomad*, op. cit., p. 137.
19. Official government reports of the time give some idea of the priorities which exercised the Manchester constabulary in those days. The police superintendent had telegraphed the Earl of Mayo the following account of the 'outrage'.
"Prisoners rescued, van horses shot, three prisoners who fired revolvers in custody."
Almost as an afterthought he had added: "One sergeant shot through the head, dead; another officer shot through the thigh and a civilian in the foot."
20. McGuinness, *Nomad*, op. cit., pp 137-140.
Here follows a fuller account of the Glasgow 'Smashing of the Van' from the local Glasgow pro-government paper – as may be easily discerned:

> ...Glasgow Scotland...1921
> "Gunfire ran out in the midday air. Children screamed and ducked for cover as the van's windscreen erupted..."
> The children making their way home from school for lunch. That warm May day would be one they would never forget. They might have noticed the men hanging around the walls of Duke Street Prison in Glasgow. They may even have detected an air of expectancy as those men anxiously watched the junction of Drygate with High Street, their hats pulled low, their hands stuffed into jacket pockets. Those children may also have noticed the sudden increase of tension as the Black Maria swung round the corner. But they would not have known what was

about to happen. For there below the section of the prison which housed the gallows, murder was about to be committed.

There were two prisoners in the rear of the police van that day, Wednesday May 4, 1921. They were being transported from the Central Police Court in St. Andrews Square to the dark and forbidding jail at the top of High Street. One of the men was a non-entity charged with indecent assault. But the other was infinitely more dangerous. He was Frank J. Carty, alias Somers – and he was a commandant in the Sligo branch of the Irish Republican Army, wanted in Ireland for theft and jailbreaking. It was his presence which made the trip so dangerous. The armed police officers inside the van fully expected his comrades to stage an escape.

Inspector Robert Johnston was in charge of the small force, and he was perched at the edge of the cab, his foot resting on the running board. Beside him were Detective Sergeant George Stirton and Detective Constable Murdoch McDonald. Two other officers guarded the men in separate compartments of the rear. Constable Thomas Ross swung the van into Drygate, flanked on one side by the Corporation Water Pumping Station and on the other by the steep prison walls. It was 12.10 pm. It was time. The three groups of men rushed out from their hiding places, surrounding the van, their guns exploding in the still mid-day air. The children screamed and ducked as the van's windshield erupted. Bullets dug themselves into the vehicle's sides and pierced the radiator with a sharp hiss of steam. Inspector Johnston tumbled from his seat, part of his skull torn off by a bullet. He tried to stand once before collapsing over the tram lines. This time he did not get up.

DS Stirton was the first to move, throwing himself from the van, his own gun out, blasting at the ambushers as he stood over the inspector's body. He was soon joined by DC McDonald, also firing his pistol, while the unarmed driver was struggling with the attackers nearest him. Meanwhile, Carty's would be emancipators were having trouble with the van's heavy rear doors. The lock would not give and they resorted to angrily firing at it in an attempt to break it. But the lock held, although the bullets bounced around the interior of the van, almost killing the man they had come to save.

DS Stirton and DC McDonald were still engaged in the fierce gunfight, while PC Ross dodged bullets and tried to get the van started again. He managed to get the engine going and steered the vehicle towards Cathedral Square. DC Stirton and DC

McDonald followed, still firing. A bullet ripped into the sergeant's wrist and he dropped his gun but continued to fight with his good arm. Finally the attackers realised their mission had failed. They began to pull back, knowing the gun battle would have alerted the prison. They split up, some making off along Rotten Row, others down the Drygate and into Cathedral Square.

An ex-nurse rushed to DS Stirton to help him but he said, "Don't mind me anymore, missus. Go and help my chum."

The woman knelt beside Inspector Johnston, who was sprawled on the ground, blood forming in a pool and flooding the tram line beneath him. With one look she knew there was nothing anyone could do.

DS Stirton set off at a run after some of the men but he had lost too much blood to pursue them any distance. The gunmen, meanwhile, had thrust their weapons back into their pockets and calmly meted into the crowds in Cathedral Square.

Constable Ross finally made it to the safety of the prison yard. When the rear door was examined, it was found the lock had jammed and it took the combined efforts of a number of big strong policemen to force it open. DS Stirton staggered into the prison behind the van, finally collapsed when the gates were swung shut. DC McDonald was miraculously unhurt in the battle. What was known as "The Glasgow Atrocity" was over – but it's effects would still be felt.

A police officer had been murdered in the city streets, and someone would have to pay. Police inquiries centred on the city's East end. Tip-offs had been received and on a day shortly after the van attack, they swooped on a number of tenement flats in Abercrombie Street. finding a variety of weapons, and arresting several people, including a Father McCrory. It was said a police officer arrested him from the chapel at gunpoint.

Later, the chief Constable would receive letters saying that the officer was a marked man for committing such a sacrilege and would not escape the consequences of his actions. But no further action was taken against him.

News of the arrests circulated swiftly and even while police officers were inside the flats, a crowd began to gather outside. Police were neither liked nor trusted in these streets and when they dragged out some of their prisoners, the mob threw stones and demonstrated their keen indignation. This time the officers managed to get away unharmed. Others would not be so lucky. That keen indignation rose steadily over the next few hours and finally there was a 2000 strong mob of men and women thronging the street. Police finally dispersed the crowd when a tram was attacked and it's windows smashed. But the trouble was not yet over.

Shop windows were shattered, police officers assaulted and finally a squad of soldiers was sent to protect Central police office from a feared attack. In all 34 people were picked up in connection with the rescue bid and the murder of the police officer, with another 12 for rioting. During a search of a cellar at 74 Abercrombie Street [editor's note: A pub] a weapons haul was found, said to be the biggest ever in Glasgow. It included revolvers, hand grenades, gelignite and ammunition. Frank J. Carty was eventually deported to Ireland.

In August, 1921, 13 people appeared in court charged with the murder. Although some of them were positively identified, none of the accused were convicted. Each of them had an alibi, and the defence were able to cast doubts on the dependability of the identification evidence as crown witnesses had been allowed to see the accused prior to a parade.

21. McGuinness, *Nomad*, op. cit., p.143.
22. Bizarrely, Kelly had apparently been captured and interrogated by Hughie Martin and his boys. He attempted to escape but was dragged back and summarily shot. His corpse was left with a sign on it explaining that he had been executed for being an informer. The next morning the body was gone. After the war, it turned out that Kelly had been wearing a bullet-proof or 'steel vest', and, though wounded, had feigned death. He later made his way to England where he survived. The only version we have of this strange tale comes from Nomad's 'memoirs' and presumably he got the story from Hughie Martin. Interestingly, as an aside in his book Nomad says, years later, regarding Hughie Martin (ibid., p. 152)

> "Hugh Martin later became a captain in the regular Free State Army. After two years of enlistment he went to Australia. In 1933 he received a severe sentence of penal servitude in Sydney for organized banditry and attempted murder. That may be true, but Hughie was a gallant Republican soldier when I knew him, and a most loyal comrade."

Well, yes, but the bullet-proof 'steel vest' somehow doesn't ring quite true.

23. Inexplicably the latest book on Irish Internment, *The Argenta* by American academic Denise Kleinrichert states that Charles J. McGuinness was one of the men arrested in Derry on internment day May 23, 1922 after the assassination of Unionist bigot and MP Billy Twaddell. This is an error. Nomad was never interned. Over twenty Derry men were interned at that time following a raid on the Erin Hall. These included: John Burke of St. Columbs Wells; James Callaghan, Fountain Hill; William Cullen, Lecky Road; Michael Devlin, Walkers Place; John Farren, Boyle Street; Arthur Patrick Friel, Nelson St; James Gallagher, Deanery Place; John Gibbons, Bridge Street; James Harkin, St. Columbs Wells; Caldwell Hyndman, Philip St; Seamus Kavanagh, Alexander Place (ended up in Frongoch); Hugh Kelly, Fountain Hill; Patrick Leonard; the three Mackey brothers of Fosters Terrace; Robert McAnaney, Bishop Street; James McCafferty, Strabane Old Road; James Moore, Nelson Street; John Mullen, Argyll Terrace and Thomas O'Hara, Bishop Street. Others were of course picked up and interned during the next two years.
24. McGuinness, *Nomad*, op. cit., p. 157.
Paddy Reilly was subsequently to attempt to escape again with another group of Republicans. The escape failed, however, and during the course of it two warders were killed. Reilly and his fellow Republican prisoners were removed to the grim prison of Peterhead in Scotland, where the dungeons were hewn out of solid rock and actually run beneath the sea. There he and others of his comrades died of tuberculosis, brought on by the damp and the barbaric conditions. Anonymous victims of the War of Independence (ibid., p. 160).
25. According to Derry man Ronan Gallagher (*Derry Journal*, 25.05.2001), during the truce McGuinness and his friend Alfred McCallion became, briefly, local heroes and annoyed the authorities by strolling around openly in IRA uniforms. McGuinness wore his ubiquitous 'brimmer'.
26. McGuinness, *Nomad*, op. cit., p.164.

Chapter 5
Germany Calling

A dispatch came from Mick Collins. "Come to Dublin at once. Full details on your arrival at Army Headquarters."

> Leaving the trusted Hughie Martin "in charge of the Column, I secreted my Colt under my armpit and set off for Dublin. *En route* I regained my clerical attire and travelled to the capital by the longest and safest way around.
>
> The address given was an empty house in Brunswick Street, Dublin. I peered into windows, and nothing but barren rooms met my eye. I stared at the address again, and verified it. What was wrong? I decided to knock. The door opened with a startling swiftness. Giving the password, I was admitted. Army headquarters were in a room in the back of the house."
>
> "Collins came into the office, shaking his tousled mane, and greeted me with an infectious smile.
> 'Mac, do you know that Scotland Yard and the Castle boys are looking for you?'"
>
> After some small chat "Collins suddenly asked the question: 'Could you bring a shipload of arms from Germany [to Ireland] in a submarine?'
> 'No,' I replied. 'The idea is absurd from any seaman's point of view. A submarine would attract more attention than a Cunarder or a Zeppelin. Why advertise what you're doing?'
> 'Just what I thought. […] I am glad to hear you veto the idea. What would you suggest?'
> 'A boat, of course: one that looks no different than a thousand others.'
> Collins face reflected approval. I went on to explain a procedure that I would follow. […]
> 'Splendid, Mac! Will you take the job?' said Collins.
> 'Yes, if you give me a free hand and enough money.'
> 'Free hand, eh? You report to no one but me, and there'll be plenty of money to buy the boat, and the ammunition.'"[1]

This is how Nomad tells the tale, in his own entertaining way, however, it seems that this account, which he gave in his book published in 1934 and in newspaper interviews in America in 1928 is not totally truthful. First off, there is no evidence that Michael Collins ever knew Nomad before 1921 – he had been 'offside' for years after all, and only joined the IRA in 1920. He was never a member of the IRB. In fact, it was Liam Mellows who suggested Nomad as the gun runner to Collins. This is confirmed by Briscoe and also by Desmond Greaves in his biography of Mellows.[2] Nomad in his account does refer to Mellows as 'a good comrade', but when writing for an American audience the name of the dead Collins was obviously more of a headline grabber than that of the murdered Liam Mellows who was, after all, little better than a communist or anarchist (he had hung out with the IWW – Industrial Workers of the World, aka Wobblies, when he was in America), whereas Collins was the fallen, lost leader.

Nonetheless, it is true that Collins did send Nomad over to London, en route to Germany, to deliver a few messages to his old O/C Sam Maguire.

Sam Maguire, after whom the Sam Maguire Cup for the All Ireland Gaelic championships is named, came from Mallabracka, Dunmanyway in County Cork. Maguire was a leading figure in the GAA, the Gaelic League and was also, unknown to British Intelligence, the head IRB centre in London. It was there that he swore into the IRB a young fellow Cork man fresh over to London, one Michael Collins. During the War of Independence Maguire, by then the IRA's chief Intelligence Officer in London was the most wanted man in England, although the British never managed to discover that, all the time, he was working in their own Post Office Civil Service.

Despite good security, the fortunes of IRA volunteers in England were not great. The young Sean MacBride recalls meeting Albert Price, veteran West Belfast Republican and father of Dolours and Marion Price, in Hyde Park where the IRA were holding an open air bomb making class – they had no premises. It was a hot July day and MacBride asked Price why he was wearing a heavy sweater. 'Because I haven't got a shirt for me back,' replied Albert.

Nomad claims that when he met Maguire, whom he admired, he was introduced to Reggie Dunne and Joe O'Sullivan. Both were Irish Republicans who had been World War I survivors, although Reggie Dunne had lost a leg on the Western Front, at Ypres. Despite this Dunne and another volunteer named Joe Shanahan had on Collins' orders previously tracked down and shot a renegade IRA man called Fouvargue who was hiding in London. Nomad claims in his book (p. 166) that he delivered personal instructions to Maguire, Dunne and O'Sullivan, who were all devoted Michael Collins men. Be that as it may, it is a matter of historical record that subsequently on Collin's orders, on June 22nd 1922, Dunne and O'Sullivan gunned down the British butcher Sir Henry Wilson on the steps of his house in Eaton Place in London. (Wilson had been the founder of the notorious 'Cairo Gang', an early British death squad and had also been found guilty by Belfast Republicans of 'war crimes' for his support for the Unionist and Loyalist murder gangs orchestrating the pogroms in Belfast. In Belfast parlance, Wilson had long been 'GFAH' or 'good for a hit' and with the truce in place and Collins anxious to capitalise on his popularity with the IRA men from the North – most of whom ended up joining the Free State Army on the promise that they would be trained, armed and then could return and 'recapture' the six counties, the operation was sanctioned.) Both men were quickly apprehended but refused to implicate Collins. Both were hanged in August 1922. Ten days later, Collins himself died in the ambush at Beal na Bleath.

But long before that Nomad had made it to Germany, via Paris.

When he arrived there were two main problems. The IRA 'agents' in Germany weren't up to much, and the arms dealers were not trustworthy.

What we know of those hectic days in Berlin and Hamburg in the summer and autumn of 1921 are based on the words of the two main 'conspirators', Nomad McGuinness and Robert Briscoe, who wrote his own self serving memoir in 1958.[3]

Bob Briscoe, from Jewish Lithuanian stock, who years later went on to become the first Jewish Lord Mayor of Dublin, was an unlikely IRA agent. In his youth however, growing up in Dublin, he had joined the Fianna. He left Ireland prior to 1916 and engaged in unsuccessful business ventures until deciding to go to Germany 'on active service for the procurement branch of the Irish Republican Army'. Briscoe found to his dismay that the person whom he was due to replace was the incompetent John Dowling, who had been in Germany for a few months with IRA hard robbed cash and managed to get himself swindled by a German conman. Meanwhile in Ireland Liam Mellows wanted the movement's money back. (Dowling apparently, keen on 'the clandestinity' used to parade around postwar Germany posing as an American 'James McGregor' and sporting riding breeches and a five gallon hat – 'a disguise which would not have fooled a Bavarian shepherd', according to Briscoe. Not that Nomad McGuinness was any less flamboyant and 'obvious', according to all extant accounts and the testimony of those who met him.)

In his memoir Briscoe clearly overstates his own importance. He was living comfortably in Berlin in a pension off the fashionable Kurfürstendamm. As 'cover' he had his wife and child with him. He was free to travel around and try to organize small arms for Ireland, posing as a representative for a straw company, Kenny, Martin & Company, which the IRA had set up in Ballinasloe, but, to date he had only managed to send a few shortarms back with sympathetic Irish sailors. And then Dowling 'lost' the £20,000.

At this stage IRA weapon procurement was at a low ebb. On November 13-14, 1920 an IRA conference approved a general restructuring of munitions provision. Jim O'Donovan, a former science teacher at Clongowes, later to become the architect of the 'S' for sabotage plan to bomb England in 1938 and who was to cross McGuinness' path in the future again, was appointed Director of Chemicals, Seán Russell was Director of Munitions and Liam Mellows the Director of Purchases. O'Donovan established a bomb factory in London. Russell visited the English Midlands seeking components for home made bombs, while Mellows was in the invidious position of having to try and scrounge some guns. To add to his problems, there was dissension in the Army Council. Cathal Brugha had insisted that the war be carried to Britain – he even had a plan to machine gun the House of Commons from the public gallery, a plan that was only narrowly outvoted, but he had got his way for arson attacks and on November 28th the IRA burned down 17 warehouses in Liverpool. But, it meant, inevitably, that security was tightened. The Irish in England were taking a pounding.

And now John Dowling had managed to 'lose' £20,000! Mellows was not happy with his 'German operatives', so he sent over Nomad, a man who he himself described as 'the most frightening individual I've ever met'.

In his account, Briscoe, hardly surprisingly, since he's writing in 1958 and all other participants are long dead, asserts that he took command. He gives himself the 'alias' of Captain Swift but, it was increasingly obvious to Liam Mellows in Ireland that both Dowling and Briscoe were out of their depth. They needed assistance, and

Germany, with its ever diminishing armed forces, its black market and steady devaluation was Europe's greatest arms bazaar. Hence the arrival of Nomad McGuinness in the autumn of 1921.[4]

What follows is Briscoe's version of the Dowling/McGuinness affair.

"Shortly after my return to Germany, Dick Kenny arrived as a courier from Collins ordering me to take over from Dowling and investigate him. Collins had already told me that Dowling was paying out large sums of money with no results whatever. If I decided that he had been dishonest, he was to be returned to Ireland for trial and execution.

Dowling made no resistance to the order. In fact, he seemed downright relieved to be rid of the responsibility. He told me quite frankly about his transactions. He had been negotiating with 'a man named Jurgens,' who, he said, dealt in wholesale groceries, mainly butter and margarine – a German butter-and-egg man. But Jurgens was also an ex-naval officer who claimed to be able to supply a large quantity of munitions and a ship to transport them to the west coast of Ireland.

Dowling had made inquiries which substantiated this story. He had then posted a deposit of twenty thousand pounds of I.R.A. money to get the deal started. That was some time before. Now Jurgens had become evasive, and complained that Dowling was being "tiresome."

I decided that Dowling was probably not dishonest – just a sucker who had been taken in by a new sort of confidence game. So I said to him, "I'll not take action against you yet, but I will have to check your story. Will you agree to remain as my prisoner in Hassenhauer's apartment while I look into this?"

"Gladly," said Dowling.

We locked him up in the bathroom of Hassenhauer's flat for several days while I made inquiries. I learned that Jurgens was in Hamburg, and decided that we would go down there to confront him. My squad consisted of Kenny, Dowling and a remarkably rugged individual who had just joined us from Ireland named Charley McGuiness [sic], of whom much more later.

In Hamburg we conferred with Doctor Schuler, a lawyer who had been highly recommended to us. He listened attentively while I told him the whole story. Then he gave us his opinion, "You have no chance of recovering this money at law. It is illegal in Germany to deal in arms, as you well know, particularly for the purpose for which you want them. If you start a suit it will be thrown out of court. You will have to adopt extra-legal methods. First let me find out about this Jurgens."

The next day Schuler reported that Jurgens was a black-marketeer. He lived an openly opulent life with a magnificent motor car and a splendid villa. He was, in fact, extremely ostentatious in a country ruined by war and defeat. Schuler called him a *shieber* – a fellow who promotes all sorts of transactions, legal or otherwise, and is willing to take fantastic risks to make a fast mark.

"I advise you to use strong methods," Schuler concluded.

It was advice right after my own heart.

Schuler asked Jurgens to come to his office one Friday afternoon, "to meet a client from abroad." The *shieber* fell into the trap. After a few moments Schuler made an excuse to leave him alone. The next thing he knew my four-man commando burst through the door. Jurgens was sitting beside the desk; a magnificently built man, over six feet tall and beautifully dressed. When he saw us, his handsome face turned olive-green.

Though I knew he spoke English, I addressed him in German. Speaking in a guttural growl, I said, "We are members of the I.R.A. Dowling here is under arrest and will be sent home and probably executed. As for you, we want our money back!"

Jurgens pulled himself together and tried to reason with us, but he kept nervously watching Charley McGuiness, who had the build of a gorilla.

"Gentlemen, gentlemen," said Jurgens, "this deal is absolutely above-board. Will you let me prove it by taking you to see where the arms are stored!"

"We'll do no such thing," I answered. "Are you going to pay us the money?"

Jurgens hesitated, switching his eyes from Charley to me and back.

"All right, gentlemen, get ready!" I said.

Kenny and McGuiness both produced automatics and pointed them at Jurgens.

"Now, look you," I said. "Nobody knows we're here. We are going to shoot you and leave you lay. Your body won't be found until Monday morning, and nobody will know what happened except Doctor Schuler, who has a good story to tell of having left you here to meet an unknown contact at your request. So you..."

At that point I was interrupted by a resounding crash. Jurgens had fallen off his chair in a dead faint!

For once I was confronted with a situation I couldn't deal with. I tested Jurgens ungently with my boot. He was not shamming. Then I dashed to consult Schuler, who was in another office: "He's fainted, what do I do now?"

"Don't let it worry you," the lawyer said. "Take this pitcher of water and throw it over him."

I went back and emptied the water on the prostrate profiteer, who came to, spluttering. We propped him up in the chair and continued the discussion. He was very cooperative. We figured out how much twenty thousand pounds was in marks – it came to billions – and he drew us a check for it. I told the boys to hold him, and took the check in to Schuler.

"This won't do," he said. "It's probably good, but the banks are closed by now. I'll draw up a document for him to sign."

He hastily drafted a paper in which Jurgens admitted receiving the deposit of twenty thousand pounds for the purchase of arms. That would at least put him in an illegal position. Jurgens was so upset at being left alone with McGuiness and Kenny that he could hardly hold a pen, but he signed. Then we let him go.

Doctor Schuler was a very astute lawyer indeed. He started a suit against Jurgens immediately, and got a judge he knew to put it on the calendar for the following morning. A subpoena was served on Jurgens that night.

Early the next morning, Schuler lodged the check at his bank, and asked them to get cash for it as quickly as possible. Then we all went to court. Dowling was prepared to admit everything, including his forged passport, as Schuler felt that honesty was our best chance. In the somber, dirty-windowed court room our names were called, and Schuler replied that we were present. Then Jurgens's [sic] name rang out. I saw him sitting in the back of the room, but he did not answer. Again the bailiff shouted, "Herr Jurgens!" Still our man sat quiet as a frightened mouse.

The court then accepted Schuler's plea to make the agreement a rule of the court. Nor was Jurgens's check stopped. We got every shilling of our money back. It is in my mind that the poor fellow thought it worth twenty thousand pounds to be rid of us.

It was just before this that our little company was reinforced by Charles McGuiness, master mariner. The dribs and drabs of arms we were sending over were not enough, and we had decided to buy a ship or two. Captain McGuiness reported to command our merchant marine. The sealed orders he brought me from Liam Mellows were most peculiar. In them I was instructed that

McGuiness had an anchor tattooed on the back of his left hand and a ring worked on the fourth finger. Since these marks were known to the British Secret Service I must have them removed.

I was further informed that though McGuiness was a Catholic, he had not been to confession for fourteen years, during which time he had committed just about every sin in the calendar. Since he was to command a desperate undertaking, Mellows ordered me not to send him into danger until he had absolution.

I was to see to it that he was put in a state of grace.

Sure this was a strange assignment for me, but it was typical of the devout and devoted leaders of the Irish Revolution. They thought nothing at all of risking a man's neck; but under no circumstances would they endanger his immortal soul.

Mellows also warned me that I must handle McGuiness gently for he had a terrible quick temper; but if once I won his confidence, he would stop at nothing to help me.

Charley McGuiness was, in fact, the toughest character I have ever met. He was a short, barrel-chested, wide-shouldered man, who always walked with his elbows out and his hands up ready for a fight. He had a big, baldish head and a great fleshy face that was scored and burned by the winds of all the oceans. The tattoo on his hand was nothing. When naked he was spectacular. From the soles of his feet to his neck he was a picture gallery, with everything from mermaids to alligators. Just to show you the kind of man he was I will tell you one anecdote.

Charley and I were in a dockside saloon in Hamburg frequented by sailors of all nationalities. I saw a man come in who looked familiar, and stared at him. There were four Swedish sailors at a nearby table, one of whom thought I was staring at him and took offense. He came over to us in a very belligerent way. It looked like a roughhouse might develop, but I explained civilly that I was looking at another man altogether. McGuiness helped placate the Swede and when he left peacefully, Charley expressed himself as being happy that he had helped avert trouble.

After a bit Charley finished his wine, stood up and went over to those four Swedes. He tapped one of them on the shoulder and said, "Well, gentlemen, if it's trouble you're wanting, I am willing to oblige."

Waiting for no more than the look of amazement on their faces, he knocked his man off his chair. The other three were up like a flash, and the fight was on. While I was still wondering whether to risk breaking security by helping Charley, he knocked down the other three Swedes. They were spread like a starfish around the table. Looking down at them, Charley said, "Now, gentlemen, I think we understand each other. Good afternoon."

You may imagine how worried I was about carrying out Mellows's orders with a character like this. I consulted a number of German doctors about removing the tattooed anchor. None of them gave me much help until finally, in Hamburg, I discovered one who was sufficiently shady for me to confide in. This chap examined McGuiness, and stated that he could do the job; but he pointed out that to do it properly, he would have to cut most of the skin off the back of the hand, as you'd cut a pattern from a piece of cloth. This would be very painful as he had no means of giving a proper anaesthetic, and a local would not help much.

With no hesitation Charley said, "Get on with it!"

We made an appointment for the next morning. McGuiness was as carefree as though he were going to a bar for a drink. In the horrid little surgery, Charley was laid out on a couch. The one cheerful appurtenance was a very pretty nurse. She stood on one side of the couch dabbing with iodine, while the doctor was making his incision and cutting off the skin.

Sitting in a chair in that little hot room, listening to the grizzily [sic] sound of scissors cutting flesh and tissue, I felt like vomiting, but Charley gave no indication of suffering. Right in the middle of the operation he winked at me and gestured with his head. I looked around, and found that he was caressing the nurse's legs under her skirt with his free hand, and evidently enjoying this counter-operation.

The doctor finished up by pulling the flaps of skin loosely together and sewing them up, leaving a straight, puckered scar down the middle of Charley's hand. The bit taken away from his finger was left to heal itself.

On the way back to our hotel, Charley seemed very irritable – he must have been in great pain. He got it into his head that the chauffeur was taking us a long way round. "We'll not let the —
— think we're fools," he said. And without any further discussion, he put his right fist through the glass partition behind the driver's head.

As a result of this, I had to take him back to the doctor, for his right arm was torn from knuckles to elbow. Then with both hands heavily bandaged, I brought him back to the hotel to lie up and cure himself for the work ahead."

[Liam Mellows confirmed this story, though he did not allude to Nomad's amatory exploits.[5]]

"McGuiness was primarily concerned with ships. He was not only to command one, but to be my adviser for the examination and selection of vessels to meet our purpose. I had already made contact with a Captain Brauner, a German ex-naval and merchant marine officer, who was now a ship's broker and chandler with an office in Bremen. Brauner slept in a bunk in his office, which was fixed up like the captain's quarters of a ship. He was a queer, gaunt, cadaverous looking man. McGuiness did not like the looks of him, but I must say he proved more than trustworthy. He kept his business with us absolutely secret.

By now I had acquired sufficient stock of munitions to fill a small boat. We told Brauner what we wanted, and he came up with an ideal vessel. She was a small trawler, with a large fish well in her bottom under the deck boards, which could be filled with rifles, revolvers and ammunition, and still leave room for her crew and the stores necessary for a voyage from Bremen to Ireland. Her name was *Anita*. McGuiness fell in love with her. The price was comparatively low because of the advantageous rate of exchange between pounds and marks, so I bought her.

We wasted no time. Charley signed on a crew and brought *Anita* around to the Free Port of Hamburg. Goods could be sent by rail or canal boat to the Free Port from all over Germany; and then shipped abroad without customs inspection. I had taken part of a warehouse there and filled it with munitions of all sorts. *Anita* was brought alongside the quay close by this warehouse, and we loaded her until she lay deep in the water with arms and ammunition.

In a matter of hours, she was ready to start down the river to Bremen which would be her port of exit. I was standing on the dock, and Charley was just going aboard, when down on us like green devils came the Gippo – the green-coated, black-helmeted police of those days. They swarmed all over *Anita*, blowing whistles and yelling – especially when they found the guns.

Charley and the crew were loaded into a big black paddy wagon and carted off to jail. Nobody spoke to me. I must have looked like the innocent bystander.[6]

Arrested on the dock with the mastermind Briscoe escaping? Doesn't ring all that true.

According to Nomad, he had proceeded to Hamburg where he purchased a boat named the *Anita*, loaded it up with cases of guns and a crew of German communists.[7]

The *Anita* voyage had, however, been dogged by ill-luck. The Bolinder engine in the *Anita* had broken down just before they were able to set out, and Nomad, after ordering his 'Red' engineer to stay on board and fix it with the aid of a mechanic summoned from Hamburg, had retired with the crew to a local Gasthaus to get refreshments. McGuinness and his motley team aroused the suspicions of the Gasthaus owner when they persisted in speaking English and attempting to pay for their drink with large denomination English bank notes, scarcely the usual tender for your average German seaman in those days. In his autobiography Nomad reluctantly admitted that this had been a 'mistake'.

By 8.00 a.m., the engine had still not been repaired and Nomad decided to set sail. He always preferred sail to steam anyway. According to him "we had not proceeded very far, however, when a customs pinnace cut across the river and swung alongside. Then a harbour launch with police aboard crossed our bow and ordered us to stop." They were boarded

> "and an important individual with a walrus moustache and a bristling Prussian haircut bellowed:
>
> '*Wo gehen Sie? Was für Ladung haben Sie?*' which means: 'Where are you going, and what's your cargo?'
>
> My German mate Ernst was a plucky fellow and he debated with the official, trying to fool him with lies."

But he was brushed aside and the machine guns were discovered hidden under many bags of salt.

> "'*Gott in Himmel!*' gasped the official, his eyes bulging at the view of four beautiful machine guns of the very latest design, and the assembling parts of four tripods.
>
> I decided to make a clean breast of the affair. Through the mate, and with my own limited vocabulary, I explained the purpose of our venture. The German official lost his Prussian pomp and bristle. He was crestfallen, and the custom authorities and police were sorry they had caught us. They had no choice now, as the Allied High Commission were very observant of exports. I was there and then arrested for violation of customs and falsifications of clearance papers."[8]

Under the Treaty of Versailles, Germany was forbidden to possess any arms, let alone export them.

The *Anita* was towed back into Baumwall harbour and 'Captain Thompson' was arraigned at the harbour police headquarters. Nomad, true to form, however, did not lose his savoir faire. He readily admitted being an agent of the 'Irish Republican Government' and convinced the German authorities to release his communist crew members whom, he asserted, had known nothing of his contraband cargo.

Justice was swift. Four days later 'Captain Thompson' pled guilty and was lectured, at great length, by the Judge about the evils of gun running and how his actions had severely embarrassed the German Republic before the Allied High Commission. He stoically bore the lecture in silence, knowing that the fix was in. Sure enough, after his tirade, the Judge concluded by fining him a mere two thousand marks (about ten pounds or forty dollars). The boat was returned to him, minus the machine guns. As he prepared to leave the courtroom, the Judge called him back into his chambers. 'Good luck on your next trip, Captain Thompson – or is it Hennessey,' smiled the Judge, shaking him by the hand.

That's how Nomad reports it. Briscoe, perhaps eager to claim credit goes into more 'detail'.

> Though I was free to go, I was badly worried. There must have been some slip, the Gippo probably had been tipped off by the British C.I.D. Meanwhile, all our work was lost, the arms gone and *Anita*, too. And poor Charley maybe sentenced to jail for years. I was determined at least to save Charley. [Cum grano salis?]
>
> Back to Doctor Schuler's little office, where we had held up Jergens [sic], I went. When the lawyer saw me, he said, "Have you been taken again?"
>
> "By the police," I answered. "We're in real trouble this time." And I told him my story.
>
> Schuler was a man of infinite resource. He immediately propounded one of his extra-legal schemes to rescue Charley. "I think we can get him out," he said. "You must pose as the Irish Republican consul in Hamburg. I think you can get away with it. We Germans are rather sympathetic to your cause, and won't ask many questions. Then we'll get him a quick trial."
>
> I put on my best dark suit and my most pompous manners and went to the jail. An authoritative manner went a long way in a

country as chaotic as post-war Germany where nobody was sure at all who would be who tomorrow. The officials were positively deferential. They took me down to a great stone barn of a room which had two big iron cages full of prisoners – men on one side, women on the other. It was like a scene from Hogarth, with doxies and filchers having a great time yelling bawdy remarks at each other from their cages.

Waving my turnkey back, I went up to the men's cage. When Charley saw me he looked thunderstruck. He rushed to the grill and said in an echoing stage whisper, "For God's sake, you vamoose!" That was a favorite word of his.

"I've come to get you out."

"Vamoose!" he repeated. "I'll probably get a few years, but if you get mixed up in this we'll both be locked up. You have a wife and child, and anyway you're much more important to the work here than I am."

This was indeed loyalty![9]

I said, "No, Charley. I've talked with Schuler, and we're going to get you out of this. He'll be coming to see you. Be absolutely frank with him. When you're brought to trial you'll have to admit that you were loading a ship with arms for the Irish Republican Army. I think you'll find that the judge won't regard that as so great a crime."

Schuler worked fast. The next morning Charley was brought to trial and made a full confession. Of course, he was traveling on a forged passport as "Captain Charles Thompson," but since it was a very good forgery we did not bother to mention that.

The judge assumed an outraged air, and imposed what he considered a heavy fine – fifteen thousand marks. That was only a few pounds and Schuler promptly paid it. But we were still out one ship and a cargo of arms.

Well, as it happened we not only saved the ship, but the cargo, too. In fact, the sympathetic authorities did not even impound the *Anita*; but, of course, under the Treaty of Versailles, the arms had to be destroyed. So they were loaded into a lorry to be carted off to a suitable place; and somehow it happened that the lorry never reached its destination; but instead went around the block to the back door of my warehouse. Those Germans did not like the British at all.

However, we were right back where we started, and very worried, too, for it was sure now that we were being watched. We lay quiet for a while, cooking up a new scheme to get a large shipment of arms out. Naturally, my small-scale smuggling racket was working beautifully;[10] but what a few men could carry on their persons was just a tiny trickle.[11]

Briscoe, though perhaps hardly a 'literary figure' has a couple of other 'Nomad stories'. This is one of the better, though perhaps fanciful one.

SAVING THE SOUL OF CHARLEY MCGUINESS

Meanwhile, I still had in mind the perilous condition of Charley's soul. So I paid a call to a Franciscan Order which had a mission to seamen. There I luckily found two Irish priests. One of them was a large robust, round-faced happy friar, and his partner the opposite of him, being thin, frail and esthetic-looking.

"Sure it is simple," said my jolly friar. "Just have a drink with him at the Triere Café. We'll come in and make your acquaintance. The rest you can leave to us."

It was no trouble whatever to get Charley into a saloon. We had been there a short time when the two friars came in. I paid no attention, until Charley noticed them, and made a joke about Brother Mutt and Brother Jeff. They stopped at our table and one of them said, "You sound like men from Ireland."

"That we are," Charley exclaimed. "Won't you sit with us, and have a bit of drink?"

Of course they did, and the talk ran on Ireland until I could see they were making McGuiness homesick. It ended with them inviting us to come to their monastery for tea the next day. Charley needed no urging.

It was a bare, dismal place where they lived; and the refreshments no more than weak tea and very hard, dry bread. But Charley enjoyed himself. We chatted some more about Ireland, and then the fragile friar asked Charley to walk around the grounds. They went out together, and I was left with my Friar Tuck.

Minutes and hours went by. I drank that miserable tea until it was up to my gullet; and we talked until the springs of our brains ran dry. But it was in a good cause. For finally Charley burst in through the door in high good humor. With a great grin, he said, "You know, Bob, I think this was something you put over on me. But you can be happy. I've made me confession, and am all right and ready for anything now. Only I hope you've been converted and confessed *your* sins. It would be only fair if you had to do penance as I have."

So there at least, was one mission accomplished. I wrote to Mellows, "You will be glad to know that Charley is now in a state of grace. But for how long – that is another question."[12]

Briscoe also (at pp. 259-260) tells a strange story of Charlie, in Berlin and while the Truce was on he and McGuinness allegedly put a tricolor on their regular table in the local coffee house which was owned an 'amiable jew'. An Irishman came in one night and insulted the Jew and when they heard this the next day Briscoe and Charlie went to his office and trashed it. When the 'jew-baiter' returned Charlie frog marched him around to the cafe to grovel an apology to the jewish proprietor. How does this gel with Nomad's blatant anti-semitism in his anti-Spanish civil War articles?

Questions were asked in the Reichstag about the *Anita* and the attempted arms smuggling with the chamber fairly evenly divided between those who wished to curry favour with their new Allied masters and those who wished the irredentist Irish revolutionaries 'Viel Glück' against the old foe. At the abortive peace negotiations which were being held in London, an apoplectic Lloyd George fumed to Eamonn De Valera about this "flagrant breach of good faith" and demanded that this "damned Hennessey" must be stopped.

But Mellows had already sent word over with his courier, the young Sean MacBride. The IRA still wanted guns.

The *Anita* had already been replaced with the *Frieda*, which, loaded to the gunwales with the biggest arms shipment ever to make it from the continent to Ireland, was preparing to make to sea. Nomad was back in business.

ARMING THE *FRIEDA*

<u>November 1921</u>
Hans Lichter was sick as a dog. Mountainous waves in the Great North sea buffeted the thirty ton tug, the *Frieda*, that had replaced the *Anita*. Most of the German crew were throwing up and the load of coal was shifting all over the deck. Lichter crawled down to the tiny cabin to confer with 'Captain Thompson', aka Mr. Hennessey, who was sitting with his feet up, a big cigar in his mouth. His boots lay on the floor and the astonished German crewman couldn't help but notice that the *Frieda*'s skipper had, tattooed on the soles of each of his feet, a faded Union Jack.

"Come in Lichter, how's the cargo?" asked the Captain, in fractured German. Lichter stumbled into the cabin, trying to avert his eyes from the skipper's feet. "All right captain, but surely we'll have to put back to Cuxhaven, we'll never make it in this weather." The skipper drank deeply from a flask of brandy. "Nonsense, seaman, I've sailed in worse weather than this, why, I remember back in 1917 when I sailed on the *Vasco Da Gama* the Indian Ocean was much worse – of course, to be fair, the ship did sink and I was the only survivor [this was really the *Magellan*], but sure a little bit of rough weather's only to be expected in missions such as these. Besides, the weather will keep the Brits on shore. Now, you're sure the cargo's all right?"

Lichter groaned. Apart from the imminent danger of the tug capsizing, the cargo, consisting as it did of 1,500 rifles, 2000 parabellums and almost two million rounds of ammunition, along with tons of explosives, did concern him. He signed on for the trip for the money, but he had not reckoned with this mad Irishman for a skipper. 'Captain Thompson' presented an awesome sight. Stocky, muscular, hirsute with a pair of vivid mad staring blue eyes. And those feet.

"Captain, do you mind me asking, why do you have those flags tattooed to the soles of your feet?" The Captain stared hard at the crewman and then seemed to relax. "Sure, I had them done years ago so that everywhere I go on this planet I'll be stamping on the butcher's apron. That's what we Irishmen call the Union Jack." "Jawohl, Kapitän," muttered Lichter, excusing himself and barely making it to the deck rail to throw up what remained of his rations into the turbulent North Sea.

In his cabin Captain Thompson, aka Hennessey, aka Charles John 'Nomad' McGuinness returned to his log.

> "Friday. Still going well, but wind and sea increasing – the latter running high. Ocean going vessels bound up Channel are making heavy weather of it judging by the way they ship water. [...] Midnight, we pass the 'Lizard' off Land's End, and head up for Irish land which we hope to pick up in the evening."[13]

On the Irish shore near Helvick Head Pax Ó Faoláin was cursing. Where the hell was McGuinness?

And, of course, Pax Ó Faoláin had been here before. Pax, later commandant of the Waterford no. 2 Brigade had spent summer nights in 1918 in a rowing boat off Stradbally, vainly awaiting contact with the Germans who were supposed to be delivering a submarine full of arms. It never showed. Nor did the 'arms ship from America'. Now Mellows was insisting on leaving the gun running to a 'mercurial' Derryman called Nomad McGuinness.

NOTES.

1. McGuinness, *Nomad*, op. cit., pp. 164-166.
2. Greaves, Charles Desmond: *Liam Mellows and the Irish Revolution*. Lawrence & Wishart, London 1971.
3. Briscoe, Robert: *For the Life of Me*. Longmans, Green and Co Ltd., London 1959.
4. It should not be thought that Dowling, Briscoe and McGuinness were the only IRA representatives in Germany in those heady days. Sean MacBride frequently came over with messages from Mellows and then there was the shadowy figure of J.T. Ryan. Ryan got to Germany in December 1920 and appears to have taken an immediate dislike to Briscoe. Ryan was a lawyer and former US Army Captain and also a major arms operator in the US who operated under a variety of pseudonyms – 'Bisonkind', 'Jetter', or 'Professor Jetter' being amongst them. In 1916 he had been the American *Clann na Gael* liaison officer with Kurt Spindler who had captained the German arms ship the *Aud* which had had to be scuttled off the southern Irish coast just prior to the Easter Rising, which had led to his indictment for treason and his flight to Mexico two years later. In August 1920 the veteran *Clann na Gae*l leader Joe McGarrity sent Ryan with $10,000 to Germany to try and get 'a good shipment of the right kind for Ireland'.
And Mellows was not the only IRA man trying to get munitions from Europe. Seamus Robinson, commandant of the 3rd Tipperary Brigade had gone behind GHQ's back and tried to get Briscoe to get arms for his men in Tipperary. Briscoe had turned

him down, but Robinson had then approached Roddy Connolly of the Irish communist party for 'procurement agents'. Connolly produced the unusual Beaumont brothers. Billy Beaumont was a polo-playing ex-British Army officer. He tried to purchase a large quantity of minenwerfer and anti-tank guns in Germany but nothing came of it. Meanwhile his brother Seán travelled to Moscow but the fledgling Comintern refused to even entertain him. *See* 'Report on the Work of Irish communist Groups'. Mac Neil (pseudonym of Seán Beaumont) to Rakosi, secretary of the Comintern, 3 September 1921, Rossiiskii Gosudartsvennyi Arkiv Sotsial'no-Politichecheskoi (Russian State Archives), 495/89/2-30/33.
We are indebted to Dr. Emmet O'Connor for this source.
See also Murphy, Brian P.: *John Chartres. Mystery Man of the Treaty*. Irish Academic Press, Dublin 1995, pp. 30-33, and Cronin, Seán: *The McGarrity Papers*. Anvil, Tralee 1972, pp. 69-99.

5. Greaves, op. cit., p. 265.
Pax Ó Faoláin (Whelan) who knew Briscoe and McGuinness, years later said "we had been trying to get someone like that. We had tried one chap here, sending him across. He went as far as Danzig and returned with a few Parabellums [This was Briscoe]. That was as much as G.H.Q. could get until they met McGuinness." (McEoin, op. cit., p. 142.)
6. Briscoe, op. cit., pp. 93-99.
7. It is interesting that in 1921-22 Nomad is a keen partisan for his 'German Communist comrades' whom he praises and, he claims helped get back home after the successful gun run. He also, according to Briscoe rallies behind persecuted Jews. How does this contrast with his virulent anti-Communist and Jewish views as expressed in his articles for the *Irish Independent* in January 1937? *See* Afterword.
8. McGuinness, *Nomad*, op. cit., pp. 168-170.
9. Briscoe, throughout his account of the German gun running always expresses a positive view of Nomad – but is this out of fear? Certainly, Nomad never mentions Briscoe even once in his memoir, apart from the odd caustic and derogatory reference.
10. Not according to everyone else, Mr. Briscoe.
11. Briscoe, op. cit., pp. 100-101.
12. Briscoe, op. cit., pp. 101-102.
13. McGuinness, *Nomad*, op. cit., p. 175.

Chapter 6
The Running Of The Guns

Anita, Frieda, Hannah & An Ancient Mariner

Estimates of IRA membership during the war of Independence vary from 3,000 to 5,000 activists, with perhaps as many as 50,000 involved in an auxiliary role.[1]

The Republicans were badly equipped when hostilities began in January 1919 but were still prepared to take on the might of the British Empire, so there was an urgent rush on to procure the necessary armaments especially during the twelve months preceding the truce in July 1921. The nine brigades later grouped into the 1st Southern Division – those in Waterford, Cork, Kerry and West Limerick – which accounted for over 25% of IRA strength and started the fight with about 120 rifles, and little ammunition. By June 1921, the 1st Southern Division had 578 modern service rifles, eleven light machine guns, over 1,000 revolvers and pistols, and a considerable quantity of ammunition. The burgeoning arsenal still lagged behind the IRA's expanding operational capacity, and quality and suitability of weaponry and mismatches of arms and ammunition remained nagging problems. Historians agree too that brigades largely armed themselves. Each volunteer paid a weekly levy to buy his own weapon, and weapons were obtained through purchases, donations, seizures, or captures. Most IRA operations were concerned with acquiring weapons. Nine hundred raids for arms had taken place by August 1920, and 2,800 by September, after which the level declined due to better security measures. British army captures from the IRA were not significant until the period from March 1921, when major seizures were effected in Dublin.

Joe Wyse,[2] later quartermaster of the (West) Waterford no. 2 Brigade, smuggled weapons from Germany and the US when working as a ship's steward. Firepower remained inadequate. In the Pickardstown ambush on 7 January 1921, the IRA's biggest offensive in East Waterford, twenty two of the fifty two snipers were equipped with shotguns.

Since 1917 Michael Collins had been building an arms importation network through the Irish Republican Brotherhood (IRB), of which he was head. Subsequently, as Minister of Finance in the Dáil cabinet, he also had responsibility for purchases. Small consignments of munitions were smuggled from Britain and, to a lesser extent, the US. Most British material was collected in dumps around Glasgow, taken by road to Liverpool, and then concealed on regular shipping services, chiefly to Dublin, but also to Sligo, Cork, Limerick, and Waterford, for receipt by sympathetic dockers. German interest in Ireland revived on America's entry into the world war in April 1917, and German agents intimated to the US wing of the IRB, *Clann na Gael*, that they would be willing to send arms to Ireland as they had in 1916. Liam Mellows, who had gone to the US after the Easter Rising, was deputed to liaise with Germans, and the Volunteers were alerted to the possibility of an arms landing on the Wexford coast.

Joe Vize[3] privately agreed with Ó Faoláin's[4] assessment of 'the mad McGuinness'. Himself a former Director of Purchases for the IRA until his arrest, he had just escaped from the Curragh jail. A cautious man, he disliked what he termed 'the cowboy element' with whom the movement had to deal. But Liam Mellows was now Director of Purchases, and he, unlike the rest of the 'bhoys' had faith in McGuinness. Liam Lynch, the third man on Helvick Head that night, shrugged his shoulders. In May he had led a deputation to GHQ explaining that the fight could not go on without extra munitions. Now he was the Divisional Commandant of the First Southern Division. He would do anything to get munitions, even if it meant relying on the likes of McGuinness. Besides, as he pointed out, for all his alleged flaws, McGuinness had been a daring operator in the past "We'll wait one more night," was all he said.

The *Frieda* had set sail on October 28th 1921 on the 800 mile trip, and, since October 30th Ó Faoláin and his team had been out on Helvick Head watching for the little tug. The nights went by but no distress flares – the pre-arranged signals – were seen which would have heralded the launching of the two fishing boats to offload the cargo. According to Ó Faoláin the password was 'Anita Ahoy' and the answering call was to be 'O'Donnell Abu!' (they were unaware that the ship had been changed).

On November 10th Ó Faoláin returned to Dublin to confer with Mellows. Gloomily, they agreed that perhaps it had been an act of desperation to entrust the vitally needed shipment to the hands of

McGuinness in a small tug with an unknown crew of Germans. The *Frieda* must have gone down.

But Ó Faoláin, like many before and since, had underestimated Nomad McGuinness. Heavy seas and dense fog had put the tiny *Frieda* off course. By November 10th, she was off Ireland, but not off Helvick Head. She was fifty miles South West, near the old Head of Kinsale and running out of coal but McGuinness, by now proudly flying a Republican flag which he had made from a spare piece of silk, was undaunted. His log reveals his cavalier approach.

> "Nothing left but to head up to eastward, aiming for Mine Head.... We have now passed well clear off the Daunt's Rock, the entrance to Cobh. Off Mine Head we open up on the light of Ballinacourty Point, and edge up to Helvick. I signal with torch, but there is no response. We cruise up and down, making signals, but still no reply. The wind is increasing from the southwest and the sea running high, making us roll frightfully. We are in awful plight, not knowing where to go and daylight drawing nigh."[5]

Disappointed at the lack of response from the shore, Nomad determined, however, to let audacity be his guide. He headed for Waterford. At the Duncannon Fort all vessels had to report and signal in but the tiny *Frieda* ignored such British regulations and, in broad daylight, sailed up the river Suir and anchored in the old channel. The *Frieda* had used up its last shovel of coal.

Decidedly annoyed that no lookouts had been left at their posts, McGuinness put a boat overside and two Germans rowed him to muddy shore. He walked for five miles across sodden fields until he reached Waterford itself. Knowing no one there he went to the parochial house and blithely inquired as to where he could find the local IRA commander.

"Why don't you ask the Mayor – he's a Sinn Feiner" was the less than amicable reply of the parish priest. McGuinness then recalled that the mayor was a Dr. White, a Republican member of the Dáil, and set off to find him. The good doctor was more than startled when a mud-stained and dishevelled McGuinness knocked on his door and announced that he had brought the gear from Germany. There's an entire British regiment and two torpedo destroyers in port right now, exclaimed an excited White. McGuinness merely shrugged. 'I don't care about that, mucker,' the Derryman said, 'I've got 1,500 rifles, 2,000 parabellums and almost two million rounds of ammunition along with a few tons of explosives anchored off Cheek Point.'

The Doctor hurriedly made a few calls. As night fell and the rain lashed down, McGuinness and the Mayor rowed back to the tug. In the darkness, it took them two hours to find it, but, once aboard, McGuinness hove up the anchor and, since they were out of fuel, warped the *Frieda* alongside the little jetty at Cheek Point. Pax Ó Faoláin, summoned by Dr. White, was there with his team. They laboured all through the night. The rifles were handed out, one at a time, chain fashion, while the heavy ammunition cases were manhandled ashore and onto the waiting lorries. As dawn came up on the Suir the last truck was loaded and sped off towards the arms dumps in the Comeragh mountains.

Only then did McGuinness and his German crew come ashore, eager for a decent meal and a bath. They had been on meagre rations and, in order to conserve their water supply, had not washed since leaving Terschelling. That night they slept in safe billets in Waterford City and the next day left for Dublin. For security reasons, McGuinness decided to split the German crew, none of whom spoke much English, into two groups, who would sit apart on the train to Dublin. Although technically a truce was in place, the country was crawling with British auxiliaries and Intelligence agents. The discovery of a German crew would have invoked the fears of another 'German plot' and would have provided the British with an excuse to launch Churchill's threatened war to the death on the Irish people.

McGuinness was therefore horrified to discover, as the train pulled out, that four Germans were missing, but it was too late for him to do anything. As the train passed Kilmacthomas, however, he saw young Pax Ó Faoláin, furiously driving in Doctor White's motor car alongside. Crouched down in the back were Hans Lichter and three terrified Germans. At Gowran Junction, the car flashed through the railway gates in a cloud of dust and Ó Faoláin delivered the shaking Germans over to McGuinness. By nightfall he had smuggled them into Dublin and they were safely ensconced in Parnell Street.

Nomad proceeded to HQ where he first encountered Dick Mulcahy, the assistant Minister for Defense in the First Dáil. Mulcahy's effusive congratulations were abruptly cut short by McGuinness. 'Where's Liam (Mellows), I want to complain about those idiots down at Helvick. I've been cruising around for days. Do you boys not want the gear or what?'

Mellows, who had given the Derryman up for dead was also delighted to see Nomad. According to McGuinness, Mellows also "deplored, and was strong in his denunciation of the military laxity that allowed us to cruise up and down off that rock-bound coast in the teeth of a southwest gale." Modestly, McGuinness was later to write:

> "He [Mellows] was emphatic in stating that, had I not been in command, the *Frieda* would either have been lost with all hands or been captured by a British gunboat. Without being unduly vain, I fully endorsed that statement."

And, obviously still disgruntled, Nomad added

> "Had I failed I should have become a national hero and, in these times of piping peace, perhaps a political success."

With the guns safely squared away and the German crew billeted with Republican sympathizers like Sheila Humphries and Liam Mellows' wife, McGuinness's next concern was what to do with the *Frieda*. An Army Council meeting was held and several suggestions, ranging from blowing her up to scuttling her in the open seas were discussed. But McGuinness would have none of it. Eventually Liam Mellows intervened. According to McGuinness Mellows ruled that:

> "McGuinness bought this boat in Germany. He bought a cargo of arms and ammunition. He has safely delivered both. Let McGuinness settle the matter in his own way. In any case he'll do as he pleases, despite this conference."

Nomad went on to say:

> "It was perfectly true! While I was a sworn soldier of the Irish Republican Army, yet I owed no allegiance nor recognized any authority higher than my own in matters appertaining to sea or ships. This fact was well understood in Dublin at the time."[6]

Nonetheless, years later there was still discontent amongst many old Republicans regarding the sale of the *Frieda* and a subsequent vessel, the *City of Dortmund*.

At any rate, the *Frieda* was refuelled, got up steam and moved to Boat Strand near Tramore. Leaving her there McGuinness set out to find a purchaser. According to McGuinness, in Cork City he located a retired sea captain (Captain Collins) whom he referred to as "an ancient mariner". The Captain was persuaded to pay a thousand pounds for the *Frieda*, which represented a rather good profit for McGuinness since he had only paid five hundred pounds for it in Germany a scant two months previously. McGuinness unashamedly remarks that he may have 'gilded the lily' slightly when he described this 'nautical treasure' to the ancient Captain Collins.

Years later, Pax Ó Faoláin, still rather jaundiced against Nomad, told how McGuinness had physically hijacked Collins, spent two days getting him soused and then conned him into parting with the money.

> "There was a bit of a hullabaloo because they were missing for a few days and Collins's wife was wondering what had happened to her husband. That was not surprising because McGuinness was a hard man for the drink, and once he came ashore he usually buried himself in some tavern."[7]

But McGuinness had use for the money. He was already planning to set up the Irish Merchant Navy and used the money as a deposit for the *S.S. City of Dortmund*, which he bought from Palgrave Murphy. He intended it to be the forerunner of an Irish mercantile marine which would render Ireland independent of foreign shipping. In the end, nothing came of this scheme and the *City of Dortmund* was constantly harassed by the British navy. Nonetheless, it didn't prevent McGuinness from smuggling his German crew back to their homeland on the *Dortmund* and, on the return voyage, bringing back the few remnants of Casement's ill-fated 'Irish Brigade' who, after the Armistice were forced to remain in Germany.

During the Civil War, the *City of Dortmund*, flying McGuinness' house-flag – "a striking device in the national colors" – was steaming up the River Lee bound for Cork City. With, what McGuinness described as "true Irish inconsistency", both the IRA and a Free State column opened fire on the one and only vessel operating as an Irish ship. The Free State forces seized the ship, and it was not until a year after the Civil War that McGuinness was able to regain title to her and sell her. (During the *Upnor* incident,[8] Nomad was in Germany which, as he modestly wrote, "prevented my pulling off this exploit myself.")

Nomad's gun running days were not over yet, however. Word came down to Dublin that an American freighter, lying at Tilbury docks in London had some Thompson submachine guns on it, a present from American sympathizers. These were supposed to have been offloaded in Cobh in Ireland, but, as usual, as McGuinness said, "the boys in Cork didn't show up in time and the Yanks had to bring them here [i.e. London]." Nomad was already in London, en route for Germany where he hoped to bring in one more shipment. Word reached him in a public house that he was to command a squad of volunteers who would be sent to him from the English Midlands and to try and effect an offloading of the machine guns.[9]

It was just another job for Captain Thompson. Masquerading as an American skipper, Nomad led his little band on board the American vessel. Laden down with two ammunition belts around his waist and six Colt automatics stuffed in his pockets he watched as the bhoys strapped the Thompsons[10] to their legs and concealed the large round magazines under their coats. Next he engaged the London bobby at the security gate with yarns about America and tales of how much he enjoyed London. Meanwhile his men shuffled past, saluting him while he roared at them in his pseudo-American accent to 'be sure and be back on ship by six a.m.'. In his *Sailor of Fortune* Nomad tells a rather fanciful story of almost being arrested with the guns in a London taxi north of Islington when the driver thought that he was 'involved with those East End anarchists' but after he had threatened the cabbie with a gun to his head, the taxi driver had said "Gor blimey, guvnor [sic]. […] My woife's [sic] half Irish so she is. Why didn't you tell me at the beginning?" By morning the guns were safely stashed and McGuinness was on his way on the boat train from Victoria. Germany beckoned.

As usual McGuinness had problems dealing with the Irish emissaries who were trying to negotiate the purchase of munitions on the continent. Robert Briscoe, who apparently still regarded himself and Nomad as old friend's was referred to by McGuinness contemptuously as 'a self-opinionated bungler', JT Jetter was 'a meddling American attorney'. But Nomad had to encounter him again upon his return to Germany.

Within a week Nomad had a new boat, a new crew, a cargo of cement and six tons of arms, ranging from Parabellums to Mausers. The new boat was the *Hannah*, which Pax Ó Faoláin would later describe as "a lovely schooner with an auxiliary motor". Nomad was less complimentary about his new command. The auxiliary motor caused considerable trouble and the German crew couldn't navigate properly. (Perhaps the fact that Nomad had informed them that their destination was Vigo in Spain where they were to offload the cement and not Ireland, contributed to their confusion.)

Nonetheless, on March 23rd, 1922, the *Hannah* sailed from Bremen. Nomad had been informed that they had enough oil and water to motor alone for ten days. Three days out he discovered that they had only four days oil and three days water and had yet to run the blockade of British vessels which sought to inspect all cargo vessels in the English Channel. On March 28th, using sail instead of the motor, the *Hannah* slipped past Beachy Head at 8.00 a.m. and laid course for Start Point. With the motor broken down they ran into a massive gale off the Lizard. As all other vessels in the vicinity headed for the safety of Falmouth, Nomad drove the *Hannah* on southward.

Well off course, the crew of the *Hannah* finally spied Irish land on April 3rd, but it was the Wexford coast, and again he had to tack south, with the wind increasing and the seas running very high. It was pitch dark and blowing a hurricane by now, a bad night to attempt a landing at Dungarvan, with its terrible entrance blocked by a group of rocks known as 'The Gainers', described locally as a death trap. Finally, just as they scraped past the Gainers' buoy Nomad spied a signal light and spotted the flares from the shore. This time Pax Ó Faoláin and his men had waited.

Despite the atrocious weather a lifeboat, crewed by IRA men appeared alongside. The *Hannah* dropped anchor and the freezing Republicans came aboard to be greeted by McGuinness with bottles of the best German Cognac. The next morning, since the motor had finally given up the ghost, McGuinness blithely sailed the *Hannah* into the tiny pier off Ring village, near Dungarvan. In broad daylight an IRA company came on board and offloaded the munitions, supervised by Dick Barrett. It seems to have been almost a Sinn Fein/IRA 'adventure weekend outing', like a Fianna camp. Vize and Wyse were there. So were Mellows, Maire Comerford, Dick Mulcahy and Seamus Woods, the Belfast O/C and his family.

It was to be the last arms shipment to make it through before the Civil War engulfed Ireland.

Triumphantly Nomad went off with the Woods in their motor car for a celebration at a local hotel and then a brief holiday in the West.

Admittedly both these voyages occurred when the truce between the British and Irish was in place. The first shipment came in only two weeks before the Treaty was signed on December 6, 1921 and the second shortly before the Civil War was to break out with the shelling of the Four Courts on June 28, 1922. Nonetheless, it can never be taken away from Nomad McGuinness that he, virtually singlehandedly, ran 90% of all the munitions the Republicans ever got into Ireland, even though half of them ended up in the hands of the 'Staters'.

But the Civil War was upon them. McGuinness naturally took the Republican side, along with Mellows, Cathal Brugha and Dick Barrett and Rory O'Connor, but he did not fight and within a year, with McGuinness back in jail in Germany, all his old comrades were dead. Brugha shot down, guns blazing, by his old comrades as he emerged from the burning Hammam hotel. Mellows, O'Connor, Barrett and McKelvey, murdered in jail as a reprisal (December 8, 1922), ordered by, amongst others, such old comrades as Richard Mulcahy, Ernie Blythe and Kevin O'Higgins, who himself was subsequently gunned down by another of Nomad's comrades, Archie Doyle in 1927.

NOTES.

1. Arthur Mitchell: *Revolutionary Government in Ireland: Dáil Éireann, 1919-22.* Gill & Mcmillan, Dublin 1993, p. 275.
2. Joe Wyse. Quartermaster Decies (West Waterford) Brigade.
3. Joseph Vize. Former British Naval officer who operated for the IRA in Glasgow up to 1918. IRB member and loyal Collins man. Worked with another of Collins' operatives, Neil Kerr, who was a ships purser and one of Collins' agents in England. 'Travel agent' for Republicans on the run, from Harry Boland to De Valera. Arrested. Replaced by Liam Mellows, May 1921.
4. Pax Ó Faoláin (Whelan) from Dungarvan, Co. Waterford. In command of the Decies Brigade. His views on Nomad McGuinness are recorded in McEoin, op. cit., pp. 140-142.
5. McGuinness, *Nomad*, op. cit. pp. 174-175.
6. McGuinness, *Nomad*, op. cit. pp. 179-180.
7. McEoin, op. cit., p. 141. Interestingly, Liam Lynch ('The Real Chief'), at the time Commandant of the Cork no. 2 Brigade and, soon, the First Southern Division, claimed that Pax Ó Faoláin had told him that "probably as a result of British Intelligence the ship and his cargo were seized" (Ryan, Meda: *The Real Chief. The Story of Liam Lynch*. Mercier Press, Cork/Dublin 1986, p. 109). Of course, Lynch apparently believed that the guns in the second cargo went North through Dick Barrett, Dan Gleeson and Seán Gaynor. In fact, most of the guns went South but maybe Lynch wasn't fully aware of this or was dissembling.

8. And poor old Captain Collins. The 'ancient mariner' had later been persuaded by the IRA to buy the *Hannah*, also for an inflated price, and he had even changed the name, yet again, to *The Warrior* but at least he must have thought that he had got rid of Nomad and the IRA. Not so. The Civil War had broken out and in the deep south each side was raiding the other. The British were delivering the Free Staters a cargo of naval arms and ammunition from Haulbowline Island to County Cork. In March IRA men Sean O'Hegarty and Michael Murphy got wind of the shipment plans and determined to hi-jack it. The first plan failed, but they improvised, marching into a pub and 'commandeering' Captain Collins and his vessel at the Deepwater Quay. On March 31, 1922, using a stolen ensign they stopped the *Upnor*, fooling her accompanying escort vessels with a false flag. A boarding party of IRA men ran the *Upnor* into Ballycotton Bay, ten miles east of Cork and unloaded the guns onto lorries.

9. This 'tale' comes from Nomad. We have been unable to obtain any corroboration of it, although that doesn't mean it isn't true. *See* McGuinness, *Nomad*, op. cit., p. 186-191.

10. For the full story of how the Thompson machinegun got to Ireland, *see* Cronin, Seán: *The McGarrity Papers*, Anvil, Kerry 1972, p. 99. Paid for by *Clann na Gael* in the United States prototypes were made in 1919 and 1920. In January 1921 Irish procurements officers ordered 100 Thompsons but only a few were smuggled into Ireland. In April 1921 two Irish American arms instructors, ex-Lieut. Patrick Cronin, who had fought against Pancho Villa in 1916, and ex-Major James J. Dineen, who had been on the Western Front, went to Ireland to train the volunteers in the use of 'the big T'. The main consignment – 495 guns, 1,392 box magazines and large quantities of ammunition was seized by US agents on 15th June 1921 during a raid on the coal boat *East Side*, docked in Hoboken, NJ, across the Hudson from New York. Ironically, in 1925 'Jetter', real name John T. Ryan, negotiated a deal through Senator Wadsworth of New York and the *Clann* got their guns back – four years too late. McGarrity finally got the guns over to Seán Russell, the IRA quarter master in the thirties and they formed the hardcore of IRA weaponry until the early seventies. By then however, the Thompson was virtually obsolete, as poor Billy Reid discovered. Oh the Radio said!

Chapter 7
With Byrd To The Pole

"The slow sad murmur of far-distant seas, whipped by an icy breeze upon a shore windswept and desolate, a sunless strand, the frightened croon, smitten to whimper, of the dreary wind."

James Stephens

The Irish Civil War, following the split between the Republicans and the Free Staters and fomented by the British, had broken out. Nomad's closest old comrades – Mellows, Brugha and Rory O'Connor were in the Four Courts being shelled and Nomad McGuinness was back in Germany trying to get more money to purchase arms. Mellows had forwarded £10,000 to his latest agent who had managed to put it down as a deposit on £40,000 worth of guns and ammunition. Of course, the Civil War broke out, the remaining £30,000 wasn't forthcoming and, according to McGuinness his "friends had become Napoleons of high finance" and "decamped for Ireland, leaving me to cajole and placate the Germans."[1]

But with the Four Courts shelled and the Republicans retreating to the South and West no word came from Ireland. McGuinness claims that in desperation he made a visit to London and was promised that the £30,000 had been raised in Cork and would be delivered shortly. He returned to Germany but when, weeks later, the delegation from Ireland arrived they were empty handed.[2]

"The deal was off. I quit the Irish movement then and there. Incompetent meddling had destroyed my gun-running organization.

Later I was arrested in Berlin on a flimsy charge of passport violation, and the more serious charge of being connected with Bulgarian revolutionaries. My previous record was against me, and I anticipated a long term in a German fortress. However, I had sufficient private means to enable me to engage the best lawyer in Berlin. My release was negotiated, but on the condition that I left the State of Prussia forever. Thereafter I retired to a monastery in the Black Forest, where I spent two months of rest and solitude.

> The year 1923 I spent in various pursuits in different parts of Europe, from Paris to the Balkans, using half a dozen passports to negotiate various frontiers. November 1923 found me at a loose end in Belgium. In Antwerp I secured a berth as second officer on a Belgian tramp steamer bound for the United States, and one cold evening in the latter part of February 1924 I walked ashore in New York determined to make good once again in the land of the Almighty Dollar."[3]

German court records of the period no longer exist and we have only Nomad's word for his wanderings through Europe and the Balkans in 1923. It can be confirmed that he did arrive in New York in February 1924 but there is one curious omission in Nomad's brief account. Four years later, in 1928 he is interviewed about the forthcoming Polar expedition with Commander Byrd. He is accompanied by his wife and his four year old son. Their address is given – 7405 5th Avenue, but Nomad gives no name of 'Mrs McGuinness' or the four year old son Patrick (whose names he never writes). Surely a marriage in Berlin to a Jewish Polish woman would have warranted a mention? But, as will be examined in the Afterword, Nomad virtually never referred to his family(ies). In actual fact, as we discovered, McGuinness met and married Klara Zuckerkandel (1902-1996) in 1923. She took the name Claire when she was with McGuinness in New York.

If McGuinness is tight-lipped about 1923 he is positively laconic about 1924-28. He says that he tried building contracting in Long Island but that:

> "a life of routine was more than I could stomach, and I was ready for the first whisper of a foreign ill-wind that boded trouble.
> My first attempt to break the doldrums was a fiasco. Chinese agents for Chiang Kai Shek in New York had arranged for me to handle a naval manœuvre of my own planning, and I was sent post haste to China. But Chinese political intrigue is even more difficult than Irish. There were internal dissensions. [...] The Canton group offered me a choice of posts, but the political change of front by the leaders reminded me too much of the Irish betrayal. I rejected all offers and returned to Los Angeles, California. After a couple of months in Hollywood, where I was employed in rigging a sailing-vessel on the lots, I returned to New York determined to settle down."[4]

McGuinness wrote this in 1935. Seven years earlier he had embellished the story of Chiang Kai Shek a little. According to the

Brooklyn Union 'he has commanded the private barge of the late Chinese Emperor and been the owner of a fleet of four ships under the name of the International Steamship company.' By the time this story got back to Ireland McGuinness had run four ships of arms from South America to China for Chiang – and somehow in the meantime managed to become President of a Latin American country.

One of the more ludicrous stories was how a visitor to the *Samson/City of New York* turned out to be a William Bull who was a member of the British court martial which sentenced Sir Roger Casement, McGuinness' old friend, to death. According to the inventive (or gullible) scribe 'McGuinness and Bull recognized each other and after the initial first shock of surprise the two became friendly enough to laugh over the coincidence of their meeting.' This is rubbish. Casement never underwent a court martial. He was tried and sentenced to death for 'high treason'. His prosecutor was the infamous F.E. Smith, a man who, only two years previously had himself organized armed resistance to the Crown in the form of the Ulster Volunteers, but his main nemesis was Chief Admiral Hall of British Intelligence who leaked genuine/forged diaries to 'prominent people' which purported to show that Sir Roger was a gay blade for those days. Casement was hanged in Pentonville Jail on August 3, 1916. There was no William Bull court martial. McGuinness was 23 years of age and in East Africa. Casement had been in Putamayo in Brazil reporting on the rubber plantation atrocities by the Imperialists from 1906 until 1911 before returning briefly to Ireland and then going to Germany to try and get guns. In short, McGuinness had never even met Casement.[5]

In all events, 1925 found Nomad, with wife and child, trying to set up as an engineering contractor in New York. He claims that he built an aeroplane factory for J.V. Martin, an ex-British sea-captain and pioneer of aviation in America at Mitchelfield, Long Island, but that 'economics had got the better of them and the venture had come to naught'. In 1925 Pax Ó Faoláin got a letter from him. In it Nomad said that he had settled down as a quiet married man. Would Pax send him a photograph of Ballynagaul, Cheekpoint and Dunabrittain? He must have been starting on his book.[6]

Nomad also apparently made several trips to Central America, probably in the eternal quest for the fortune he never made. He used to send postcards to brother Hugh. One of his nieces recollects being a small child and asking Hugh innocently what one card meant. It was a picture of a Mexican street with the comment 'Dear Hugh: not much doing here, only two dogs fucking in the street.' And two copulating canines didn't pay any bills.

Then came the news over the radio. Admiral Byrd was planning to fly over the South Pole and was looking for experienced volunteers.

Byrd's 'trip' to the South Pole – which he only flew over, was primarily a publicity and fund raising venture. The heroic Norwegian Amundsen had already made it to the Pole – on foot, in 1911. One month later the brave but rather dim Captain Scott and his men were lost near the Pole. The Irish explorer Ernest Shackleton made four epic trips in the region, including escaping from the *Endurance*, which was trapped in the ice.

In short, there was no need whatsoever to fly over the Pole. But Byrd had raised the money and he had to deliver. Capitalists like Ford and Dupont expected to have icy mountains in remote Antarctica named after them and perhaps lodge a bogus claim for any mineral wealth possibly discovered in the future. But big money meant they could buy a lot of good publicity. The patriotic American citizen, soon to suffer in the throes of the stock market crash needed a popular hero and Byrd fitted the bill. That plus the presence of a camera crew meant that for the first time the public could see reasonably clear film footage of the mighty icebergs and gallant and well equipped crews.

McGuinness applied at once.

> "Antarctica had always interested me. It was off the beaten track. Brave men had perished trying to wrest secrets from its icy bosom. To gain first-hand knowledge of any place there is no better method than to go there."

> "'It's no use, Tim,' I said [to my partner]. 'I've got this wretched wanderlust. That Antarctic expedition has thrown me out of gear.'"[7]

In an interview he gave shortly before his departure on the expedition to Harry Goldberg which appeared in the Metropolitan section of the *Detroit News* on October 7, 1928, under the title 'Byrd's Mate, Shipwrecked, Shot at, Sentenced to Death, Chased by Leopards, Expects to Find Peace at the South Pole', Nomad poses in furs for a picture which accompanies the rather garishly illustrated article. Goldberg describes McGuinness as "a Conrad rover come to life. Only 35 years old, his twinkling blue eyes and jaunty face have crowded more excitement into the last 20 years than an army of average men see in their lifetime. [...] Bullet scars on his left hand, hip and right leg are an indication of an adventurous career."

But Goldberg discovers a softer side to McGuinness.

> "'Haven't you had enough excitement, putting yourself in constant peril, and want a house and home?' he was asked.
>
> 'I have a family,' replied McGuinness, his voice for the first time losing its even tone. 'I was married to a Russian woman in Vienna. [Klara was Polish and they married in Berlin]. I have a boy past three and I'm devoted to them.
>
> 'But I can't stand the grind of civilized life. I owned a motorboat on Long Island Sound and I did about everything you can do with a boat. I've been in this country for four years and I've tried many things.
>
> 'Suppose I stuck in a commonplace job. What memory of his dad is that to give to a boy?[8] And your neighbors have such a narrow view of life. They judge everyone by their own mean standards. [...] If you don't live according to their conventions you can't be tolerated at all.
>
> 'I had to get away from all that. When I'm home I'm restless to get somewhere there might be something stirring to be done.'"

And so McGuinness had applied for a position with Byrd's expedition and, in due course had been interviewed by the Commander in his suite in the Biltmore Hotel. Commander Byrd has not left any memoir of this interview but McGuinness has.

> "'Why do you want to go on the expedition?' Byrd quickly asked.
>
> 'I'll tell you why, Commander,' I said. 'There seems no hope of a decent war breaking out in the near future. Piracy is difficult to organize, and it's too hot in Nicaragua for comfortable revolution.'
>
> Byrd burst out laughing. 'That's the queerest reason that's been put up to me yet. Say! What do you consider the best jobs you've yet accomplished? I want the truth!'
>
> 'Breaking Frank Carty out of prison under a death sentence. Escaping myself under similar circumstances. I consider those two good jobs.' [...]
>
> 'I see by your papers you're a good sailor, have held three commands. Guess I'll take you.'"[9]

Newspaper reports and subsequent legend named Charles McGuinness as 'Byrd's number 2' and would have it that without McGuinness Byrd would never have made it over the South Pole. This is, to say the least, piling Ossa upon Pelion. Nomad was taken on to patch up and re-rig an ancient Norwegian whaler, the *Samson*, which was already fifty years old and only weighing 500 tons – compared to the whale factory ship the *Larsen*, which weighed 18,000 tons and was to play a more important part on the expedition than the McGuinness' *City of New York*, as the *Samson* had been renamed.

The unpopular Captain Melville was appointed skipper and McGuinness made 'Chief Officer'.

McGuinness explains that this was because

> "Not being an American (in truth I had no nationality) Commander Byrd regretted that he could not give me command. But the public would not have tolerated a foreigner in command of a ship sailing under the 'stars and stripes' on a mission of national importance. For myself, I would have sailed as bos'n and been glad of the opportunity."[10]

McGuinness' first job was to make the elderly barquentine sea ready and this in itself was quite a task. But after a few months at the Tebo Yacht Basin in Brooklyn, the old and worm eaten spars had been taken down and replaced, the jib boom had been unshipped, the hull recaulked and new sailing yards crossed on the mainmast. The *City of New York* was ready to play its part in Byrd's national extravaganza.

For that's what Byrd's expedition was really all about. That and personal glory for the commander.

At the time of the expedition (1928) Admiral Robert Evelyn Byrd was 40 years of age. Born in Virginia in 1888. (McGuinness was to claim that Byrd was 'half-Irish' but the family genealogy doesn't confirm this). A graduate of the class of 1912 from the U.S. Naval Academy, he served in the battleship fleet until being invalided out in 1916. He went on to win his wings as Naval Aviator 608. When the war ended he was Commander of the U.S. Naval Air Forces in Canada.

From 1924 on he became fascinated with transpolar flight. In 1926 he took leave of absence from the Navy and organized a privately financed expedition based in Spitzbergen. Supported financially by John D. Rockefeller, Edsel Ford and the *New York Times* Byrd and his pilot Floyd Bennett claimed to have reached the North Pole on May 9, 1926, although later explorers were to cast doubts upon their claims.

Nonetheless, Byrd returned a hero and was given the Congressional Medal of Honour. A newsworthy public figure and with more commercial sponsorship he next completed the first multi-engined airplane crossing of the Atlantic and then had turned his attention towards the South Pole.

Polar expedition was a dangerous trade. All remembered Captain Scott who had perished near the South Pole in 1912, after being beaten to it by Roald Amundsen, and Amundsen himself, who had helped advise Byrd, himself died in 1928 shortly before Byrd's departure, on a polar flight searching for the Italian aviator Nobile[11] whose airship was missing. But Byrd was the popular hero, and with the backings of the newspapers this expedition was to be the best financed yet.

Three boats plus the assistance of the large whale ships the *Larsen* and the *Sir James Clark Ross*. Four airplanes. 86 crew, 94 dogs, most of them brought in from Labrador and tons of supplies, navigation and photographic equipment, for this expedition was going to be covered by the press.

On September 9, 1928 Charles McGuinness wired his brother Hugh at the Main Street in Buncrana, Co. Donegal: "Enroute Antarctic. Write back City of New York. Dunedin. N. Zealand. Greetings. Sheilah family and yourself – Charlie." The message was sent by wire from station WFBT – 800 miles N.E. Colón (Panama Canal Zone).

Several days previously, just before the *Eleanor Bolling* towed the newly refurbished *City of New York* and her crew of 31 out from her moorings in Hoboken the local media had informed their readers that '5 of the crew were all Brooklyn boys, including tough guy Charles McGuinness'. There was a touching personal human interest paragraph in the *Brooklyn Union*'s effusive piece.

"Farewell Scrawled on Byrd Ship's Lifeboat by First Mate's Wife. 'Don't forget us. Your wife and child. Auf wiedersehen.' – this message scrawled in pencil on the keel of the aft starboard lifeboat of Commander Richard E. Byrd's ice-breaker, the *City of New York*, will probably often remind Charles J. McGuinness, first mate of the vessel, of the pretty Russian girl he married in Vienna and who, with their child, is now beginning a two-year wait in her little apartment, at 7405 Fifth Ave., until her ship comes in. Mrs. McGuinness, with wives of other members of the crew and officials sailed down the Bay on the *City of New York* on Saturday. Just before the ship pointed her nose out to the open sea, there were fond and tearful farewells between members of her crew and their wives who then returned to the city on the tug *Macom*. The wife of the Fightin' Irishman wept a little at parting. Just before she left the vessel she scrawled her farewell message on the lifeboat."

The small *City of New York* and the *Eleanor Bolling* (formerly the *Chelsea*, originally a British mine-sweeper it had been turned into a rum running ship and then seized by the U.S. customs)[12], left from New York in early September because it would take them much longer to reach the rendezvous point in Dunedin, New Zealand. Byrd himself departed with 14 crew members from San Pedro, California aboard the giant whaler *Larsen*. Byrd had with him the four airplanes, 5 tons of dynamite for blasting through the ice, 75 sheep, several milch cows and about 9,000 tons of supplies. They left California on October 11, 1928 and reached New Zealand in three and a half weeks without adventure. Unlike McGuinness' *City of New York*.

The crew were a motley bunch. Nomad immediately clashed with Captain Melville.

> "Melville was a schooner man, and wanted only the fore and aft sails set. On a square-rigged ship this was heresy, and I said so.
> We were opposite types. The ballyhoo of the expedition and the recent elevation to naval rank had gone to his head. But press clipping was his hobby, and dreams of eclipsing everyone in the ocean kept him so busy that I had no interference in running and handling the ship."[13]

Amongst the crew were three professors, a millionaire 'tourist', a Paramount film expert, some ex-US Navy mariners, 3 Norwegians and a six foot tall Boy Scout – Paul Siple, representing the adventuresome youth of America. Lumbering at no more than 6 knots per hour the clumsy bark took 20 days to reach Colón at the Panama Canal. There Captain Melville discovered to his dismay, and perhaps Nomad's schadenfreude, that the canal officials demanded money from the skipper for toll and fuel. 'No money, no transit, and no coal.' An embarrassed Melville had to borrow the money from one of the crew. Melville incurred more wrath from McGuinness when he threw three of the crew and a black stowaway off the boat and ordered that they be deported to the U.S. They passed through the canal and cleared Balboa on the Pacific coast but developed engine trouble and had to put back for repairs. Nomad and two other crew members nearly got left in a bar in Balboa when the boat sailed without them and they had to chase after it in the pilot's launch.

Melville was developing almost Queeg-like tendencies if McGuinness is to be believed.[14]

> "The skipper's fetish for economy, discipline, and sanctity became unbearable. He refused to recognize the time-honoured custom of 'splicing the main brace'. This practice calls for a glass of rum after heavy work in stormy weather. Sailors, tired and soaking wet, expect this reward; but Melville would not permit the 18th amendment to be violated. He refused to permit any coffee to be made or served in the galley at night or before breakfast time – a strange rule to enforce at sea.
> Then the fun began. Someone took cacao from the supplies, and broke into a case of *Klim*, which is powdered milk. Mixed with hot water, it made a palatable drink appreciated by the night watches and the men in the stoke hold. One day the skipper trained his glasses upon a can floating beside the ship. He read 'Klim' distinctly and doubtless felt the same thrill of discovery experienced by Balboa 'upon a peak in Darien'. [Secretly] he dosed the cocoa supply with a violent purgative [and] half a dozen men were in the throes of dysentery the following day."[15]

The *City of New York* was again running out of coal and McGuinness had to fight to refuel in Tahiti and not the far less appealing Pago-Pago.

The *Eleanor Bolling*, which had left New York a full month later than the *City of New York* still reached Papeete in Tahiti a week before the *City*, and, despite the disapproval of Captain Melville the two crews partied with the locals. Nomad claims that he met old friends from when he had last been in Papeete 14 years previously.

> "It was a sailors' dream come true – champagne, tropic moon, guitars, singing and dancing. [...] The party was a splendid bacchanal."[16]

Ninety days after leaving New York the former *Samson* spied Otago Heads and limped into Dunedin to be reunited with the *Bolling* and Byrd from the *Larsen*.

But the expedition was cumbersome. The *City of New York* was holding them up and they now realized that without the assistance of the *Larsen* and another Norwegian whaler, the *Sir James Clark Ross* it would be impossible to transport all the planes and the dogs, not to mention the personnel from America.

It was decided that the *Bolling* was now to tow the bark down to the ice-pack. At the edge of the ice the *Larsen* would take over and tow the *City* through the hundreds of miles of floating ice. Nomad was transferred to the *Bolling* and away from the hated Melville. On December 2, 1928 they set sail for the Bay of Whales.

The *Bolling* was a better boat than the *City of New York*. Commander Byrd took charge and morale improved. Captain Brown was far more reasonable than Melville who had been quietly left in New Zealand. But the *Bolling* was only 800 tons and the task of towing the *City* through mountainous seas towards the icebergs was frightening.

> "The *Bolling* was like a submarine; seas came rolling on board and stopped on board. Our rooms were full of water and the common mess-room, situated in the most sheltered part of the ship resembled more a swimming pool than a dining-room."

> "The hero of the occasion was […] Dick Perks [sic], a hard-boiled seadog from Liverpool [who] toiled and slaved at his greasy chores in rubber sea boots that reached clear up to his waist […] swimming round in his kitchen in a welter of pots and pans. [But] never once […] were we without a hot meal."[17]

About 63 degrees south the vessels encountered the first icebergs and truly mountainous seas. Men were swept overboard – McGuinness saved the cook Perks when a large wave almost threw him over the rail. Things were even worse on the *City* when the bridle of the steel hawser snapped and they had to spend over two hours in the howling gale trying to haul the cable in. Eventually the damage was repaired and both vessels made it, on December 10, 1928, as far as Scott Island, two huge basalt rocks emerging from the ocean. Their existence had been in doubt since only one man, Lieutenant Colbeck had sighted them while on Captain Scott's 1901 expedition.

Meeting up with the *Larsen* the *Bolling* left the *City* with them and returned back to Dunedin for supplies.

New Zealand obviously suited McGuinness. The expeditionary forces were popular with local society and much sought after. McGuinness revelled in the 'social life'. But by January 1929 they were refurbished, "loaded down below the Plimsoll mark" and steaming south again for the Bay of Whales. Despite heavy seas they reached the Barrier and then had the difficult task of discharging the

Ford airplane ashore where it had skis bolted to its fuselage.

It was at this time when the press back in the States began to really lionize the heroic Commander Byrd that an avalanche of over a hundred tons of snow suddenly collapsed on top of the *Bolling*. The bark heeled over at a 30 degree list, but somehow righted itself. In the meantime seaman Benny Roth was thrown into the water. He clung to a cake of ice but was being swept away when Byrd threw himself into the water to try and rescue Roth. The freezing water numbed him instantly and he too started to founder. McGuinness, Captain Brown and crewman Joe de Ganahl had to rescue the would-be rescuer while Lieut. Harry Adams, mate on the *City of New York* launched a dinghy and saved Benny Roth. According to McGuinness "part of this episode was captured by alert movie-men, but their request for several re-takes to complete the scenario were repulsed by the commander." That's how McGuinness saw it, but by the time the trip's syndicated reporter, Russell Owen had written it up and spread it around the world Byrd was the hero, even though he'd had to get rescued himself. 'Byrd has medals for saving five men from drowning' claimed Owen. Perhaps interestingly Owen names ten of the sailors who effected the rescue of Byrd and Roth. McGuinness' name does not appear amongst them.

There was actually not much for McGuinness and the crew of the *Bolling* to do on shore. Their principal job after all was as coal delivery men – albeit in the most inhospitable conditions. They watched the Norwegian whalers as they harpooned dozens of whales with their Svend Foyn gun and laughed at the penguins but on February 2, 1929 they were on their way on the 2,300 mile journey back to New Zealand. The ship being empty bobbed along like a cork on the water. The return trip took only 13 days.

It took only 36 hours to load further supplies and then the *Bolling* was off to sea again, this time with a strange passenger named Richard Gale Brophy on board. Back in New York Brophy had been a man of influence and power. He had interviewed John D. Rockefeller and the rest of the Captains of American Industry; he had raised huge sums of money for the expedition and a grateful Byrd had appointed him second in command. Brophy had finally made it to New Zealand and was now intent on joining his leader in 'Little America' as Byrd had renamed the Barrier berg at Whale Bay. But he was decidedly eccentric.

For once Nomad is not too censorious of Brophy. "The strain of his position had created a mental disorder." "Brophy was now developing strange ideas. He sent voluminous radiograms to Byrd [that] Byrd told him to stop." Brophy then took a dislike to both Byrd and Captain Brown and tried to enlist McGuinness in a mad plot to run a counter-expedition, take over the boat and make for Scott's old headquarters on McMurdo Sound.

> "[We have] an aeroplane, plenty of dogs and sufficient stores. I listened politely, but took no heed. I knew he was unwell.
> Then he succumbed to the obsession that [Captain] Brown was going to shoot him. Taking a small bell tent he moved aft and pitched on the after hatch, exposed to wind, sea, rain and sleet. [...] With bedding and a typewriter he disappeared from sight and occasionally we would go aft to see if he was still aboard [in his airy wigwam]."[18]

But the weather worsened and Byrd ordered the *Bolling* back to Dunedin as the ice-pack was closing fast. Having failed to discharge their cargo the disgruntled crew of the *Bolling* turned around and made it back to Dunedin. There Brophy was relieved of his position. The ordered return of the *Bolling* apparently engendered some rivalry and bad feeling with the crew of the *City* who were staying at the Barrier. Many of the *Bolling* crew felt that they had been slighted and should have been there in 'Little America'.

Back in 'Little America', from March until September, Byrd and his party bedded down for the Antarctic winter in atrocious snowbound conditions. In New Zealand however, apart from general marine maintenance Nomad and those of the crew who had not been sent home by the parsimonious Melville enjoyed themselves 'hunting and sticking pigs'. They were to make one more coal delivery trip in the late summer of 1929 but when it came to leaving New Zealand McGuinness was to write 'we felt that we were leaving home rather than going to one'. And after spending Easter week in Papeetee on the return trip he adumbrated 'had there not been urgent reasons to the contrary I would, I frankly confess, have stayed there for good'. This hardly squares with missing 'the little Russian wife and dear child.'

But all good times must come to an end. On Thanksgiving Day, November 28th 1929, the Fokker *Floyd Bennett* set off to fly over the South Pole. The famous Bernt Balchen was the pilot; Harold I. June was the radio operator; Captain Ashley C. McKinley was the official photographer and cartographer and Admiral Byrd was along for the ride. Finally, at 1.25 on November 29th 1929 Byrd radioed 'My calculations indicate that we have reached the vicinity of the South Pole. Flying high for survey.' Byrd dropped a Norwegian flag in memory of Roald Amundsen; a British flag in honour of Captain Scott, an American flag in honour of America and another American flag in honour of Byrd's former pilot Floyd Bennett.

The two year expedition had been indeed dangerous. Men and dogs had died and gone mad. Planes had been lost and large sums of money expended so that Byrd could fly over the Pole and name a range of mountains after his chief sponsor John D. Rockefeller. But back home in the U.S. all was euphoria. After all, didn't the citizens need circuses to take their minds of the Wall Street crash of the previous year.

The Mayor of New York, Jimmy 'Johnnie' Walker, set aside June 19th 1930 as the date of the official reception, so the vessels, which were for once ahead of time, had to drift around aimlessly for a few days. This suited McGuinness who must have been one of the very few people who went to Antarctica and returned home with a case of malaria, which he'd contracted on the return voyage. But by June 19th he had recovered sufficiently to be on the deck when the *Bolling* and the *City of New York* sailed into New York harbour to a huge display of flags and hooting horns and whistles. As he went ashore Nomad was greeted by his "old friend Count Felix von Luckner" who in his splendid uniform of a German admiral "made a striking picture, bellowing out a thunderous welcome to the Irish rebel turned explorer."

After a civic reception at City Hall it was on to the luncheon at the "Advertisers' Club" (this is surely a Nomad misprint for the Adventurers' club) where he rubbed shoulders with James J. Corbett, former world heavy-weight champion and the famous travel writer Lowell Thomas.

That night it was off to Washington DC for a trip around the city, the highlight being presented to President Hoover and members of the Senate in the gardens of the White House the next day.

Back in New York McGuinness and another crew member, Jack O'Brien, were accorded an official and public reception at City Hall by Jimmy Walker, the Mayor. "I presented him [the Mayor] with an Irish flag that had been flown over the South Pole. The Mayor received the flag, to present it later to De Valera, leader of the Irish Republican Party in Ireland." Alas, no Irish flag actually flew at or over the South Pole. But perhaps DeV never knew that this was just another of Nomad's little instances of being careless with the facts.

(His wife Klara/Claire and beloved little Paudeen were not brought to these celebrations, Nomad was apparently bringing 'some other woman' of unknown identity).

Similarly, he claims that a few months later he received "telegraphic information that the Secretary of the Navy would present me with a gold Congressional Medal for Services Rendered. I accepted the medal."[19]

Nomad was to find accommodation not in the small apartment with 'the little Russian wife and dear child' on 5th Avenue but at 486 Prospect Place in Brooklyn. From there he wrote his brother Hugh on August 27th announcing his return and relaying some scéal about former Derry denizens whom he'd met in New York.

Byrd had returned in glory and was soon made a rear admiral. He went on to make four other Antarctic expeditions, spending the winter of 1934 alone in a meteorological hut 100 miles into the interior and almost dying from carbon monoxide fumes. His expeditions claimed hundreds of thousands of square miles of territory for the United States. He died in 1957.

Nomad McGuinness went from the 'honour' of meeting President Herbert Hoover to humble rum running off Rockaway Beach. He had had his brief moment of fame and then found himself out of work in the midst of the depression. A different line of work would have to be found.

Notes

1. McGuinness, *Nomad*, op. cit., p. 208.
2. The murky financial dealings of the 1920s are lost in the mists of the Civil War. Who lied to whom? Who ripped off whom? McGuinness' story may well be true. Certainly Ernie O'Malley was to subsequently probe the missing money, without apparently coming to any definite conclusion. (*see: Papers of Ernie O'Malley* (1916-1956), IE UCDAD P17a/4).
3. McGuinness, *Nomad*, op. cit., pp. 208-209. Why does Nomad lie? The vessel was not a Belgian tramp steamer – it was the *SS Dorelian*. It landed in New York on February 8, 1924. A look at

the manifest shows that he was listed as an AB – Able Bodied Seaman, not a ship's officer. The ships' manifest also describes him as "British, 5 ft. 6 inches and 148 lbs" (Source: Tim McGuinness).
4. McGuinness, *Nomad*, op. cit., p. 210. It is most unlikely that he actually did go to China in 1927 as he claims.
5. To be fair to Nomad he does admit that when being interviewed by the gullible and sensation hungry New York press "I witnessed at first hand the American love of publicity exploitation and general hokum. We were photographed, we told lies of former adventures, and reporters added reams of falsehoods to those given so lavishly. […] I was credited with having commanded the Chinese Emperor's barge. A lady reporter asked me to tattoo a full-rigged ship on her arm. I compromised with a small anchor and made her the happiest girl in New York." (McGuinness, *Nomad*, op. cit., pp. 213-214.) *See Brooklyn Union*, first week of September 1928.
See too, for instance, Bell, J. Bowyer: *The Secret Army. The IRA 1916-1979*. The Academy Press, Dublin 1979, p. 221.
6. McEoin, op. cit., p. 142. The next time Pax was to hear from McGuinness was three years later, in 1928, when he told him how he'd signed up for the Byrd expedition in which he was "second in command" and invited "me and some of the lads from Ballynagaul to come along". The boys of Ballynagaul declined.
7. McGuinness, *Nomad*, op. cit., pp. 211-212.
8. Several years later McGuinness was to write *Behind the Red Curtain*. In it there is no mention of his dearly loved son – or wife. The book is dedicated 'to Anita, in the hope that when she is old enough to read, the world will be a brighter and happier place.'
9. McGuinness, *Nomad*, op. cit., pp. 212-213.
10. ibid., p. 213.
11. Umberto Nobile (1885-1978) was an Italian aeronautical engineer. He flew across the North Pole with Amundsen and Ellsworth in 1926. A general in the Italian air force and professor of aeronautical engineering at Naples, in 1928 he was wrecked in the airship *Italia* when returning from the North Pole and was judged to be responsible for the disaster.
After having a major public argument with the hero Amundsen, Nobile had raised the money for a new airship himself and was

the pride of Italy. Six of his crew died on the way back from the Pole when they came down in bad weather with the airship iced over. The rest, led by an injured Nobile survived for over forty days before being discovered by the Italians, who crashed their rescue plane. Six nations raced for the kudos of rescuing the Polar explorer and it was the Russian icebreaker the *Krassin* which finally saved Nobile and 8 crew. But Amundsen and his rescue party of 13 were all lost without trace. Public opinion, ever fickle, turned against Nobile – there were even rumours (totally unsubstantiated) of murder and cannibalism amongst some of the survivors. After the war Nobile was 'rehabilitated' and continued making airships until his death in 1978.

12. The *Chelsea* had been renamed the *Eleanor Bolling* in honour of Byrd's mother – Eleanor Bolling.
13. McGuinness, *Nomad*, op. cit., p. 215.
14. In fairness to 'Captain Queeg' Melville there is a story in the McGuinness family of how Charlie started out with the expedition as first mate, chief officer. At Panama City during the first leg of the expedition Charlie missed the boat and had to be ferried out to catch it because he was off on a bender with two cohorts. In port, drunk, he and a woman he brought aboard fell off the barquentine. Acts like these undoubtedly didn't endear him to Captain Melville, a hard-line naval mariner. Charlie was switched to the *Eleanor Bolling*, which never got the credit or the publicity that the *City of New York*, the expedition's flagship did.
15. McGuinness, *Nomad*, op. cit., pp. 219-220.
16. ibid., p. 222.
17. ibid., pp. 227-228.
18. ibid., pp. 237-238. Brophy turned up again in equally bizarre situations. Having been adjudged mentally incompetent in New Zealand he was deported, after he insisted in wandering around Dunedin in Antarctic clothing in the town's hotel dining rooms. Upon his return to America he next staged a fake suicide, leaving his clothes and an enigmatic note informing the world that he 'was going to take a long, long swim until the waters closed over my head,' in a bathing cabinet on Coney Island. A search produced nothing and the story was an overnight sensation. A week later however Brophy was spotted in disguise on Broadway. He'd been doing 'a B. Traven' (perhaps this gave Nomad the idea 18 years later?). Brophy was next sighted

writing about the expedition for the *Omaha Bee* but then disappeared again from public life. McGuinness however claims that when, after the expedition had returned and he was in the White House garden to meet President Hoover he saw Richard Gale Brophy standing apart, lonely and morose but clearly a part of the entourage. (ibid., p. 248.)

19. ibid, pp. 248-249. Originally, in the beginning when we were researching the book we were unfair to McGuinness.

"Friday, 23 May 1930

Joint Resolution Authorizing the presentation of medals to the officers and men of the Byrd Antarctic expedition.

Resolved by the Senate and House of Representatives of the United States of America in Congress assembled, That the Secretary of the Navy be, and he is hereby, empowered and directed to cause to be made at the United States mint such number of gold, silver, and bronze medals as he may deem appropriate and necessary respectively to be presented to the officers and men of the Byrd Antarctic expedition to express the high admiration in which the Congress and the American people hold their heroic and undaunted services in connection with the scientific investigations and extraordinary aerial explorations of the Antarctic Continent, under the personal direction of Rear Admiral Richard E. Byrd, said medals to be suitably inscribed.

SEC. 2. That such amount as may be necessary for the cost of said medals is hereby authorized to be appropriated out of any money in the Treasury not otherwise appropriated.
46 Stat. 379"

Notes: There are no people listed in this Act except for Rear Admiral Richard Byrd. He personally chose who would receive the medals and *The New York Times* of 3 August 1931 page 19 prints the listing of the gold, silver, and bronze medal expedition members. According to CRS Report RL30076, there were 67 medals minted, but according to this list, 66 were given out. Without a definitive list from the Naval Office, this is the best list available to me at this time.

(We are indebted to Dr. Tim McGuinness, Nomad's grandson for this information and we have additional confirmation in a letter from Nomad to his brother Hugh, dated September 1932.)

Chapter 8
That Illegal Smile:
Rum Running On Rockaway Beach

The fame of the Antarctic expedition faded soon. Byrd of course remained a household word, but the lesser members of the expedition, such as McGuinness, had their few moments of fame and then returned to relative anonymity. McGuinness had split from his wife Claire and son Patrick/Paudeen and was living at a different address but as usual he was planning something.

He apparently conned a 'friend', New York stockbroker Ralph de Milhau into partially financing an expedition to recover the lost Incan treasure which supposedly lay at the bottom of the sacrificial lake in the Venezuelan interior, but times were hard (the depression was on) and suckers were few and far between. And de Milhau wasn't a complete fool.

Another even more ludicrous venture – a pleasure cruise to the Bay of Whales with his 'chivalrous friend' the gallant Count Felix von Luckner[1] and McGuinness as tour guides fell through. Nomad claims that it was because the yacht *Mopelia*[2] was too slow for the lengthy and hazardous voyage. No tickets sold and it was back to the drawing board. But:

> "As a result of the publicity of these proposals my name came to be bandied about as that of a competent seafarer. I was not unduly surprised, therefore, when one evening a mysterious 'phone call summoned me to a shipyard in the environs of New York Harbour.
>
> I was not surprised when I received an offer from a rum-running syndicate – already I had turned down several such offers during the past few years. Would I take over command of a rum boat equipped with three 'Liberty' motors? She was about sixty feet long with a capacity for 600 cases. I accepted with alacrity. Like most of the veterans of the Byrd party, I was almost destitute of funds. That state of affairs did not exist for long. One week with the rum syndicate and I made more money than I received for two years under the banner of science!"[3]

Nomad was about to play his part in 'the noble experiment'.

National prohibition of alcohol (1920-33) – the 'noble experiment' – was undertaken to reduce crime and corruption, solve social problems, reduce the tax burden created by prisons and poorhouses, and improve health and hygiene in America. The results of that experiment clearly indicate that it was a miserable failure on all counts.

Although consumption of alcohol fell at the beginning of Prohibition, it subsequently increased. Alcohol became more dangerous to consume; crime increased and became 'organized'; the court and prison systems were stretched to breaking point; and corruption of public officials was rampant. No measurable gains were made in productivity or reduced absenteeism. Prohibition removed a significant source of tax revenue and greatly increased government spending. It led many drinkers to switch to opium, codeine, patent medicines, cocaine, and other dangerous substances that they would have been unlikely to encounter in the absence of Prohibition.

Prohibition fell far short of eliminating the consumption of alcohol.

Second, consumption of alcohol actually rose steadily after an initial drop. Annual per capita consumption had been declining since 1910, reached an all-time low during the depression of 1921, and then began to increase in 1922. Consumption would probably have surpassed pre-Prohibition levels even if Prohibition had not been repealed in 1933. Illicit production and distribution continued to expand throughout Prohibition despite ever-increasing resources devoted to enforcement. It was all too reminiscent of today's ludicrous 'drug wars'.

Third, the resources devoted to enforcement of Prohibition increased along with consumption. Heightened enforcement did not curtail consumption. The annual budget of the Bureau of Prohibition went from $4.4 million to $13.4 million during the 1920s, while Coast Guard spending on Prohibition averaged over $13 million per year. To those amounts should be added the expenditures of state and local governments.

And then there was the 'illegal smile'. Alcohol became exciting. Slightly – only slightly dangerous. Just as in the seventies and eighties, and still today, everyone in the know has 'their connection' who can supply illicit drugs, be it cocaine, heroin or even the beneficial herb. So too, in the twenties the bourgeoisie would flock to the clubs and shebeens, to the Cotton Club where they could hope to rub shoulders with Owney Madden,[4] Walter Winchell, Lucky Luciano, and their gunsels, be overcharged for rotgut liquor or really overcharged for the real thing brought in from Canada, and listen to the new black singers of jazz and blues. Hi-de-hi! What fun! Or they could go to their nearest mean dive or 'blind pig'.

And people had to help supply the demand. And Nomad was one.

By the time that McGuinness got involved the main route for alcohol for thirsty New Yorkers stemmed from the small French island of St. Pierre et Miquelon, south of Newfoundland or from Nassau in the Bahamas.

At St. Pierre the liquor was taken out of cases and wrapped in burlap, to facilitate the handling on schooners, speed boats and trucks.

> "When I made my debut into rum-running in the summer of 1930 the profits to be made were substantial; but the stuff was gradually falling in price. Economics are more effective in curtailing liquor consumption than all the revenue agents and coastguards in the country."[5]

And there were by-products to the rum-running rackets.

> "Chink smuggling is a riskier business than liquor smuggling, and many a Chinaman lies on the bottom of the ocean not far from New York.
>
> When the Chink runner reaches the danger zone, the yellow freight is manacled together in groups of six by leg- and hand-irons. Should a revenue cutter heave into sight, the wretched Chinamen are jettisoned without compunction. This abhorrent racket flourishes off the coasts of New York, Cuba, and California. The price for smuggling a chink is usually from five hundred to a thousand dollars a head. It is paid by a Tong leader. If the Chink comes through the ordeal he is a serf until he pays his master back in wages earned in a restaurant or laundry chain."[6]

> "As a rule, rum-boat skippers are just good boatmen. My crew were all men of high calibre. The chief engineer was formerly the chief on an oil tanker running from New York to Buenos Aires, and he knew how to get the most out of our two Diesels. The chief's assistant was an aviation mechanic who had resigned a commission in the naval flying division. The radio operator served eight years in the United States Navy as a chief petty officer. He was constantly on the alert, despite the terrible weather, maintaining a constant liaison with the operator on shore.
>
> Life on a rum boat is no sinecure. There is no haven against dirty weather, and the majority of our operations needed the cover

of fog, storm, and darkness. Our men drank champagne to conserve the fresh-water supply, which was needed for cooking, but in all my experience of rum-running I never drank a thimbleful of liquor myself."[7]

Well, maybe?

During this time McGuinness is alleged to have augmented his income by penning a series of articles on rum-running under the pseudonym 'Nighthawk'. These appeared in five parts in the *New York Evening Graphic* (*see* Chapter 9).

As for the name 'Nomad'.

Most people do not get to chose their own nickname, as many a would-be 'Champion' know to their cost. Prior to the writing of his book *Nomad* or *Sailor of Fortune* McGuinness was called 'Charles', 'Charlie', 'McGuinness', 'Captain Hennessey' or 'Captain Thompson'. During his rum running days he used the pseudonym 'Olson'. His old IRA friends wouldn't have recognized his new soubriquet since Nomad didn't come up with it until 1934-35 when he wrote his book. Even then, he was not totally original. 'Nomad' had been the *nom de guerre* of none other than General George Armstrong Custer, he of Little Bighorn fame (or infamy). In Victorian times there had been at least two books about a romantic adventurer called 'Nomad'. But it was a catchy title, and McGuinness made sure it stuck in every interview he gave thereafter.

But while penning his autobiography McGuinness still had to make a livelihood and rum-running was the quickest way.

Nomad's first boss was Walter 'Bimbo' Waddel, one of Owney Madden's top men, who was described by McGuinness as 'boss of the shipyard and all booze operations in this section of Long Island'. A Swede, Tom Swanson was his chief mate. His boat was to be the *Voltaire*. She was a 'dollar and a quarter' – a 125 ft. long speed merchant with two large diesel engines fitted so that she could carry a large load at a cruising speed of 14 knots and when chased could get up to nearly 20 knots, giving it an edge on the coastguard cutters. But it would take a few months to fit out the *Voltaire* and in the meantime McGuinness had to get some experience in.

Nomad describes his first landing.

"Jumping out [of the truck], I saw the beach black with moving figures, sharply etched on the background of smooth white sand. It was freezing and the hard sand and ice crystals, reflecting the rays of a crescent moon, caused ripples of light and shade to flow over the surface like undulations on a silken robe. [...]

Away off in the distance, where the ink-black sea cut the horizon, the three occulting flashes of the Ambrose Lightship were visible, silently and demandingly domineering the channel leading to the harbour of New York.

But the most striking feature of this *nocturne nauticus* was the slim, pearl-grey yacht riding to anchor out beyond the booming surf. She lay like a ghost, not a light or sign of life visible. [...] The voice of Swanson, at my elbow, dragged me down to earth.

'Going to be tough getting through the surf, cap. I don't think we'll make it; the wind's going round to the southard of east.'

'I thought that the minute we hit the beach, Tom,' I replied. 'Guess we'll take a shot at it anyway.'[8]

Inevitably, disaster struck. The first run was, to be frank, not a success.

"We lined the boats up about a hundred feet apart. Danny Krebs, engineer on the *Voltaire*, took the first dory, Swanson the second, myself the third, and Pete, one of the sailors and a skilled boatman, the fourth.

Waiting a favourable chance, I sang out: 'Let's go, boys.'

With the aid of three men, we ran the boat out into the water until we were submerged to the waist. We allowed a couple of big rollers to get by, holding desperately. Then I jumped into the dory, which became a live thing once in its natural element, and grabbed the oars. The three gangsters gave the boat a short run and a shove seaward to get me started. I buried the oars in the boiling water and strove to get clear of the surf. I was making good headway, too, endeavouring to keep the bow of the boat head on to the breakers. Two more hills and I'd be clear of the surf.

Suddenly it seemed that the whole ocean came rushing for me. The dory was thrown bodily up into the air on the apex of a roaring, hissing geyser, and I flew over the stern into the boiling confusion of water. I was buffeted, blinded, and all but suffocated in the seething swirl. Like a thunderbolt from the sky, I sensed rather than saw a massive body descend on me. I threw up my hands, preferring to drown rather than be split in two with the falling dory.

I remembered nothing more until I came to on the beach, dazed and shivering with the cold. Danny Krebs commandeered a car and drove me to his home, where a hot bath and a change of clothes soon made me fit as a fiddle.

Swanson was the only man who got his boat through."

But of course everything had to be called off.

> "We decided to do this [the next job] with a newly outfitted speed-boat capable of carrying four hundred cases. It would mean, of course, running the gauntlet both going out of Rockaway Inlet and returning.
>
> Rockaway Inlet, the entrance to Jamaica Bay, was well patrolled by coastguard cutters, besides being overlooked by the coastguard station at the Point. The Bay is a veritable maze of creeks and channels, and once in these no coastguard could ever hope to catch us. We had a special pilot for this tricky part – Dominick, a clever Italian seaman, whose skill had bested the coastguards through ten years of liquor smuggling."[9]

Shortly thereafter a radio message instructed them to rendezvous with the Canadian yacht *Semiramis*. Their new boat the *Lynx*, with its three 'Liberty' engines flashed out into the open ocean, went alongside the yacht and loaded up to capacity with bootleg whiskey.

They crept along at about 14 knots (the *Lynx* could do 35 if needed) and successfully unloaded at a coal dock. Within minutes several trucks of booze were trundling their way to the New York warehouses and the *Lynx*, now empty, was back to sea to meet up with the *Semiramis* again. But tragedy struck. From out of the mist came a revenue coastguard cutter and they were firing. A burst of machine gun fire cut through the upper corner of the wheelhouse, ripping away the angle iron binding the corner. This struck McGuinness on the forehead, blinding him and throwing him overboard. Here follows his account of his miracle survival.

> "The *Lynx* was disappearing in thick sleet and snow. The coastguard cutter roared past, not twenty feet away, without seeing me.
>
> I had joined the rum racket for excitement. I was getting it. Clad in oilskins and sea-boots, with heavy woollen clothes underneath, swimming was out of the question. Moreover I could see with only one eye.
>
> With much manœuvering I managed to shake off one boot. This helped a little, but made me side-heavy. Of rescue I had no hope, but at regular intervals I shouted 'Help'. There was quite a sea running but not enough to worry a good swimmer. As I rose on the crest of a wave I could see the shore-lights of far Rockaway ['the Irish Riviera' as locals called it then] sometimes breaking through the mist of snow and rain.

Was this to be my end – to drown like a rat in the ignominious profession of rum-running? I was working under an assumed name and it flashed on me that my passing would go unnoticed. I thought of all my previous escapes, but was convinced that in all of them there had been a sporting chance. I had to shout less frequently now to conserve my breath.

I felt myself growing weaker; it was more difficult to keep my head clear of the water. My mind was extremely active at the beginning of the ordeal, but I was gradually becoming resigned and lethargic. Then, just as my arms refused to paddle longer, I heard a sound that electrified me. It was the rattle of davit blocks – some one far-off lowering a boat. The *Lynx* had no boat davits; she carried the dories lashed on the after-deck. It must be the coastguard.

I waited for the splash of oars, but nothing happened. Then, horror of horrors, I heard the rattle of the blocks again. They were hoisting the boat back on board. I knew the full meaning of the word despair. But the good Guardian Angel must have been standing by. I heard the splash of oars and a faint hail in the distance. I answered 'Help' as loudly as I could, and kept repeating it at regular intervals.

A couple of minutes later the high bow of a Canadian dory pushed out of the gloom and headed straight towards me. I was saved!

I was too heavy with sea-water to clamber into the boat, so I hooked my arm over the gunwale and in this fashion was towed back to the *Semiramis*.

On the way back, Blackie, the supercargo and representative of the rum barons, told me what had transpired. When I was shot overboard [...] Swanson [had] eluded the coastguard, cruised inshore and picked up the yacht. He went alongside and told them of my mishap. Old McDonald, the skipper, and Blackie ordered a boat over. They attempted to launch a light dinghy, but in the long ground swell the rolling yacht made this a feat of rare skill. In the rush to get the boat quickly in the water the after boat-falls jammed while the forward tackle went by the run. As a result, the boat hung perpendicularly from the after davit, swinging and crashing wildly against the side of the *Semiramis* until the dinghy was smashed to pieces. After some delay in casting the wrecked boat adrift and clearing tackles, another boat was hooked on and with more caution safely put over the side. Blackie took command, and to his perseverance and promptitude I owe my life.

The crew of the yacht hauled me out of the water on board. They were astounded that any one could have remained afloat so long under such conditions of wind and weather. [Note: Bear this in mind when we come to the final chapter.]

A seaman tied a rude bandage tightly round my head to keep the eyebrow in position and stop the bleeding. Now that the ordeal was over, my head throbbed violently; I felt half frozen and utterly wretched. The *Lynx* was now alongside loading. I went on board. Down in the engine-room I discovered a quiet corner out of the way, where I sat on the warm copper motor exhausts and thawed myself.

Soon we were racing home. Luck was with us this time, and we reached the inlet without seeing another craft of any description. A quick run up the channel and we were alongside the drop discharging our second cargo. When the last case was put on the last truck seven o'clock chimed in a nearby church. Dawn was streaking the sky in a pale orange tint and the familiar sounds of a new day being born sounded vaguely in the cold bleak morning. The wind had subsided, but the snow fell thick and silently. Houses and trees were covered under the soft white mantle. Even the *Lynx* looked beautiful amidst these new effects.

A jarring note came from the twoscore and ten gangsters on the dock. Guards were being allocated to each motor-truck. One riding in front with the driver was armed with a sawed-off shotgun and a Colt .45 automatic. Two thugs rode in the body of the truck with the liquor. They had a Thompson machine-gun and an automatic apiece. The danger lay, not from the law, but from hijackers, for these desperadoes asked no quarter nor gave any. As 'killers' they had a high social standing in the gang and received a steady wage from the rum directorate for their murderous abilities.

The rank and file piled into waiting autos and the whole cavalcade drove off citywards, spreading out fan-wise as they left the environs of the dock. To avoid undue suspicion I waited until 9 a.m. before proceeding to the hospital, where eight stitches were put in my wounds. My baptism in the rum racket was certainly thorough. Others I knew were not quite so fortunate. They did not escape."[10]

On its first, successful, trial the *Voltaire* was stopped by the coastguard but since they were not as yet loaded with contraband they were permitted, grudgingly, to proceed. McGuinness claims:

> "I was sailing under the *nom de guerre* of Olson. It would be embarrassing if I was captured under my own name after being recommended for the highest honour the United States Government allows a distinguished citizen. The coastguards knew full well the nature of our mission, but there was no evidence they could pull us in for. The petty officer in command, who was a Scandinavian doubted the authenticity of my accent, which has a decided Celtic flavour. 'You speak damn funny for a Swede,' he said.
>
> 'So would you,' I replied, 'if you were married to a woman named McGuinness.'"[11] [So much for 'security'.]

The first run of the *Voltaire* was a success for McGuinness. The new boat performed well. They made the rendezvous point with a Canadian schooner from Nova Scotia 75 miles south of the Ambrose Lightship and loaded 5,000 bales of Scotch, Rye, Wine, Champagne and Brandy. They left the schooner at five in the evening and headed for Long Beach, where both the Mayor and the Chief of Police were notoriously on the take from the gangsters. A coastguard cutter fired on them with its one-pounder and its machine gun, but the *Voltaire*, under McGuinness' command outran them and unloaded the haul into the dories and away in the lorries.

> "At 5 a.m. every case was ashore and we were speeding back to the schooner for another load. The night's work netted me twenty-five hundred dollars. I received 50 cents for every case landed – more, that is, for landing one load of booze than was paid to most members of the Byrd expedition for two years' service under the banner of science."[12]

The second trip proved more fraught with danger. "Sneaking out of the mist like a grey wolf" came a 75 ft. coastguard cutter while they were unloading from the *Voltaire* to the *Semiramis*.

Nomad, in the faster boat was able to escape, but 'old MacDonald', the man who had saved McGuinness' life but a month previously was captured in the slower *Semiramis*. McGuinness passes no comment on this – nor a word of sympathy. The *Voltaire* had, however, been shot up, and needed repairs. And the booze hungry clientele had to be satisfied. Another 'vessel' was procured.

Reminiscent of the strange cobbled together Chinese junk which McGuinness claimed to have sailed in the South China Seas, he recounts how his boss Bimbo wanted him to try out "the greatest freak in ship-construction ever perpetrated on the Atlantic seaboard".

"This ungainly tub could attain the speed of 35 miles per hour with three powerful converted aeroplane motors, but these motors were placed so far forward that, when running, the *Maureen* (as she was named) ran with her head well down and her stern sticking up, like a bull charging in a ring. As a result of this peculiar construction, the exhausts were clear of the water when running, but submerged when stopped, thus allowing the water to back up through the pipes into the motors. At sea the motors had to be kept going all the time to save the vessel from swamping.

I was by no means enthusiastic about going to sea in such a craft. It was midwinter, freezing hard."[13]

After one nightmare trip, when the *Maureen* froze over, Nomad, who may not have been quite so 'skeely' a skipper as he always claimed to be,[14] ran the 'monster' on shore –

"'Do your best Harold!' I shouted in the howling wind. 'Ten minutes will see us ashore or in hell!'

At last! We were in the surf and racing shorewards like an express. The nightmare of the breakers was past."[15]

Nomad and his crew fled as the boat split in two.

McGuinness' rum running career, short though it was, was coming to an end. Six weeks later the *Voltaire* was involved in offloading a cargo in the Rockaway Inlets when they were surprised by armed coastguards.

"'Come on, throw 'em up, everybody!'

I looked up at the dock and saw the uniforms. The load was grabbed all right. Well, they wouldn't grab me, if I could help it.

The motors were turning over dead slow as they always did at an unloading. Dominick was sitting on a case of champagne when the first commotion arose. He jumped to his feet and grabbed the wheel. We looked at each other and smiled. I grabbed both handles of the engine-room telegraphs and rang – 'Full speed ahead!'

There was a roar of command from the dock, but too late; we snapped the ropes as if they were a spider's web, and shot into the midstream. The liquor raiders opened fire with their revolvers, but we laughed at these weapons. The *Voltaire* had survived tougher barrages than that. Out in the creek a launch was cruising. They whistled for us to stop, but we dashed madly past and round a little island. It was low water at the time and we took the turn too sharp. The *Voltaire* came to a shuddering stop, with the launch close behind. The jig was up. Deserting the unhappy rum-boat to her fate, we all jumped over the side and swam the few yards to the shore. Luckily we grounded on a bank on the mainland opposite the little island, and in a district where Dominick was well known. Soaking wet and shivering, we ran through the marsh grass to a small shack, where the occupants were wide awake.

We were made heartily welcome, and while waiting for the automobile to warm up we all took generous draughts of rye. Pete, Dominick, and everyone, with the exception of myself, had managed to salvage a couple of bottles apiece.

The cargo was confiscated in its entirety, as was the boat. All my savings were in this last load. I took this as retribution for trying to get rich quick, but no one can say it was the easiest means.

The Rum Barons offered me a larger and better boat to continue but I turned down their offers. I had sampled the Rum Racket. I had enjoyed the excitement. I had liked the fellows on the boats. […] But there was something about the whole thing that disgusted me. Risking your life for an ideal is satisfying, but risking your life to make money, especially for others, had no point."[16]

It perhaps slipped McGuinness' mind when he penned the above that the Volstead Act was repealed in 1933. Prohibition was over. McGuinness had got into 'the rum racket' too late.

Yet, with amazing *chutzpah* he concludes *Nomad* and *Sailor of Fortune* with the modest lines: "The problem the proletariat in Soviet Russia had set out to solve, made a strong appeal to the rebel in me. I went to Russia."

Notes.

1. Count Felix von Luckner is one of the few persons whom Nomad ever calls a friend. They had quite a lot in common as adventurers, since von Luckner was successful in promoting himself as a world famous flamboyant German war hero and buccaneer – 'the scourge of Allied shipping in the Pacific' during WW I.
Born Phelax Lendige on June 9, 1881 in Dresden he was destined for a life straight out of 'Boys Own'. Sickly in his infancy he was in later life, for a time, a circus strong-man, a wrestling champion and, even when well past his prime, continued to delight audiences with his feats of strength.
He joined the Freemasons at the age of forty after the career which sealed his fame and made him a household name throughout the world. At age thirteen, 'after being captivated by the menu of a luxury liner', he ran off and shipped as an unpaid cabin boy on a Russian sailing ship bound for Australia. Life aboard was very different from the pictures evoked by the aforesaid menu. And he was lucky to survive a fall overboard.
He abandoned ship in Freemantle and for seven years he roamed the world in a plethora of jobs, including selling the Salvation Army's *War Cry*, assistant lighthouse keeper, kangaroo hunter, circus hand, professional boxer, fisherman, seaman, Mexican army guard for President Diaz, railroad construction, tavern keeper and barman. He spent time in a Chilean jail accused of trying to steal pigs; won a wrestling competition in Hamburg; twice suffered broken legs, was thrown out of a hospital in Jamaica for lack of funds, but was lucky enough to be befriended by some German sailors. Aged twenty, and with less book knowledge than an average ten year old, he entered a German navigation training school. After qualifying and serving on a South American liner, he was eligible to become a reserve officer in the German navy. In 1912 he entered the German navy for active service in the ship *Panzer*. A visit to German territories in Africa saw him engaged on an elephant hunt. World War I broke out in 1914 but the British blockade of German ports severely limited the German navy's capabilities. In the battle of Jutland, von Luckner commanded a gun turret on the *Kronprinz* with 'skill and cunning'. These attributes, combined with the fact that he was

apparently the only German naval officer who had served 'under sail' singled him out for a unique command which sailed him into the history books of the world' (at least according to his colleagues in the Masons).

The *Seeadler* (Sea Eagle), a 1570 ton three masted sailing ship, built in Glasgow in 1888 and captured by the Germans while under a British flag, was converted under von Luckner's directions to an auxiliary cruiser, heavily armed and equipped with two 500 H.P. engines, but carefully disguised inside and out as a Norwegian timber ship *Inna*. Von Luckner managed, during a violent gale in the North Sea 23 December 1916, to break the British blockade – the *Inna* was inspected and passed – , and sailed north around Scotland into the Atlantic. Over the following 88 days his ship, renamed the *Seeadler* or *Sea Eagle*, disguise removed, captured eleven Allied ships in the Atlantic, and sank ten without a single loss of life, crew or captive. In April 1917 he rounded Cape Horn and entered the Pacific where three more ships were sunk. On 2 August his good fortunes ran out and the *Seeadler* was cast ashore by a tidal wave onto remote Mopelia Island in the Tahiti group, inhabited only by three Kanaks left by the French to catch turtles.

Von Luckner was involved in more adventures before returning to Germany as a hero. The highest award made to him was an honour placing him above the scope of German law, usually the prerogative of only the German Royal family. He was summoned to Rome by the Pope who called him "a great humanitarian". Between the two world wars, von Luckner and his wife Countess Ingeborg travelled throughout Europe and the United States.

Some, however, felt that he was a propagandist for nazism, a charge that he denied, claiming to be an ambassador for peace only. Although too old for active service in World War II, Hitler attempted to use him for propaganda purposes but demanded that he renounce Freemasonry. He refused. He also refused to renounce the various honorary citizenships granted him in the United States.

Hitler made life difficult for von Luckner, and his bank account was stopped. In remote Halle, where he was living, the citizens seemed to feel that their relative immunity from air-raids was due to the presence in their midst of the Count, who had been given the freedom of so many American cities. In the closing stages of the war refugees from other areas crowded in. The Count was asked by the Mayor and others in April 1945 to seek out the approaching American troops and seek terms. The German General in command disclaimed any responsibility, but permitted him to try. The control officer from Berlin remarked disdainfully: "There's another international Freemason." He did manage to find and negotiate with the Americans, among whom were Masonic friends, and they agreed not to bomb the city. He was able to so advise his friends in Halle but, on the advice that Hitler had condemned him to death, he was forced to flee into hiding. Count Felix von Luckner died 14 April 1966, in Malmo, Sweden.

A brother mason wrote: "His last wish was that it should be said of him, as it had been said of his own hero, another Mason, Buffalo Bill Cody: 'He was a great white scout, a loyal and honest man', and this wish was fulfilled in Lodge White Lily, 16 April 1966." (This account is taken from a rather strange Masonic site dedicated to 'a hero'. The basic facts check out however.)

Is it too far fetched to suspect that the success of Lowell Thomas' biography of von Luckner *Adventures of the Sea Devil*, published in New York by Doubleday in 1932, may have inspired McGuinness to put pen to paper to earn a crust with his memoir *Nomad/Sailor of Fortune*?

2. Mopelia – named after the small Tahitian island where von Luckner had been cast ashore.
3. McGuinness, *Nomad*, op. cit., pp. 250-251.
4. When Nomad took the job running rum onto Rockaway Beach he was, whether he knew it or not, and it would be a miracle if he didn't, working for the New York king of the rum runners, Owney Madden (1892-1964).

English-born New York bootlegger, gangster and killer, Madden, a leader of the lethal Gopher Gang on NYC's west side, was involved in hundreds of gang fights from 1903 to 1914. He was an expert user of the blackjack, brass knuckles, and his favorite weapon, a lead pipe wrapped in newspaper. By the time he was 21 he had been arrested more than forty times, charged with robbery, assault and murder. In 1914, he was convicted of killing 'Little Patty' Doyle, a rival gang leader and sentenced to 10 to 20 years in prison. Released on parole in

1923, Madden had learnt well. He never went back to prison and survived the internecine mob wars, dying with his boots on in Hot Springs, Arkansas, where he had opened up profitable resorts and casinos for the well-to-do who wished to rub shoulders with the gangsters.

Madden had become an important bootlegger and speakeasy owner in NY and worked with such top criminals as Dutch Schultz, 'Lucky' Luciano, Meyer Lansky & Abner 'Longy' Zwillman. He also owned the Cotton Club. He died in 1964.

5. McGuinness, *Nomad*, op. cit., p. 253.
6. ibid., pp. 253-254.
7. ibid., p. 256.
8. ibid., p. 260.
9. ibid. pp. 261-262.
10. ibid., pp. 265-268.
11. ibid., pp. 268-269.
12. ibid., p. 270.
13. ibid., pp. 274.
14. Nomad admits, almost casually, that on one of his voyages he 'misread' their position 'by making an error in the carry over figure in adding the zenith distance to the declination to get the latitude.' As a result they found themselves off Atlantic City in the midst of the coastguard's heaviest patrols. In Boys Own fashion they escaped by throwing fishing nets overboard to foul their pursuers' propellers as well as kegs of malt whisky, which would stave in a cutter's bow if it struck them.
15. McGuinness, *Nomad*, op. cit., pp. 277.
16. ibid., pp. 279-280.

Family photograph, John and Margaret McGuinness with their children including the baby Charles John, 1893.

RUNNING DONEGAL FIGHT.

Ardara Raid Frustrated.

POLICE FIND IN DUG OUT.

The manager and cashier of the Ulster Bank at Ardara, county Donegal, were held up by four armed men with revolvers shortly before three o'clock on Thursday afternoon. The bank was searched, and the raiders then demanded the keys of the safe, but this demand was refused. The raiders failed to secure any money, and left. A party of police on patrol from Glenties under a head-constable arrived on the scene, and came in contact with the raiders, who fired on the police.

After a running fight for three miles through sandhills along the sea coast, the police wounded two of the raiders, one of whom was captured, and gave his name as Charles Hennessey, of Drogheda.

The police searched the neighbourhood, and found two dug-outs containing bedsteads, bedding, seditious literature, a police pouch, a lamp, and provisions. The contents were seized and the dug-outs were burned.

The police then searched the house of Patrick Harkin, of Rosbeg, and found four rifles and 460 rounds of service ammunition, khaki uniform, and putties, a number of haversacks, five bicycles, five bombs and a number of trench coats and field glasses, which they seized. Harkin was arrested by the police.

Francis Gallagher and Patrick J. Reilly, of Ardara, who were wanted by the police, were found in the vicinity and arrested. There were no police casualties.

Report in the *Derry Journal* on the raid in Ardara and the arrest of a 'Charles Hennessey' (Charles McGuinness), June 1921 (*see* p. 57-58).

Wedding photograph Charles and Claire McGuinness, Berlin 1922.
(Photo Copyright © 2000-2002 Tim McGuinness)

Charles and Claire McGuinness in Berlin, 1922.
(Photo Copyright © 2000-2002 Tim McGuinness)

Radiogram to Hugh McGuinness, September 9, 1928 (*see* p. 103).

Moscow I'll immediately return the jack. I've been over six weeks here in New York and it costs like hell to live and appear decent. The European trip cleaned me well out to help matters. Sorry to impose Hugh but you know how these situations arise.

I should like to hear from the remainder of the family and I shall write them all before I leave Sed.

I guess I've told you nearly everything so I'll bring this to a close with love to Sheilah the family and yourself

Your loving brother

Charlie

Leningrad s/s Saguache Moore & McC.
Moscow Hotel Metropole Sverdlov Sq.
V.S.S.R.

PS this is being mailed rather late write the Moscow

Letter to Hugh McGuinness, September 25, 1932 (*see* pp. 138-140).

SAILOR
OF FORTUNE

CHARLES JOHN McGUINNESS

ADVENTURES OF AN IRISH SAILOR, SOLDIER,
PIRATE, PEARL-FISHER, GUN-RUNNER,
REBEL AND ANTARCTIC EXPLORER

Illustrated

A. L. BURT COMPANY, *Publishers*
New York   Chicago

PUBLISHED BY ARRANGEMENT WITH MACRAE SMITH COMPANY
PRINTED IN U. S. A.

Charles John McGuinness

Frontispiece of the American edition of *Sailor of Fortune*, 1935.

The *Isallt* off the Ballymoney Rocks, Co. Wexford, December 6, 1947.
(Photo Copyright © 2000-2002 Tim McGuinness)

CHAPTER 9
WELCOME TO MURMANSK, TOVARICH!

AUTHORS' NOTE:

Why did Nomad go to Russia? What did he find there? This is a difficult question. For ninety per cent of the 'Russian years' we have to rely upon Nomad's brief memoir – never a necessarily wise thing for an historian to do.

Originally it was thought that his undated 124 page book *Behind the Red Curtain* was published in Dublin between 1937-1939. It was published by Grafton Publications, which gave an address of 270 North Circular road, Dublin and has not only no ISBN number but no date of publication. It is virtually impossible to obtain these days. It was almost certainly a vanity publication by Nomad himself. Surprisingly it is not recorded either in the British Library or the Irish National Library. There may have been another edition of this published under the pseudonym 'Peter Dawson' but we have been unable either to acquire a copy of this or even a verification that it ever existed.

Nomad has also, it has been alleged, written several children's books using the 'clever' pen name 'Damon'. No trace of such literary works could be found until just before we finished this book. Then, to our amazement we discovered that the old 'folk story' that we'd heard in Derry years ago about Nomad publishing under the name of Damon was confirmed by Patricia Bryce, née Doherty, who remembered as a wean seeing copies of at least one other book in her father's room. She would even recall the pseudonym 'Peter Damon'. Later that very same night we tracked down three books by 'Peter Damon' published in Dublin by an apparent vanity press in 1946 and 1947. (For more, *see* Afterword and Appendices.)

Also, later, Nomad allegedly told stories about mythical 'Nomads' to his oldest son Patrick. Additionally, on the frontispiece of the copy of *Behind the Red Curtain* in our possession it states that Captain Charles J. McGuinness is the author of *Nomad* and *The Odd Button* 'in preparation'. Alas, we do not know if the *Odd Button* ever saw the light of day. Perhaps some reader could help?

After researching the matter the authors believe, for reasons which are explained in the Afterword why we think *Behind the Red Curtain* was really written during WWII (possibly while Nomad was in Arbour Hill Jail) and not published until 1946 or 1947 (*see* Afterword).

WHY RUSSIA?

In the memoir McGuinness gives various reasons for his decision, in the autumn of 1932, to take ship from New York to Leningrad.

> "When I gave up a life of security and comparative ease in the United States for one of uncertainty in Soviet Russia I was doing precisely what millions have tried to do before: kill two birds with one stone.
>
> The fact that the Soviet Union claimed to be a Workers' Republic shorn of all the faults, anxieties and greed fostered by capitalism and imperialism, filled me with a determination to find out if Utopia had really been attained at last. […]
>
> One of the driving forces behind much of my restlessness had been an enthusiasm for Polar exploration. So I wanted to see at first hand how the Soviets tackled the vast problem of their Polar coastline."[1]

Elsewhere he claimed

> "I was obeying a call – an urge to investigate at first hand the most sensational social experiment attempted in modern history. That Bolshevism was universally questioned, contradicted, argued and puzzled over, had made me all the more anxious to serve in the ranks of the proletarian army which was said to be fighting the evils of World Capitalism."

This is a rare piece of left wing political rhetoric from McGuinness. Indeed, the only other reference he makes is in the introduction to *Behind the Red Curtain* where he briefly, very briefly, states that he "found capitalism in its worst form – State Capitalism – ruling the Soviet roost."

However, as usual with Charlie it was almost certainly not true. In an unpublished letter to his beloved brother Hugh in Derry, dated September 25th, a week before he left for Moscow via Leningrad wrote, *inter alia*:

"I sincerely hope that Sheilah, yourself and the family are well. The family must now be well advanced with Moppa and Sean of an age I vividly remember you and I going through even though we were but fledglings then. I would give anything in the world to see you again as it certainly seems a long time since we last met. During my last trip to Europe I didn't have much time for writing but next time I'll be more settled and will keep in constant communication. On Wed. September 30th I leave for Leningrad en-route for Moscow to take over a government post in the Zovtorgflotte or in English, the ministry of Marine. Zov, who is the head of all marine and shipping affairs has personally sent for me and I am led to believe it is some honour, but I'll soon find out. Conditions are lousy in the U.S.A. and a revolution would be no surprise if something doesn't roll along to improve things. The domestic situation by me is about ended and although regrettable it is or was inevitable. Darling Paudeen [his son Patrick] is really the one who suffers most but he is now in a convent school to which Claire sent him so he is, in a fashion, well looked after. I should like to have him with me in Russia where he would receive the proper doctrines from the beginning. He is going to be a little warrior and is crazy about ships and the sea. I look to a kind fate to straighten the whole business satisfactorily. I can get Claire a divorce as soon as I get established in Moscow to put her right."

He goes on to reveal how he has sold some ghost written articles under the name 'Nighthawk' for *The New York Evening Graphic*, a 'New York scandal sheet' about rum running. 'Everyone is trying to find out who 'Nighthawk' is .... The Editor adds the blood and gore to a few stories I give him.'

He then returns to his aspirations in Russia.

"I have introductions to all the worthwhile people in Russia and hope to carve a name for the illustrious clan MacAongusa. In Irish circles here they are all emphatically aware of the fact that the McGuinness is the oldest and noblest family in Ulster and there are occasions when I take some pride from that belief."

After the patriotic sentimentality he suddenly becomes bitter with America.

"On returning from Europe I received the Gold Congressional Medal, the highest honor in the United States. It is a pretty bauble about the size of a dollar piece cast in pure gold and worth $45. The ribbon is blue and white. The medal was accompanied by a letter from Hoover, one from the secretary of the Navy, and a long flattering effusion from Byrd asking me to join him in his next expedition, promising me a command and a commission. He knew that I was already hooked up with the Russians and his offer is to keep me placated."

It is true to say that 'the commodore' was known to have a close affinity for Capt. John Barleycorn, and this may account for Nomad-Byrd's 'on-off' relationship.

Then alas, as some may have expected, comes the touch.

"In my preparations to vacate here Hugh I've exhausted every resource I have and will be leaving here pretty near bankrupt. If you could possibly dig up a couple of pound and send them to me c/o *SS Saguache*, Moore McCormack Line, Leningrad. They may catch me on arrival. That is the steamer I shall travel on. They maintain a direct service between New York, Helsingfors and Leningrad. As soon as I get settled in my job in Moscow I'll immediately return the jack. I've been over six weeks here in New York and it costs like hell to live and appear decent. The European trip cleaned me well out to help matters [sic]. Sorry to impose Hugh, but you know how these situations arise."[2]

Faithful brother Hugh. While Nomad was on his Polar exploits he was sending very little money back for Claire and 'darling Paudeen'. He regularly writes to Hugh asking for 'a loan' but unknown to him Claire had got fed up waiting for him, penniless in a hostile Brooklyn slum. She had been secretly writing to Hugh also, requesting 'a little money' and speculating and hinting how wonderful it would be if she and little Paudeen – 'who resembles your children so much, Hugh', could come to live in beautiful Donegal with the wonderful McGuinness family minus that miserable so-and-so husband of hers. Somewhat poignantly she asks whether 'it is Derry or Londonderry, I do not understand.'

Incidentally, when Claire arrived in Derry for the first time around 1922 she could apparently barely speak English. But, seven years later she could speak and write pretty good English and has 'a fine fist', as a schoolteacher like Hugh might have noted.

She was forced to move to another slum – 470, 74th Street – and apparently led a life in straitened conditions while Nomad was off in Russia and Spain until she met and married a Mr. Eigen. She lived on into her 90s in New York, not dying until 1996.

But, regardless of whether any money from Hugh got through or not, for Nomad the die was cast. Would Russia prove to be a 'brave new world' where he could bring up his son?

Unfortunately, he was to be sorely disappointed. But it should, really, have come as no surprise.

Years earlier, the *Buford* generation' – European 'reds', who lived in America, had been rounded up in the infamous Palmer raids, and on December 20, 1919, under the beady eye of a young J Edgar Hoover, 249 'reds' (most of them anarcho-syndicalists), including such luminaries as Emma Goldman and Alex Berkman, were forced onto the *Buford*. 'The Soviet Ark' departed Ellis Island with the deportees bound for Russia.

"They should be put on a ship of stone with sails of lead and their first stopping place should be Hell" claimed General Leonard Wood, a former military governor of Cuba who came down to the dock to 'see the anarchist bastards off'.

Emma only lasted two years in Russia however, and was able to get out and travel Europe, publishing her influential anti-Bolshevik book *My disillusionment*. Many other exposés of the new Soviet tyranny appeared throughout the twenties and it seems unlikely that by 1932 Nomad had not learned that all was not milk and honey in the land of the muzhik.

So was it just Wanderlust? To the 'Ends of Earth'? What was he hiding from? Family? Personal demons? And what was going on in the USSR?

The late 1920s were epic times for Russia. New power stations, steel plants and engineering works sprang up out of nowhere with a phenomenal speed of growth and Russia's output of coal, iron ore, oil and non-ferrous metals was rapidly increased. The original figures for the First Five-year Plan as worked out by relatively cautious economists in 1929 were soon discarded in favour of more ambitious targets which were then repeatedly raised; the slogan of the day was that 'there are no fortresses which Bolsheviks cannot take', according to a historian of the period.[3]

Before the year 1930 ended, an order was issued to extend the plans and speed up their application. The fixing of new objectives to be attained in production and in construction work became an all-absorbing everyday task, a kind of collective mania. The First Five-year Plan was no longer mentioned. No doubts were allowed as to it being accomplished, and even surpassed, in four years. Everyone was plunged into calculations concerning the Second Five-year Plan, to cover the period from January 1933 to the end of 1937. During that period all the capitalist countries, including America, would certainly be left far behind. The future was read in figures, as playing cards are used for fortune-telling, and the figures docilely obeyed the desire of man.

But the peasantry called a halt to these soaring flights of the urban imagination. Their active resistance to collectivization was indeed crushed; thousands of recalcitrants were killed and hundreds of thousands were deported to forced labour camps or dumped on the outskirts of the new industrial cities such as Magnitogorsk to live in tents and shacks – there was no housing for them – and provide the cheapest of cheap labour for building projects. But if the peasant could not oppose the government in arms he could practise a passive resistance and he did. Vast numbers of horses, cattle, sheep and pigs were killed and eaten so that they were no longer there to be handed over to the collectives, and many of those which were handed over soon died of neglect as the peasants took no further interest in them. By the end of 1932 famine had returned, particularly to the Ukraine, the USSR's food basket, and during the winter and in the spring of 1933 great numbers of peasants starved to death. It was the peasants who died and not the workers in the towns, for the state continued to take out of the countryside enough to meet a basic food ration in the towns – and also something for export. And then Stalin's purges began in earnest.

In January 1934 the Seventeenth Congress of the CPSU (the Communist Party of the Soviet Union) was held in Moscow. There was, apparently, a complete unanimity of members of the Congress in support of Stalin and his policies. Several former leaders of groups within the Party which had been at one time or another opposed to Stalin – Zinoviev, Kamenev, Bukharin, Pyatakov, Rykov and Radek made penitent speeches in which they admitted that Stalin had always been right and they had been wrong. But behind the appearance of what had come to be styled the 'monolithic unity' of the Party there was still conflict, and a conflict perhaps more dangerous to Stalin's supremacy than the overt opposition with which he had previously had to contend, because resistance to his arbitrary personal rule was now coming from within the *bloc* of those who had hitherto been his supporters. Schapiro thus explains how this new situation had arisen:

"As the years wore on [from 1929] to an ever-mounting crescendo of self-congratulation from the Party leaders, exaggerated claims of success, faked statistics and exhortation to yet greater efforts, the more sober realities of the situation produced a corresponding depression. In place of the promised plenty, there was food shortage, accompanied by strict rationing, especially marked during the famine year of 1932-3. The rapid influx of the peasants into the towns, which were unprepared to receive them, contributed to the lowering standards of living which had advanced under the NEP. Absenteeism, unemployment, hunger and real famine began to stalk the vast land."[4]

And it was at this very time that Charles 'Nomad' McGuinness, having no financial resources, no friends in Russia and unable to speak any of the languages prevalent in the chaotic Motherland chose to arrive at the Finland station. "A bleak grey morning in Autumn heralded our approach to Leningrad." The voyage from New York had taken 21 days. Just so, but why then does Nomad, when complaining about his lack of funds bemoan the fact that he had 'wasted good US Dollars having a good time in Copenhagen and Amsterdam en route?

First impressions of Leningrad were not good. The 'customs men from the GPU' who came on board robbed the passengers. McGuinness lost his treasured 'leather bound set of Dickens'. Bribery and poverty were rife. The Nevsky Prospekt was disappointing.

"A cold drizzle of rain oozed from a leaden sky; it dripped down the facades of dingy four storied tenements. The once-stuccoed fronts were leprously scaled, over all hung the pallor of sodden decay.
The footpaths on the long street leading from the port resembled duck board passages in the flooded trenches of a battlefield. [...] It was penetratingly cold. [...] The passing faces were broad, high cheekboned, and blue. [...] Long queues of hooded workers, men and women, waited apathetically outside the stores. At intervals figures emerged tightly clutching to their sides chunks of black bread. Tearing pieces of the soft warm mess out of the middle they stuffed them into their mouths. High overhead bright red streamers crossed the street. They read "Workers of the World Unite." "Long live the Dictatorship of the Proletariat."
But no one looked up. [...]

A jostling preoccupied crowd surged along what had been formerly the gayest boulevard in Europe. Where formerly the Czarist rulers trod in selfish majesty the bewildered proletariat uneasily promenaded."5

In between detailing how he was mugged, robbed – on trains, in bars, Pivnayas (beer cellars) and in every low dive he, foolishly, at times at least, entered, McGuinness 'elucidated' about his new country.

"It is estimated that more than 165 different languages are spoken in the Soviet Union; but Russian is the official tongue. [...]

The Russian peasant is a striking paradox. He is the weakness and the strength of Russia. The thought that their beloved village will come under the heel of an invader produces a savage spirit unrivalled in any country. Stalin and his cohorts well understand this; and thus a continuous stream of propaganda floods the land. They are told through the press, the flaming posters, over the radio, that the forces of capitalism are always on the frontiers watching for the slightest weakening in the defences of the Red Army to sweep in and confiscate the land. [...] Stalin's words strike a heroic note among industrial workers: "We do not want an inch of foreign country but we shall not part with an inch of our own.

He forgets the half dozen or so small nations in the Caucasus annexed by the Red forces in 1924, his native Georgia being one of them. He forgets the case of Latvia, Lithuania, Esthonia, Poland, and those tortured territories east of Berlin."6

And almost as an afterthought McGuinness claims that when he first went to Leningrad he was expecting a job.

"In New York I had been led to believe that in Leningrad my arrival was expected; that all necessary arrangements had been made to secure me an appointment with Soviet Antarctic waterways. [...] Though my credentials were beyond criticism, no one in Leningrad dare take the initiative of helping me either financially or in any other way without sanction from Moscow."7

So it was off to Moscow, having cadged 'a small loan from an American engineer', and onto the train. Third class. Atrocious conditions. Robbed of course by these 'damned muzhiks'.

In Moscow, the money he was expecting had not, naturally, arrived. But fortune favours the sailor. A brief affair with the delectable Xenia Andrievna 'you must look after yourself, Carl Ivanitch' she sighed as the Derryman was forced to take his leave.

He touches lucky and gets a billet run by the party. And so experiences how the 'aparatchiks' live. The head of the Sovtorgflot finally returns and gives McGuinness some money and a temporary appointment – not as 'harbour master in Leningrad' but as a 'Port Inspector', a sinecure.

Before he leaves Moscow there is a visit to the Bolshoi Theatre (he liked it) and to Lenin's tomb: "he looked like a small Mongolian-eyed, middle-class shopkeeper." And to the slums of Moscow. There he managed to get himself nearly killed and lost all his worldly possessions after being drugged in a lowly vodka shebeen into which he had foolishly entered after being suckered by a cab driver. He was only saved by 'a flaxen-haired little boy whom his parents had put into my bed to warm me up after dragging my unconscious body in from the landing before I froze to death.'

And then back to Leningrad, this time not third class but first class.

> "My return to Leningrad was something in the nature of a triumph. Moscow had phoned Sovtorgflot acquainting them of my appointment as the city's Port Inspector. […] I was treated with marked consideration, a thing that is unfailingly reserved until the new arrival has given proof of political stability." [sic]

He lands a good billet, formerly a banker's residence which is reserved for the party faithful.

> "I paid 90 roubles a month for my little komnata. This was approximately one third of the wages I was to receive for the same period. […]
>
> I looked forward to an interesting month or two before the port froze solid for the winter […].
>
> I was given a table desk, a bentwood chair, a pen, a glass ink pot, containing some gelatinous residue of purple ink, some paper, a heavy metal stamp, which made an impress of a hammer and sickle pennant encircled by the legend: "Inspectora Porta Leningrad," and an ashtray and tea pot. The tea pot was by far the most important item."[8]

But Nomad's days in Leningrad were not happy. The port was, in his eyes, incredibly incompetent. Any suggestions he made to improve conditions and turnover were enthusiastically praised and then ignored. He became disillusioned by the squalor, poverty, greed, bribery, corruption and social inequalities. There was no idealism left. It was a dog eat dog world. Apart from famine being endemic there were rumours about cannibalism in the Ukraine and the Black Sea territories. Nomad spoke to a young girl whose husband had been shot for 'stealing Trevelyan's corn that the children might see the morn.' It was darkness at noon for him as it had been for many before and would for many subsequently. A diet of cheap rotgut vodka and 'machorka' ersatz cigarettes wrapped in newspaper were the only 'treats'.

Nomad sat in as a 'judge' on some 'disciplinary hearings' although, as he admitted, his Russian was extremely rudimentary.[9]

But when the winter ended and the ice melted the Soviets found something for Nomad to actually do. They sent him to Murmansk.

Murmansk. North West Russia. 125 miles (200 km) north of the Arctic Circle on the Eastern shore of Kola Bay, 30 miles from the ice free Barents Sea. Climate: Winter – extremely severe (i.e. -50 °C), Summer – short and cold.[10]

When Nomad arrived in the late summer of 1933 Murmansk was a wooden town of about 40,000 occupants. The town was snow free for only three months of the year.

"It was late summer in the period of perpetual daylight when I came one evening to the narrow footbridge spanning a gully which I had to cross to reach my lodgings. A crowd of ill-clad Russkys [sic] were lounging against the protection of the wooden rail that surmounted the gully for about ten feet each side of the bridge approach, a string of horse-drawn wagons had been backed up close to the edge of the gully, and the drivers were busily engaged shoveling the loads of horse manure and refuse into the pit. [For more on manure, *see* Afterword.]

When the last wagon was unloaded the driver yelled "poslednye tovarische" (the last, comrades) and cracked his whip. With a ringing shout the loungers swung into action. They rushed down the steep sides of the gully like a herd of mountain goat. Out into the steaming surface of the manure heap they dashed and with a skill begotten of practice these homeless people burrowed deep and well like Siberian huskies in a snow drift. In a twinkling they vanished from sight, only their faces showing here and there at the base of a smoking machorka cigarette. I recalled the bourgeois apartment house in Moscow. I thought sardonically of how the rulers of the classless state ensured their own comfort."[11]

But all was not doom and gloom. McGuinness records attending with his girl friend Xenia Andrievna a wedding of his friend Kola, a Russian sailor. Space was at a premium, but they managed to get a room big enough to hold a wedding party of twenty.

> "Everyone was dressed to kill. Most of the men, who were seamen, were dressed in checks, mauves and skyblues, that went with flame-red neckties or scarves, and topped bright yellow boots. The girls were less gorgeous, but not unduly so. I felt like a veteran stable sparrow intruding in an aviary of exotic tropical birds. Only one girl was plainly dressed. She had on a suit of blue dungarees, a pair of men's boots – small size – and a glazed fireman's cap. But she wore a red scarf and flashed two shining gold teeth. The neighbours were flabbergasted at the elegance."

After 'gallons of vodka' are consumed Nomad ends up with the gold toothed dungareed guest. His innate chivalry is perhaps typified by his account, for 'Nat's' recollection(s) are lost in the miasma of time.

> "The lady in blue overalls could speak some English of a nautical nature.
> "I am a donkeyman on a God-damn coal burner" she said brightly to me. "My name is Nadezshda but this lousy crew call me Nat."
> "I am glad to know you Nat," I replied, and flattered her by adding: "You speak very good English for one so young."
> "I got it off a blasted American engineer" said Nat calmly as she piled my plate with Bitotchki Zapusta and fried potatoes. "That son-of-a-bitch put my sister and me in the family way and then beat it home to America and never paid us a cent."
> She had much to say about that astonishing man but nothing that redounded to his credit. [...]
> Nadezshda said: "Living with any son of a bitch is a crazy idea. Give me enough to eat and plenty of vodka and I'm satisfied."
> "A simple and strictly moral creed, comrade," I told her."[12]

Like the gentleman he was, Nomad draws a veil over the rest of the evening.

Another interesting tale which Nomad spins concerns how a Russian 'friend' of his, who was being transferred out of Murmansk but wanted to retain the tiny shack that he and his wife Natasha lived in 'got me drunk and proposed that I move in with Natasha who would look after me' and that would mean that because they were a couple they would not be evicted. Alexander might, or might not return, sometime. Natasha was all in favour.

"Alexander called loudly: "Natasha prikhoditye."
The door opened immediately and Natasha entered, her ear scarlet from being pressed tightly against the keyhole.
She smiled knowingly, ingratiatingly, and, was I seeing aright, coyly. To me Natasha was dead sea fruit – green gooseberries. She was short and heavy-footed, though the soul of good nature.
I was getting no bargain even with the temptation of food thrown in and immediately decided to exercise great caution."

Nomad's rejection of the fair, or not so fair, Natasha was, he says, to redound on him. He fell into poverty in the bitter Murmansk winter and, stumbling around the streets encountered the spurned Natasha who had in the meantime shacked up with 'a scrubby-looking little militia man' but

"over her plump arm she carried a basket of assorted fish heads fresh from the sea and bloody from gutters knife. She smiled scornfully at my gaunt cheeks and then let her eyes droop caressingly on the sleek well proportioned heads with their tender white mouths and red gills. The blow was physical and mental, for I knew well the savoury fish soup that would emanate from that basket under her dexterous ministrations. That night, to combat the vision of steaming bowls of fish soup that harassed me, I wrote a long plaintive missive to Xenia Andrievna."[13]

Xenia comes, rescues him and goes back to Leningrad. He returns to nine months of misery.

"When it became known that sausage and mincemeat made of human flesh were being bootlegged in public markets the Kremlin issued a decree against the offering for sale of all cooked meats in public places. […]
In Murmansk where nothing edible could grow except Arctic moss, our plight was not enviable; but it was paradise in summer for famine-stricken refugees. Fish could be got and there was a steady though limited supply of black bread and vodka. For nine months or more I existed on one meal a day that consisted of one raw salt herring and a chunk of black bread. Sometimes I could get a glass of weak tea sweetened with a sticky piece of candy to vary the menu."[14]

Towards the end of his memoirs Nomad reveals his complete disillusionment with 'the workers' paradise. And Murmansk. 'A winter in latitude 70 degrees north, in summer underwear (most of my clothing was stolen while absent on work of building up socialism), hardly recommends itself to Russia's image.' Building up socialism? At least Nomad managed to get out of the Soviet nightmare just before the advent of comrade Stakhanov and his campaign.[15]

Interestingly, he describes a Russian 'Gulag' near Murmansk called 'Soloviki' as

> "a fearful inferno of death and decay in the Arctic circle. [...] So-called political and criminals [...], professors, priests, engineers, artists, writers [...] nuns and women of high birth [...] were sent north. Large groups of depraved criminals of both sexes accompanied them to act as spies and keepers [...]. They died by the thousands. The criminal element was the last to perish. Cannibalism was rife. They slaughtered and ate each other. Then monster rats arrived and overran the island. They ate what was left of the corrupt and wasting humans. The island was picked clean. The first major convict settlement in the new Workers' Republic had been exterminated!"

The area had been visited by a British Commission of well meaning but deluded British Labour party members like George Lansbury. They'd been ferried around the Kola peninsula and easily duped, wined and dined. They had seen the Workers' paradise![16]

Perhaps Briscoe's actions on behalf of Mellows and the service of the good priest in Berlin all those years ago did something for McGuinness. At any event, his final comments on the state of religion in Russia in the two and a half years he was there deserve memorializing.

> "Most of the churches I visited had been converted into what were called Anti-God museums. The term "Anti-God" always puzzled me. Why not Anti-Sun or anti-Moon or anti-everything including the whole solar and a million other systems? Anti-Religious one could, at least, fathom in their fanaticism to make Russian Communism a universal creed. But to declare war on the Divine Creator of all things from primroses to planets was a mighty ambitious undertaking."[17]

And then he gives as his reason for leaving Russia that 'I was bored'. This comes just after he has casually slipped in an aside that

> "I had been hurled down a ravine in a truck as a prelude to spending a spell in a hospital where rats as big as terriers gambolled without hindrance in the corridors and primitive lavatories. [...] Badgered by friend and foe and eager to escape, I pinned my hope on the North-East Polar passage."[18]

He went on a trip back to Moscow to beg for an appointment. He took a brief and depressing trip down the Volga. Then it was back to Leningrad and Murmansk where

> "I was presented with what virtually amounted to an ultimatum: to make the complete voyage which was to circumnavigate Asia and Europe, and therefore be most of the time through foreign waters, I must become a Soviet citizen. That was something I was not prepared to do. [...] I was adamant on that point – and because of that was obliged to leave the ship. [...] I made up my mind to get back to the United States. And began the round of the Bureaux again."[19]

The Russians apparently seemed rather relieved to get rid of 'the mad Irishman'. There are stories of his name being inscribed on a plaque in Red Square in Moscow along with that of Jack Reed and other 'foreigners who came to help us in our hour of revolutionary need'. There is a story about a plaque put up in his honour in Murmansk harbour. But there is little evidence for these tall tales. Similarly, in 1930 when Pax Ó Faoláin, Sean MacBride and Bob Briscoe were reminiscing in the Savoy restaurant in Dublin about that old rogue McGuinness:

> "*Oh*, said MacBride; *He is Harbour Master now in Leningrad. And what of the wife and children?* said I [Ó Faoláin]. *Oh you know McGuinness: never behind the door where women are concerned*, said MacBride. *He probably now has a Russian wife. Along with that he got a very high decoration recently, the Order of Lenin or some such thing!*"[20]

It may be hard to comprehend why McGuinness, hardly a diehard revolutionary, went to Russia in the first place. It is surely not hard to understand why he wanted to leave it. He had achieved no decent job or been able to advance his polar expeditionary aspirations. He'd seen, and experienced, extreme hardship, famine and the disintegration of a society in the midst of mass terror and self destruction. Anyone from a Western European background would want to get out. But Nomad did it because he was 'bored'?

He concludes his account in a rather bizarre flight of whimsy.

> "So one fine, starry September night, I stood full of thought on the Soviet steamer "Sverdlov" watching the last ropes being hauled aboard. The port looked drear and forlorn; [...] The dome of St. Isaac's surmounted by the cross of an unwanted God still dominated the Soviet stronghold.
>
> A group of weary men pulled a heavy gangway clear of two lines of railway tracks. As they hauled they cried "Raz, dva, tri." Out in the stream the G.P.U. men gave me a final salute. [...]
>
> I looked up at the stars; and an odd, crazy thought struck me, mixed up with a toneless voice that echoed over the years –
>
> "Who belongs to dees?" demanded the voice.
>
> "God" my mind answered. "The God of St. Isaac's, of St. Basil's, of all the Russians."
>
> The stars looked down ... and I felt unutterably glad."[21]

So he left because he couldn't take it any more – and that is no reflection on Nomad, or because he was bored, or because of some kind of religious rebirth in the old heathen?

But where was he going?

He says he left on a Soviet steamer and was intent on going to America. But he ends up in Spain, then Ireland.

Writing in January 1937, when he was back in Ireland before most of the International Brigade had even got out there, Nomad was to write:

> "There was a war in Spain! Inactive, in the warlike sense, since the Chinese campaign of 1926, I decided to investigate Europe's most complex fracas.
>
> After studying the leading Press reports, like most people, I came to the conclusion that the Government forces were losing. This, then, was the side I should support. It was obvious the other could get on quite well without my services.
>
> Not exactly the fervid motives of the average volunteering Galahad, but, as it was to be my fourth major campaign, I may be excused sentimentalism in choosing sides. I have found little sentiment in war."[22]

He then recounts how he went to Spain, not direct from Russia with a cargo of guns for the Republic but via the Communist party in London (*see* Chapter 10).

So the Soviet steamer *Sverdlov* did not take him to Russia, or indeed Spain. He ended up in Paris, intent on wandering, this time to the Iberian peninsula, *terra incognita* for Nomad, the world traveller.

Notes.

1. McGuinness, Charles John: *Behind the Red Curtain*. Dublin, undated, p. 3.
2. Private Letter to Hugh McGuinness, 25.09.1932. In possession of Patricia Bryce.
3. Basily, Nicolas de: *Russia under Soviet Rule*. Allen and Unwin, 1938, p. 263.
4. Schapiro, Leonard: *The Communist Party of the Soviet Union*. Eyre & Spottiswoode, London 1960, p. 378.
5. McGuinness, *Behind the Red Curtain*, op. cit., pp. 16-17.

6. ibid., pp. 10-11.
7. ibid., pp. 18-19.
8. ibid., pp. 55-57.
9. Several sources talk of McGuinness being 'multi-lingual' and speaking 'at least six languages'. This is nonsense. Nomad himself admits that he had barely a few words of Russian and German. He couldn't speak Irish, and never even claimed to have mastered any African or Far Eastern tongues. This is not to denigrate the sailor of fortune, but merely to show, yet again, how legends spread.
10. The description comes not from Nomad but from the Murmansk Chamber of Commerce, 2001.
11. McGuinness, *Behind the Red Curtain*, op. cit., pp. 87-88.
12. ibid., pp. 97-101.
13. ibid., pp. 104-106.
14. ibid., pp. 110.
15. Stakhanov, Alexey Grigorievich (1906-1977). Coalminer and legendary worker from Sergo (renamed Stakhanov in 1978), Ukraine – Stalin territory. In 1935 he started an incentive scheme for exceptional output for Soviet worker heroes who would slave away for little or no pay for Stalin, 'the little father' and were called 'Stakhanovites'.
16. McGuinness, *Behind the Red Curtain*, op. cit., pp. 114-118.
17. ibid., p. 119 – under the chapter heading 'Show God Who's Boss'.
18. ibid., p. 125-126.
19. ibid., p. 127.
20. McEoin, op. cit., p. 142. In fairness to Sean MacBride, it should be mentioned that McGuinness himself, in his introduction to *Nomad* 'modestly' states:
    "In omitting a hunt for buried treasure or the rescue of a beautiful maiden in distress who turns out to be an heiress or a princess, I may be unorthodox. In the former case, the treasure I know of still remains to be salved, but nothing would tempt me to cut through malaria-infested jungles for the sake of gold. And as to the latter and romantic omission. I must truthfully state that any distressful maiden who crossed my path attributed to the author a goodly portion of her distress."
21. McGuinness, *Behind the Red Curtain*, op. cit., p. 128.
22. *Sunday Independent*, January 4, 1937.

Chapter 10
Blood and Sand –
The Spanish Civil War

"There was a war in Spain! Inactive, in the warlike sense, since the Chinese campaign of 1926 [he's already claimed it was 1923, or 1927], I decided to investigate Europe's most complex fracas. After studying the leading press reports [in Murmansk!], like most people, I came to the conclusion that the Government forces were losing. This then was the side I should support." [Government forces were not losing in early 1936 at the onset of the war.]¹

There was always some kind of mystery about McGuinness' activities in Spain. The authors spoke to almost a dozen Spanish Civil War veterans, including those who attended the veterans rallies in Barcelona but none recalled him. There was amongst some an undercurrent that Charlie had 'disgraced himself' but no one wanted to talk about it. The truth, when we found it was, as things often are, more prosaic. The reason that Republican veterans did not meet McGuinness was that the very first did not arrive until November 1936 and went straight to the front – where Charlie never saw action, let alone visit. And Nomad left at the end of 1936, because he was back in Dublin by the 1st of January 1937.

The fascist led revolt against the democratically elected government of Spain exploded on July 17-18, 1936. The insurgents seized power in Morocco, Navarre, Galicia and Seville but the key cities of Madrid and Barcelona remained faithful to the government. While the fascists of Germany and Italy provided planes, tanks and guns, supplies from 'allies' like Russia were slow to arrive. To make matters worse, in August the French government reversed itself and stopped further sales of arms and munitions to the lawful Spanish government, starting the Non-Intervention policy of Britain and America.

By October 10, 1936, the hard pressed bourgeois 'socialist' government of Largo Caballero was forced to announce the creation of the Popular Army, incorporating Army units still loyal to the government and the left wing militias like the anarchist FAI, the Trotskyite POUM and the communist Party (Marxist-Leninist-Stalinist).

Overseas International Brigades were being organised in Ireland, England, America, France, Poland and Germany.

According to McGuinness he went armed with an introduction from the Communist Party of Great Britain to Paris in September 1936 where he was directed to the Bureau D'Aide de l'Espagne who sent him over to the Spanish Embassy on the Avenue V. Charlie claims he was initially engaged to run guns and planes from the United States via Mexico but plans were changed and he was advised to proceed to Spain.

He travelled south to Marseilles in a train full of volunteers of the International Brigades.

The next day he sailed from Marseilles on board the *Cuidad de Barcelona* with 2,000 other volunteers to the southern Spanish port of Alicante. There Charlie claimed to be the only Irish man amongst the 1,200 international volunteers, being joined six weeks later by Bill Scott, a member of the Irish Communist Party.[2]

From here he travelled by train to the town of Albacete in the Province of Murcia, 150 miles from Madrid. Volunteers were pouring in from France every day, travelling from Perpignan to the Spanish assembly point in Catalonia. When the first British volunteers arrived they were accompanied by Tom Patton, an Irish man from the Achill Island.[3]

By November 1936 guns and ammunition from Russia started to arrive in serious numbers, machine guns of the Vickers type mounted on three wheeled carriages, tanks and a few aircraft.

It was at the Playa de Toro that Nomad saw his first bull fight. He didn't like it. He thought it was cruel, and his dislike was compounded when the volunteers were forced to eat boiled beef for several days after the fight.

Nor did he have much time for his fellow volunteers, most of whom were risking, and were to give, their lives fighting against fascism. Charlie was later to claim in his *Irish Independent* articles that 'fifty percent of the French Volunteers were not communists (neither was Nomad) or Socialists (neither was Nomad) but were merely unemployed soldiers (sounds like Nomad). The barracks in

Albacete turned out to be a deserted monastery about which, it seems, Nomad explored his fantasies when he sold his 'story' to the proto-fascist *Irish Independent*.

Stuck in war torn Albacete for nearly three weeks awaiting a chance to use his navigational skills, Charlie saw no direct action and never saw the front. With no apparent socialist commitment to the cause he was alarmed by the raggle-taggle band of volunteers who were beginning to form the International Brigades. He made up his mind to desert. Nomad of course would not use that word, but that was what he did – he prepared to run away.

Just before he could leave he was told to proceed to Madrid. He headed out one night on a convoy of ten Russian three ton trucks loaded with American Remington rifles, Russian Maxim machine guns and ammunition for both. Nomad alleges that he survived yet again when the convoy was strafed by German Messerschmidts.

Fifty miles outside Madrid they pulled up and were billeted until further orders. Charlie could not come to terms with the lack of military training of his 'comrades' and regarded them inferior, in his own words, to the other side. He seemed to have forgotten his time with the Derry dockers and Donegal farmers when he was robbing banks around Ballybofey.

Nearly overrun by Moorish troops who had attacked their position Charlie reported a full company of 'green' comrades being wiped out by machine gun fire. Charlie had strategically 'taken command from behind a hillock of earth and rock'.

In the mayhem that followed the attack Charlie scattered with the rest of the 'comrades' and made his way, alone, to Madrid.

Arriving there, Charlie found the Ministry of Marine had been evacuated to Valencia and 'at this stage decided to leave Spain by any means possible.'

However when he demanded to be allowed to leave Iberia he was placed under arrest until a suitable train could take him back to the coast. There was the little matter of desertion. But they were short of men and Charlie seems to have escaped with a lecture and a slap on the wrist. He 'hi-tailed it' for Barcelona.

There his first stop was not the International Brigades HQ, the CP, the FAI or even the French Embassy. Instead he headed for the British Embassy, home of 'his old foe', where he sought an emergency passport to prove his nationality as British! He left Spain and crossed the Pyrenees with his new papers and reached Perpignan in France. From there he took a train to Paris.

In his glorified account of his last days in Spain and his reasons for leaving, which appeared in the *Irish Independent* Nomad claimed:

> "I fancied now and then that the beautiful pale faces of the Spanish senoras wore looks something like that of our womenfolk when the 'Tans' went swaggering through semi-demolished towns in Ireland in 1921... I had witnessed executions in China, saw firing squads in East Africa, but never saw anything as wanton as this [This is his evil comrades, not the fascist enemy]. 'My God,' I prayed [that must have made a first], 'Get me out of this accursed land. Nothing in the world, no cause, can justify this.'"[4]

"This dramatic account is, however, contradicted by a British consul official in Barcelona who reported that McGuinness was deserting for the rather more mundane reason that he found the conditions 'appalling owing to lack of organization, want of training on the part of the troops and a fairly complete absence of any attempt at sanitary precautions'."[5]

What follows, word for word, is Nomad's 'account' of the Spanish Civil War as printed in the *Irish Independent*. We have inserted historical data where appropriate or available and comment briefly upon the possible veracity – or lack thereof – of this tawdry piece of hackery, a product of Grub Street if ever t'were one.

NOTE:

The first article is dated January 4, 1937. By his own account Nomad did not arrive in Spain until September/October 1936 and spent his time idling around Albacete. He was only in Spain some three weeks when one considers the travel time each way, never saw action at the front and disgraced the 'good name of MacAonghusa' as well as all Irish freedom fighters.

The articles do not read well chronologically – though they are obviously not helped by the sub-editing and the repetitions but we print it here, as is, more in sorrow than in anger.

The Trailer.

January 2nd 1937 – January 8th 1937.
True Story That Will Thrill You!
"I Fought with the Reds…"
An Irishman's Adventures
Our Great New feature

An Irishman's hair-raising adventures with the Spanish Reds are described in "I Fought With The Reds in Spain" by Captain Charles J McGuinness, exclusive publication of which commences in the *Irish Independent* on Monday.

This is the most amazing narrative of real-life adventure ever to be published in an Irish newspaper.

Telling his thrilling story with a gripping realism, the author takes YOU with him to see the red reign of terror in action. Suppressing nothing, he reveals how the ruthless war on religion is waged…

"I Fought With The Reds" is a sensational document … **Don't miss it! Order your copy NOW!**

A LIFE OF THRILLS

A glance at the following story of the author's adventurous career will give readers a foretaste of some of the thrills in store for them in "I Fought With The Reds".

Captain Charles J McGuinness is the embodiment of the spirit of adventure of the Twentieth Century.

He has had a truly amazing career. He has roamed the Seven Seas and there would appear to be few countries in the world that he has not trod. [sic]

A restless nomad, he has sought adventure in every quarter of the globe. Sailor, soldier, rebel, pearler, gold digger in Australia, polar explorer, gun-runner, jail-breaker, rum-runner – he has been all in turn – and a few more besides.

Captain McGuinness is a Derryman, who has the sea in his blood, for he comes from a seafaring family. He was born in 1893 and since he was 15 years of age, when he ran away to sea, he has allowed his roving spirit full freedom. Wherever adventure loomed he has packed his kit and made for it.

FOUR SHIPWRECKS![6]

That early escapade of making off to the sea was quickly followed by a shipwreck in the South Pacific in 1909, when, after 15 days in an open boat, he was rescued.

This was not his only taste of shipwreck – three times subsequently he was on ships that came to grief and, in one instance, he was the only survivor of the entire crew.

He did pearl fishing in the South Seas, and visited the Near East, Africa, West Indies, Central America, China and Japan.

BROKE PRISON

He joined the British Navy at the outbreak of the Great War, and was two years in the service. He was transferred to the army, and saw fighting in German East Africa. There he was captured, but escaped from the prison camp, travelling on foot alone for 200 miles through swamp and jungle.

The war over, he turned his attention to his native land, where plenty of adventure at the time was to be had.

He carried out gunrunning for the IRA and took part in the fighting against the Black-and Tans in Donegal. While awaiting court-martial in Derry, after being wounded in the hip, he escaped from prison, and made his way to Dublin.

He brought considerable quantities of arms into the country for the IRA.

WITH BYRD EXPEDITION

In the subsequent years his adventurous spirit brought him to many other countries, and the next highlight of his career was when he was appointed Chief Navigation Officer,[7] for the Expedition to the South Pole, commanded by Vice-Admiral Byrd. 'An adventurer of a vanishing type,' he was described by Admiral Byrd.

He played a big part in the success of the expedition, and when he returned he presented to Mr James Walker, Mayor of New York, an Irish Republican flag, which had been carried over the South Pole by vice-Admiral Byrd.[8]

Captain McGuinness designed the emblem of the expedition, the members of which received a remarkable demonstration when they returned to New York. Lectures on the expedition were given by Captain McGuinness before many organisations and clubs in America.

That expedition over, this nomad was at a loose end. But not for long – for he had turned almost immediately to another field of adventure – rum running from Canada to [the] United States.

In this escapade he had many amazing adventures and escaped from the United States authorities.

Under the nom de plume of 'Night Hawk' he described his rum running exploits in American newspapers.

From rum running in America his wanderlust brought him to Soviet Russia where he spent some time.

His experiences in many countries he published in a book, 'Nomad', published a few years ago which created the greatest interest in these countries and in America, not only because of the amazing exploits of the man himself, but because of the disclosures it made.

And then Spain called him – for there was adventure there.

Don't miss his own story of his exploits in Spain, commencing in the *Irish Independent* on Monday.

IT WILL THRILL YOU!

THE ARTICLES.

ADVENTURES IN WAR-TORN SPAIN
MONASTERY USED AS A BARRACK
Reds Orgy in A Chapel
Shocks On Way to Front
"I SWORE TO DIE CLEANLY"

By Captain Charles J McGuinness, 4th January 1937

There was a war in Spain! Inactive, in the warlike sense, since the Chinese campaign of 1926,[9] I decided to investigate Europe's most complex fracas.

After studying the leading Press reports, like most people, I came to the conclusion that the Government forces were losing. This, then, was the side I should support. It was obvious the other could get on quite well without my services.

Not exactly the fervid motives of the average volunteering Galahad, but, as it was to be my fourth[10] major campaign, I may be excused sentimentalism in choosing sides. I have found little sentiment in war.

MY RECEPTION IN PARIS

Armed with an introduction from the Communist Party of Great Britain, I proceeded to Paris in the beginning of September. Arriving at French headquarters on the Rue Lafayette, I pushed my letter of introduction through the steel wire meshes of the bomb proofed reception office. A surly attendant examined the note.

'More damned English,' he muttered courteously. 'Just wait a minute.'

He disappeared up a caged-in staircase. In a few minutes the surly attendant returned, opened a steel door, and admitted me through the barricade.

Without interest, and certainly without any display of enthusiasm, he advised me to go to the 'Place du Combat.' He gave me a rough chart for street direction, and a slip on which was written: *Comrade Garcia, Chief of the Bureau for Spanish Aid.*

'Why do they all come here! He whined as he ushered me out. I didn't know, but I told him in good French that he was an unfriendly, stupid lout.

Credentials cause a Surprise
The initial reception was not inspiring, but in Soviet Russia I had experienced a liberal education in proletarian bog bureaucracy.

The 'Place du Combat' was a huge square surrounded by dilapidated, dirty buildings, covered in all kinds of flaring red placards, the Hammer and Sickle predominating. These buildings were the revolutionary headquarters in Paris.

In the middle of the Square stood a wooden shack surrounded by a nondescript mob of the proletariat. They eyed me curiously. Over the door of the shack was written the legend: BUREAU D'AIDE DE L'ESPAGNE. I entered!

My credentials caused quite a flutter when I presented them. Comrade Garcia turned out to be a little Spanish Jew with Harold Lloyd spectacles and a huge portfolio. He was suspicious, as most communists are of anything beyond their ken.

'You had better go to the Embassy. They can deal with your case. I know nothing about ships,' he added, with a false smile.

'Arms and 'Planes from USA'
'And less about war,' I thought, 'but you are the makings of a successful Proletarian general.' He then gave me a letter of introduction to the Spanish Embassy.

At the Spanish Embassy on the Avenue George V, after interminable conferences, I was definitely engaged to secure and bring arms and 'planes from the USA via Mexico. My experiences and knowledge of the Americas would be invaluable. There was an unlimited supply of gold, I was informed, and already 40 aeroplanes had been purchased. When they were flown to Mexico, I should make arrangements to have them shipped to Spain.[11]

I was highly interested in the project. It would be gunrunning extraordinary. But there is many a slip... At the last minute all the plans were altered and I was advised to proceed to Madrid. I was astounded and disappointed but determined to see the thing through.

En Route For Marseilles
The following night I boarded the midnight express for Marseille. The Gare du Lyon was crowded with drunken candidates for the Spanish International Brigade, and the whole reminded me of a very sordid counterpart of Victoria or the Gare du Nord during the World War.

One group of about ten stood apart, looking stiff and out of place. They were Oxford and Cambridge 'comrades' out to save the world for democracy! I think they had all hoped to get good jobs in the Labour Party after they had all written books about their adventures. Poor chaps, few would survive!

As the train pulled out of the station the seven hundred volunteers for Spain lustily sang the 'Internationale.' The leaders expostulate, trying to maintain the farce of secrecy.

'Silence!' they shouted. 'Discipline!'

But the drunken legionnaires only moved to a higher and more maudlin key as the train rolled though the suburbs of Paris.

In my compartment was a select group of French Foreign Legionnaires. There was an ample supply of wine, and they sang all through the night, or held heated harangues on Communism, Fascism, the Legion, and Spain. They reviled German and Italian intervention.

'Wait until I turn this loose,' said Souchez – a tough looking hombre just home from China after completing 12 years in the Legion. He patted with his foot a long, heavy package which protruded from under the seat.

'Rat-a-tat-tat!' he further emphasised and then burst into a North African Legionnaires marching song.

By Liner to Spain

Arriving in Marseilles, we repaired in groups to various friendly Communist cafés to await orders. As I was to assist the captain of the transport, I was immediately driven to the docks, where I boarded the luxurious liner *Cuidad de Barcelona.*

The Captain explained that in the event of the ship being chased off her course and out of sight of land by the enemy I was to take command.

'I have only sailed on the coast,' he explained. 'I don't understand navigation.'

That evening and all the next day the departing legion thundered down to the ship in a fleet of taxis. No one took any notice, though it was quite evident we were a Spanish ship, and bound for Spain. There was no passport control – nothing. A couple of Gendarme patrolled the dock, and no one was allowed to go on shore. At the same time we loaded an assorted cargo classified on the manifest as 'general.' Then, at dusk one evening in late September, we sailed for Barcelona.

Off the Chateau d'If (famous fortress of 'the Count of Monte Cristo'), as we sailed south-west, the crew painted over the ship's name and port of registration '*Cuidad de Barcelona*, Palma, Majorca,' also the red bands on the funnel. At night all lights were switched off, and the 2,000 Legionnaires squatted all over the ship, the political leaders, of course, annexing the cabins-de-luxe.

No Irish in first Detachment
I was assigned a luxurious stateroom, with bath, in accordance with my rank. I felt self-conscious at this mark of esteem, and gladly allowed two Yugoslavs and two Czechs, all of whom spoke a smattering of Russian, to share the cabin. The British minority slept, or, at least, lay down in a forward alleyway. From first to last this forlorn contingent led a lonely existence in the Brigade. The barrier of language kept them apart. There were not enough of them to form a separate contingent, so they were shuffled back and forth. None of the other national groups would have them, – until on the final day, when they attached themselves to a French company and entrained for the front.

There were no Irish in this first detachment of the International Brigade with the exception of myself. I stood alone at all times, and had the distinction of having served in more campaigns than any other member.[12] Bill Scott, the only member of the Irish Communist Party, arrived in Albacete, the base for Madrid, six weeks later. He had been jettisoned in Barcelona, and was on the point of returning home when he was moved frontwards.

We Arrive in Alicante
Six hours out from Marseilles we received radio instructions to proceed to Alicante, a port on the south Spanish coast. The passage was uneventful. Off Barcelona we spotted two Italian cruisers, but they paid no heed to our passing. Our great risk lay in approaching Alicante, where insurgent battleships were reported active. As we approached the entrance at day break we steamed slowly past German, Italian, French and British war vessels, but not a sign of the enemy, for which I was devoutly grateful.

Without the cup of coffee which had been our breakfast since sailing, we disembarked in Alicante in the group formation leaving Paris. A brass band led us through the beautiful city now draped with red banners and slogans.

An Oxford-Cambridge Yell
It has been the communist policy to make the Spaniards believe that Russia was helping with men and munitions, when the truth is that French Anarcho-Communism is the power behind the Red Government – even the well-bred and out-of-place Oxford-Cambridge contingent gave a college yell: 'Red Front! Red Front! Red United Fighting Front!' Their clear and superior enunciation fell on desert [sic] ears. They only yodelled once.

Our First Meal in Spain
Late in the afternoon we were issued tinned fish, dry bread, and a mug of wine – not so good for the first day in Spain! In the evening we fell in

and marched back to the City Hall. Two hours of standing in the Square listening to the same prattle and we marched off to the railway station en route to Madrid, or so we thought.

The railway journey into the interior was a masterpiece of triumphal propaganda. Every railway station was festooned with flowers and red banners. The platforms were thronged with wildly cheering citizens shouting 'Viva Russia!' Brass bands played the 'Internationale' and the 'Red Flag.'

The now partially revived foreign brigadiers entered anew into the spirit of the Russian hoax and sang in languages any one of which was Russian to the simple peasantry. Gifts of fruit and wine made us all feel better, and many of us drunk.

I was still with the French group of legionnaires, and benefited from their skilful foraging. At the beginning of our journey one untoward incident was typical of the type. Four British 'comrades' tried to hog a whole compartment by putting out the light, pulling down the blinds, and strewing the seats with baggage – and this on a train packed to suffocation.

An 'Attack' on British 'Comrades'

I led the French attack, talking easily understandable English. We soon ousted the cultured Communists. They were wroth [sic] to leave, and said: 'No true Communist gets drunk. You are breaking 'pawty' rules, and you are lowering British communism in the eyes of foreign comrades.'

'That's too bad,' I answered, as I chose a corner seat. 'I am not a Communist. Even worse, I suppose, as far as you Drawing Room Reds are concerned, I am an Irishman, and none too fond of Britishers of your type.'

Only fifty percent of the French in the Brigade are Communist: the other fifty are just plain unemployed ex-soldiers. As results have shown, the soap-box soldier is the first to fall; a good soldier can generally get cover if any at all is available. The death rate in the international brigade is high as a result of politics over military skill. Few professional Communists are good soldiers.

About 3 a.m. we came to a stop in a brilliantly lighted station, where we left the train. Lined up in straggling formation we marched off behind a band, accompanied by the curious townsfolk. No one knew the name of the town; some thought it was Madrid. We marched though stately streets until we came to a smaller one.

'Right turn!' we marched into our latest barracks.

A Monastery as a Barracks

Once inside I realised that I was in a religious building – a monastery or convent, perhaps. A huge statue of Our Lord lay broken in the patio.

Altar candelabra was strewn everywhere – surely a strange setting for a military barracks.

The patio was surrounded on all four sides by a two-storied building, situated between two streets. One side, formerly a school, was now converted into a huge dining hall, wooden tables running its full length. On these were strewn tin dishes, our second meal in Spain – a piece of pork fat, a chunk of dry bread, and a mug of strong wine.

In spite of our hunger few made a hearty meal. Sleeping quarters were provided in a cellar underneath and in the violated chapel adjoining and at right angles to the dining room.

Loath to sleep in either, with a French chap, who was as much disgusted as myself, I found a small nook on the top floor. There we spent the night in anything but comfort.

Revolting Scenes in Violated Chapel
In the morning we descended to wash to find the troops up and about exploring the monastery and having a rare orgy of blasphemy. We had to pass through the chapel to get outside. Here a most astounding tableau met our gaze.

A group of Poles and Italians were marching round the church attired in sacred vestments. A group of Jew boys were swinging incense burners. On the altar another group were mimicking the Mass. Up in the organ gallery a Frenchman was playing the 'Internationale' in slow time. All were chanting an accompaniment.

In niches in the chapel wall stood bold Hebrew legionnaires attired in clerical robes. The displaced statues lay broken on the floor beneath.

Near where I entered, close to the dismantled altar, a depraved-looking Slav was in the act of breaking the cover off the Mass Book, laughing like an idiot the while.

I pushed him to one side. 'You swine,' I said, 'I hope you will be as tough when you get to the front and your opponent tougher.'

Latrines Draped with Vestments
To cover up my effrontery, which might easily have meant death amongst such depravees, I spoke sharply in Russian: 'Don't you know, you fool, that looting merits the death sentence on active service? I shall report all this to Brigade Headquarters'.[13]

Other decent chaps were also showing signs of disgust, but they were easily in the minority. Later on in the day I spoke with a Spanish Miliciano who informed me that but a week prior to our arrival 40 priests, nuns and lay brothers had been executed in the Patio where lay the broken statue of Our Saviour [sic – or sick?].

Housing such a crowd, the Chapel barracks soon became intolerable. A faint trickle of water from one surviving spigot was the sole source of drinking water. Vandalism had destroyed the entire plumbing system. Latrines were erected in the square, huge wooden tubs, guarded by a wooden railing on which were draped altar cloths and vestments.

Sleeping accommodation was of the foulest. Imagine 200 men of all nations laying on the stone floor of one damp cellar on dirty pallets of straw. Imagine them eternally coughing and spitting, wrangling and sweating, discussing the virtues of Communism, cursing fascism, until daylight steamed in through the barred windows.

One such night and I swore to die cleanly rather than undergo another period of such degradation. There was, and is, no medical supervision in the brigade. There is only room for Communist propaganda. Many suffered from pernicious and contagious maladies. Sleeping on stone or tiled floors (wood is scarce in Spain) soon left its mark.

FOUL WAR ON RELIGION
Communists' Trail of Sacrilege
Not a Single Church Unmolested
Blasphemous Periodicals on Sale

Charles J McGuinness, 5th January 1937

After my first experience I found a room in town. The town, we discovered, was Albacete, in the province of Murcia, about 150 miles from Madrid. There was much criticism of my superiority complex by the British. They, in the ignorance of a first military venture, considered dirt and vermin the hallmark of really roughing it.

They boasted of not having undressed since leaving Paris. As I had come to Spain to go to Madrid on a special mission, I ignored all criticism. One thing I stipulated definitely, I would in no way become attached to or assigned with any group of British Communists.

A week in the barracks of the 5th regiment, as the transformed monastery buildings were now officially dubbed, a general shuffling of the Brigade took place. The German group being the more disciplined, and looked up to as military models, were accorded a barracks to themselves. The remaining conglomeration moved to the barracks of the old Garda Nacional. This was a huge roomy structure, built in the usual style, enclosing a spacious square. It was soon packed to completion, and a bit over.

Another Irishman for the Brigade
Contingents were arriving daily from France – Perpignan and Marseilles being the concentration points. From Perpignan troops and material were brought to a point near the Spanish frontier by motor lorries. Then they

marched across the border, carrying baggage and equipment. Spanish motor lorries concluded the transit by bringing the new arrivals to Figueras, the Spanish concentration point in Catalonia.

Another small group of British arrived, this time a really decent bunch of ex-Army men and a couple of officers. Amongst them was an Irish lad from Achill – Tom Patton. There were now two Irishmen with the Brigade – a very small percentage then out of 8,000 diverse nationalities.

A month later, when Bill Scott arrived, Ireland's only Communist representative (Patton was an English Communist Party member), there were three Irishmen in a Brigade of 12,000 men.

Patton was a decent chap. I told him of the executions and stupid vandalism and asked how he could reconcile such actions with his faith.

'No matter what I am, or where I am, I shall always be a Catholic,' he replied. 'I can't help the actions of those scum.' He was eventually attached to the British group, who were attached to nobody. If they had left Spain with any degree of secrecy they would never have been missed.

Arms from France and Russia

Up to this time, no member of the Brigade had laid hands on rifle, machine-gun, mortar, or grenade. There were a few old sporting guns and some Spanish Oveido rifles to give guards and sentries the appearance of the real thing. Later a consignment of about 5,000 Remington rifles with ammunition arrived from France. Then came a few Lewis guns, but it was not until the beginning of November that Russian armaments came on to the scene.

These were mostly machine-guns of the Vickers type, mounted on a three-wheeled carriage, and good copies of the Lewis gun. But it was the aircraft and tanks that roused the hopes of the International column.

Truthfully speaking, the foreign Communists had little sympathy with the Spanish people. They blindly worshipped Russia. Spanish Milicianos and Legionnaires did not fraternise. On one occasion when a large draft of Valentian Militia, mostly Anarchists, were approaching Albacete, rumours were adroitly spread that they were Fascists on the warpath. The International Brigade were confined to barracks until the Spanish Anarcho troops had gone to the Front.

Women in the Brigade

Fraternising with Anarchists was strictly taboo, and yet the war was being fought by the Anarchists. Only a small percentage of Spain follows the teachings of the third International (Russia). Trotsky has more followers, while the Syndico-Anarchists easily outnumber all the Radical groups. Thus it will be seen that, no matter how this conflict in Spain is settled, there will be warring forces at large for another decade at least.

Occasionally, women came with the various drafts from France – Hungarians, Poles, Romanians, and Germans. Mostly all were Jewesses; they looked absurd trotting around in uniforms with Sam Brown belts and revolvers. As with many of the effeminate males, quite a few wore bracelets of revolver cartridges.

For amusement there were never-ending harangues for new arrivals, and send-offs to the Front. Andre Marty, noted French Communist Deputy, and leader of the Black Sea fleet mutiny, was the principal speaker.

Marie Nicolette ('Nicko') was next in point of favour. The 'Internationale' was sung on all and every occasion. 'Reveille' was played on a concertina by an Italian ex-circus clown. His repertoire was limited, consisting only of the 'Internationale' and 'Bandera Rosa' [sic], the Italian Red Flag hymn.

My First and Last Bull-Fight

The first and last bullfight I attended was one given in our honour in Albacete.

The Plaza de Toro (of unhappy memory), or Bull Ring, was a huge ornamental arena situated close to our barracks on the fringe of the town. Before the so-called amusement started the International brigade marched around and though the arena to give the Spaniards a treat. Clad in various designs and colours of uniform, from artisans blue overalls to a job lot of British khaki, newly arrived from Valencia, the effect was colourful – but as the rank and file included some of France's submerged citizenry, native and adopted, they were anything but specimens of physical fitness.

Their physical vagaries ran the gamut of the average freak show. Marching behind a burly, shapeless, Italian 'comrade', who rolled and lurched like a tug in a cross-sea, keeping step was difficult. Away off to starboard was an ex-French soldier with one leg at least six inches shorter than its pal kept the company busy changing step. Some executed a few steps of a jig trying to do this difficult military feat, invariably landing back on the same mis-step.

How the half of them were accepted is a mystery. What the thousands of physically fit and of military age Spaniards thought was strictly their own business, but anyhow, the spectators cheered loudly. If they could cheer a bull being tortured to death, cheering us was not quite so difficult.

The Parade over, we got what seats were left. Then a beautiful black bull was released into the ring. Five toreadors were mincing around waving red banderos – there were no horsemen. The bull apparently thought it was a game and began to romp with his torturers. Even when a dozen darts had transformed him into a cavorting blood fountain he seemed more hurt than angry.

The crowd were delighted. Beautiful senoritas clapped their hands, 'Brava, mi brava!' they shouted. Then an assembled downtrodden Spanish proletariat.

A graceful matador approached the now bewildered, panting bull. Draping his red bandero round his sword he waited the feeble rush. A quick side step; then with an affected nonchalance the brave matador drove the sword down behind the bull's shoulder.

The poor animal dropped on its knees in a pool of blood. It struggled desperately to rise, slipping pathetically in the blood-soaked turf. The crowd now jeered the matador for bungling his stroke. He drew a long bladed dagger from its sheath and at last finished his unsavoury job.

A pair of horses dragged the bleeding carcass across the ring at full gallop as another victim entered the place of slaughter.

'We Are All Damned Fools'

Seated on my right was an ex-French soldier of the World War and later a Sergeant in the Foreign Legion. 'Armande du Bois' was my closest friend and a most loveable type of fellow. I had noticed he was extremely nervous during the bullfight, occasionally clutching my arm and shuddering.

Jerkily he jumped to his feet. 'Come, let's go. Vite, vite!' I arose and quickly followed him up to the terrace surrounding the amphitheatre. Two other Frenchmen also left their seats.

Clear of the howling mob, Armande spontaneously burst into tears. 'They are not human,' he moaned. 'Such barbarians.' We were all affected, and gladly exchanged the remaining contests for the solace of a bodega.

The Leaders Behind the Lines

Said Jacques Renaud, a cashiered officer of the Armee Nord Afrique, 'Spain is but a French-Russian pawn. Look at the leaders behind the lines. Who are they? Leon Blum, in France directing the stream of International political refugees across the Pyrenees, in Perpignan the Socialist Mayor turns over the huge military hospital and grounds to the Communist Party. Everyone there sees the contingents arrive and leave for Spain almost daily. Then we have Leon Braunstein [sic] (alias Trotsky), Finkelstein (alias Litvinov), and Rosenburg, Soviet Ambassador to Spain united in fighting for the Spanish Government!'

One Certainty: The War on Religion

This angle opened a new train of thought, and opened a floodgate of dangerous criticism. The fact that Trotsky's forces, the POUM, the largest Communist organisation in Spain; the Freemasons of the Anarcho-Syndicalist groups, and the Soviet Third international were working together was not loudly advertised.

We discussed the Basque Catholic situation and their adherence to the Red Government.

One thing we knew of for certain – that nowhere we had been stationed was there a single Catholic church unmolested and free for Divine Service.

And we saw ample evidence of the war on religion everywhere – the horribly indecent blasphemous periodicals openly on sale. These filthy journals are flaunted before the eyes of Spanish youth to inculcate in them a hatred and loss of respect for the Church. I have some of these journals here in Ireland to prove that they are directed solely against the Catholic Faith and the authors are mostly non-Catholic.[14]

January 6th 1937

Massacre in A Cemetery
Outburst of Reds Bloodlust
Hundreds of Soldiers Nauseated
Murderers Work in Secret Now

Reverting to the Plaza de Toro at Albacete. This magnificent arena may have the advantage of providing the bloodthirsty citizens of Albacete with amusement, but when we were forced to eat the bulls, and in the Bull Ring, the place became revolting.

Underneath and behind the concrete stands and directly facing the latrines, long tables were stretched, flanked by crude benches. This was the mess hall, called upon to feed over a thousand or more troops daily. It was a shocking fiasco. Organisation was so infantile that no proper preparation was ever made to feed the tens of thousands of troops passing through the town.

A couple of days would have sufficed to build fireplaces and ovens. Instead, all food was cooked in huge boilers over a wood fire burning on the ground. As the tables could only accommodate about four hundred at a sitting, getting to the Bull Ring late was a tragedy. It was not uncommon to wait two hours to consume a meal in ten minutes.

First Real Taste of War
Breakfast consisted of black coffee and dry bread. Dinner: Beans stewed in rancid olive oil, a piece of boiled bull and a tin mug of red wine. Supper was much the same as dinner.

At 8 p.m. there was a complete blackout of the town as a protection against air raiders. Late diners gulped their beans and bull in the dark. Luckily the keen invigorating air of the central Spanish plateau bred vigorous appetites, and personally as the food

[Large piece of original text missing]

'We Are Going to The Cemetery'
I noticed the direction we were heading. I knew of the murder in the barber's shop. I had seen the trucks drive off and I felt our destination was similar to where they went.

'We are going to the cemetery, I imagine,' I said. But as none of the column bore arms I did not grasp the real meaning of our mission.

An hour's march brought us to the cemetery gates. As in all Spanish cemeteries today, sentries were posted all around. We passed through into the beautifully kept central walk and soon arrived at the further wall. We halted in marching alignment, three deep, facing inwards.

'About turn!' we turned about —

A Line of Bleeding Corpses
A ghastly spectacle was revealed. At the base of the whitewashed wall on the ground lay a line of bleeding corpses. Twenty metres long was that line. The bodies lay singly or crossed, one above the other. Pale hands and faces, bloodstained, shattered, made vivid splashes in the sombre grisly line.

I felt horribly sick. The deep trench between us and the wall yawned gaping. To left and right were mounds. What they covered was grimly portrayed lying under the wall.

Above a cloudless blue sky looked down pure and serene: little birds were pecking for twigs not a metres length away from the body nearest to me.

I had witnessed executions in China; saw firing squads during the World War in East Africa, but never anything so wanton as this.

'Tomorrow Fifteen More Will Be Shot'
It seemed there was no limit to the accumulation of horrors. Taking advantage of the gruesome moment, an oily Hungarian Jew, a political group leader, jumped upon one of the mounds. 'Comrades,' he cried, 'There lie the enemies of the proletariat. This is the only answer to Fascism. Death to the traitors.'

He held forth on the slavery of the working classes, spoke of the broad highway of Communism leading upwards.

The impious swine waved his hand skywards.

I refused to listen to such muck and left with hundreds more who had immediately fallen out of the line after turning about. 'Tomorrow fifteen more will be shot.' We heard this bandied around as we left. Thirty five workers murdered to build up Socialism. A good day's work.

Executions Carried Out in Secret
I might explain that in Albacete the Policia are armed with Italian big game hunting rifles, double the calibre of an ordinary service rifle. The bullet fired is nothing short of a small projectile, and inflicts an awful wound, the rough base spreading fanwise and serrated on leaving the gun barrel.

A closing note. At present no one is allowed admittance into a graveyard except those directly interring a body. Executions are carried out in secret by a trusted and hardy group well primed – secrecy robs them of nothing of their terror. The following day fifteen 'Fascists' were executed according to plan.

Three days after the execution in the cemetery, at least at night, we had an air raid. A solitary bomber flew over the city bent on bombing the Government hangers. He dropped a couple of bombs and retreated, chased by three Red 'planes, firing bullets of machine gun fire. It was thrilling to watch, and spoke highly of the nerve of the sole aviator to venture so far over enemy territory. The bombs dropped out on a saffron field, making two small craters.

Disgusted With The Campaign
The following day I was summoned to Headquarters and told to prepare to leave for Madrid that night. At last I was to proceed to the capital, and in doing so, pass mighty close to the firing line. By this time I was utterly disgusted with the campaign, but determined to stick it out until I had first-hand experience at the front.

For weeks columns of the brigade had been leaving for the Front line, but still the commander of the Brigade, Kleber, remained in Albacete, riding round on the proverbial white horse. He was a Russo-German, speaking both these languages perfectly.

Russian aviators and engineers were now making their appearance in connection with deliveries of trucks and 'planes, but no Soviet citizens or soldiers made an appearance. There was no reason why they should. The Government had more man power than they could cope with economically. It amused me to watch the thousands of young men of military age who were more mentally and physically fit than the flotsam and jetsam of the International Brigade.

Orders to Proceed to Madrid
The solution to this seeming paradox is simple enough. France gets rid of an embarrassing section of her population. Spain will see that they are exterminated in the campaign, thus solving the problem of their absorption if the Government wins. The Brigade has been formulated to act as the spearhead of attack wherever they were in action. This is clear to almost everyone with the possible exception of the poor political

refugees who imagine a land of milk and honey to exploit when they end their victorious war.

Even if they win, I cannot see Trotsky, Stalin, Blum and the Freemasons[15] and, the most important factor of all, the Spanish people, forming a Coalition Government to rule a land of milk and honey.

On my reporting to Headquarters that night ready to move, I got the surprising order to proceed to Madrid, acting on the way as a guard of an ammunition convoy bound to the front en route Madrid.

January 7th 1937

Under Fire by the Enemy
Thrills in Night Attack
Reds prove to be poor fighting men
Authors Dramatic Getaway

The ammunition convoy was speeding along the Aranjuez - Madrid road. Ten Russian three ton trucks loaded with American Remington rifles, Russian Maxim machine guns and .303 ammunition for both.

I was riding on the first truck, together with two French men and a Bulgarian refugee long resident in France. No one spoke, and in the bitter cold we crouched down on top of the hard angular cases.

The section of the road we were transversing was well known to the Insurgent bombers and guards covered the important railway junction close by zealously.

A Journey of Fear and Dread
They had repeatedly blown up the railway tracks after each fresh repair job by the Red railwaymen. At any moment we might be ambushed, either from above or below. Then I would probably have to fight – for my life – in a cause with which I had lost all sympathy.

The lure of adventure had called me hither, and the odds against me ever escaping from the adventure were many. I scanned the bleak and black expanse into which the dimmed headlights of the convoy shone feebly.

'Here, Comrade, Have a Drink'
Noting but an opaque wall and the monotonous drumming of the engine. Since the horrible spectacle of the mutilated bodies in the churchyard my nerves were shaky.

Now I dwelled morbidly on the fact that at any moment a withering blast of machine-gun fire might rake the convoy or a mine explode and blow us into eternity. Or – out of the inky sky a winged monster might appear and attack us from above. Or –

Groe, one of the Frenchmen, broke in on my meditations.

'Here, comrade, have a drink.'

He proffered a bottle of cognac, I noticed that his hand was shaking. The hand I stretched forth to meet the bottle wasn't too steady either.

I drank a generous draught, so all the others, but we might as well have drank water for all the stimulus we obtained.

Air Attack on the Convoy

Suddenly the harsh bark of a klaxon and a shrill whistling. The alarm signal. 'Halt.'

The convoy ground to a stop and all lights were switched off.

In a silence and darkness that seemed solid, the hum of powerful aeroplane motors came out of the western sky. We dismounted and retreated a short distance form the explosive cargo on the trucks.

The roar of the 'planes drew nearer until they were directly overhead, but still invisible.

From the direction in which we came a blinding flash cut the darkness, followed by a deafening roar. We dropped flat on the ploughed earth.

A couple of seconds and there came another explosion nearer and more terrifying. A shower of earth and stones flew over our recumbent bodies. No one was seriously hurt.

Glass in Every Truck Shattered

We lay for another couple of minutes until the disappearing hum of the bombers faded away to a thin drone.

Every truck had the glass in its hood windows shattered, and one refused to start. After repeated failures to function, we divided the load amongst the nine remaining trucks and set off for the front.

Daybreak found us not far from Getafe, where the Red Army held a line cutting across the Toledo-Madrid road.

Do not confuse this with your ideas of the World War front. The troops, Spaniard and foreign, were scattered irregularly over the countryside, occupying farmhouses, outhouses, sheds, and shelters of all kinds.

There were often wide gaps on either side, but no portion of an army will pierce these gaps deep enough through fear of being cut off.

There are also pretences of modern fortifications in the shape of crude barricades of stone and earth. Here and there were concealed machine-gun nests and an odd, very odd, dug out completed the military structure.

Well to the rear were a couple of German 7 millimetre light field pieces. When we drove up with our precious load there was no enthusiasm.

A Dissertation on Food

'Better leave the boxes on the trucks,' said the wise Spanish Commandante. I got his meaning without the aid of an interpreter. I also took in the graceful lines of his Hispano Suizs, and gave it the odds in beating all in the field in the race to Madrid or elsewhere away from this mala guerra.

There was no opposition. I asked the Commandante where we ate. 'Come with me,' he said. Linking his arm with mine he led me to his own billet which was also company headquarters – a small dirty room adjoining an odoriferous goat house. I enjoyed a good meal of beans, meat and fish stewed in olive oil.

Here I must explain that having travelled considerably my tastes in food are catholic, but I have a weakness for olive oil, garlic, macaroni, rice, and I even find the Spanish oddities of octopus or octupi and garden snails savoury tit-bits [sic]. But woe to those living in Spain who care not for such food.

Frenchman Who was a Philosopher

I was anxious to proceed to Madrid, but all cars were requisitioned for local service, so I had to wait the Commandant's pleasure – and, believe it or not, I had to wait with a group of French and Poles holding this particular section of the Front.

One of the Frenchmen humorously remarked when I complained of the delay: 'Oh! I shouldn't worry, Comrade. You stay with us and you will get to Madrid fast enough. Wait and see.'

This philosopher had reason to know. He explained that the present rout had started in Toldeo some ten or twelve days ago and was but temporarily hung up. 'We'll be on the move soon,' he promised, scratching himself vigorously.

During the day a shabby-looking shaven brigand allocated to each group their stand-to stations in case of a sudden attack.

Assigned to Outpost Duty

A Moorish battalion covered this section of the Line, so I was most assiduous in selecting a spot that would offer the most safety from direct or enfilading fire. I was much more particular about selecting a safer line of retreat. I was keenly conscious of the inferiority of our command in general – officers and men, armament and tactical. They did not seem to co-ordinate.

There was no mental bond – everything done was singularly amateurish. The few who knew a little of military matters either made a terrific fuss or concealed their knowledge entirely.

At dusk I was assigned to outpost duty. Upon this plateau the wind was cold and penetrating. Wrapped in none too fleecy blankets, their living content gave us the only source of warmth in scratching fits, but this could not be maintained indefinitely. All the troops not on outposts or patrols sheltered in barns and sheds, packed together like sardines.

Wide Spaced Flashes of Fire

There was little sign of life from the enemy. Sporadically up and down their line ran wide-spaced flashes of rifle fire, just to show us, as it were, that they were on the job. The Red troops fired at the flashes, and thus each side had a vague idea of each other's position.

I earnestly prayed that I might get through to Madrid without stopping a bullet or a bayonet. At about 10 o'clock we were relieved, and I went back to the high powered goat house, where I ate a satisfying meal of raw bacon and bread washed down with wine. Then I lay down on a pile of straw between two Polacks (Poles) and fully attired, soon fell asleep.

'The Moroccans are Upon Us'

I awoke to the shrilling of a whistle. 'Assemblement, assemblement! Vite, vite! The Moroccans are upon us!' we rushed out in the darkness, each group going to their stand to position fully equipped. I reached the small earthwork barricade and lay down behind a well-reinforced parapet of my own construction.

The ground in front was scrubby and strewn with boulders. It would prove a difficult terrain for a sweeping charge, but such was the weakened morale that the red Army tactics were at that time concerned with defence. The others could do the charging.

Along a distance of about five hundred yards a steady stream of fire poured into our lines. It took a couple of minutes before the answering fire checked some of this. Then the Moors dropped to desultory firing.

Company of Recruits Decimated

Was the attack off? Away to the right of our earthwork barricade a group of Milicianos were firing regularly in a long line of flashes. I remembered the low ridge there, or small dyke, that the Company Commander allocated to a 'green' company just arrived from the base. Their firing died down and little was happening on either side.

Five or ten minutes of tense waiting. Then suddenly as if operated by one switch, a dozen blinding searchlights lit up our positions as brightly as by noonday sun. Simultaneously a terrific gust of withering machine-gun fire burst forth in a deafening crash. Sheltered and temporarily out of danger behind the hillock of earth and rock, I looked over to the strategic ridge. To my utter amazement I saw the defenders of the ridge like chaff literally blown away in the leaden storm.

'I Picked out the North Star and Ran'
The poor 'rookies' had draped themselves over the ridge to get a better firing stance, or for some other reason (there were no survivors to explain), instead of taking advantage of its proper element of shelter.

The line broke and ran, closely followed by the shouting Moors. I ran crouching to a barn two hundred yards away. From one side extended a low adobe wall, part of a yard enclosure. Near a small wooden gate I dropped flat as a torrent of lead whined over me.

I waited for a moment – then dashed through and ran behind the building. Everyone was running wildly. I ran towards the Commandant's Headquarters adjoining the goat-house, but the Hispano Suiza was gone, so had our trucks, and so had the artillery.

Then I picked out the North Star, laid a course Nor' Nor' West and ran.

Irish Independent, 8th January 1937

AMONG THOSE ABOUT TO DIE

Condemned Priests Blessing
The author leaves war torn Spain
'Without one pleasant memory'

The rising sun threw a pale light on the roofs of the small town to the south. I was on the main road to Madrid and travelling with an assorted company. Milicianos on trucks, on foot, and officers in cards went flying past – some with arms, some without. I picked up a rifle that some weary or frightened soldier had dropped on the route, and marched on. Again unattached!

My side felt chafed and raw; possibly my belt with the heavy ammunition pouches. I threw them away. Then I noticed two neatly drilled holes in the side of my tunic.

I Arrive in Madrid
I had a look inside. Sure enough, a bullet or something had grazed me, scarcely breaking the skin by the sheerest of good luck. I felt devoutly thankful, and then threw away the rifle. As one army retreated, a new one was rushing along the road collecting arms and men to make a further stand – further on.

Arriving in Madrid by way of the Princesca Bridge, I discovered that the Minister of Marine had left for Valencia. If I wanted to see him I must go there. I certainly wanted to go to Valencia, to any seaport or outlet where I could leave this unhappy land. Any move I had made up to now seemed to get me deeper in the toils, and again I prayed hard for delivery.

How the Spaniards Are Insulted
Columns from the International Brigade were now arriving to stiffen the defence of Madrid and were being concentrated in the Casa de Campo. How the Spaniards swallowed this gratuitous insult so meekly I cannot understand.

The Communist (Russian) organs were forever lauding this band of very mediocre conscripts and unemployed as a modern military achievement. Trotsky's crowd will say anything so will the Anarchists of Catalonia and, of much more portent, so will the Spanish people when they are called upon to meet the bill.

At this stage I don't intend to enlarge further on my experiences, but will deal with the few remaining unpleasant episodes that marked my departure from Spain.

Permission to Leave Spain
Back at Brigade headquarters I demanded to be returned to France. Would I accept command of a gunboat? No. A cruiser? No. I knew they had no commands to offer and this was but a stall to coax me into the Artillery or Flying Corps. All right. Marty agreed with bad grace and I received permission from the Frente Populaire to leave Spain.

My papers were in order, I was immediately put under police supervision – until a suitable train left for the coast. There were four of us returning, two French, a Hungarian and myself.

The night before our departure was spent in the guardroom of police Headquarters in an atmosphere of smoke and garlic. Now and then prisoners were brought in, singly or in batches, after the approved midnight forays.

Talk with a Condemned Priest
In the morning I went out into the prison yard to get a sluice of cold water. I was half-drugged and stickily dirty from grime and smoke. About twenty prisoners were walking about the yard or standing in little groups. They looked pale and wan and were conversing in low tones.

A few were at the water spigot, washing. I divested myself of upper clothing down to an armless sports singlet and commenced to wash. Alongside I noticed a gentle-faced young Spaniard.

'Good morning,' he said in Spanish, as he moved aside to give me more room. 'Quite well,' I replied, 'How are you?'

Then looking cautiously around, he added softly, 'I see you are a foreigner, and', looking at a tattooed crucifix on my forearm, 'a Catholic.' 'Yes, I am a catholic and an Irishman,' I also spoke quietly.

'Tomorrow I go to the Cemetery'
Our conversation was a dangerous one. Why, he might have been a spy, for all I knew, but his face was reassuring, 'and', I further remarked, with

a note of satisfaction in my voice, 'I leave for France today.'

'May God go with you, my friend,' he barely breathed. 'I am a Catholic priest and the day after tomorrow I go to the cemetery.' Everything went blank before my eyes. A cold hand touched my heart. The grisly terror that lurked everywhere, robbed me of understanding.

I turned to ask the young priest if it were really true – but he had gone. A guard approached. 'Don't listen to these Fascists, Comrade,' he said. Then he remarked pointedly, 'And don't ask or answer questions. We'll do all that.'

I took the hint, and also understood why the priest so quickly left me. He feared the danger I might have got into through conversing with him.

Barcelona Today is Sovietised

I dressed quickly and, as in a trance, walked though the heavy iron grille back to the guardroom. I understood later that most of the prisoners were 'Fascists' awaiting execution or imprisonment in the hulks of Barcelona or Valencia.

I saw touching scenes as relatives brought the prisoners food. Mothers, wives, sisters – they smiled bravely; but when the visit was over I saw them weep unrestrainedly.

I will omit details of the journey to Barcelona, via Valencia and Tarragona, and deal directly with this once beautiful and prosperous capital of Catalonia.

Barcelona today is the capital of a partly Sovietised Province. It is a glaring nightmare of red banners, placards, slogans, and slovenly disorder.

'The Anarchists Rule Supreme'

The Anarchists rule supreme, backed by Trotsky's Communists. Tramcars and buses are painted the diagonal red and black of the Anarchist flag, so are trucks and automobiles.

Every faction has a different coloured flag, and some cars and buildings fly the lot. The effect can well be imagined.

As Barcelona was formerly the industrial centre of Spain, so it was the revolutionary or separatist centre. But it was rather a contradiction of Anarchism (which is individualist!) to see the wholesale collectivisation of factories, hotels and transport.

As in Russia, the people must become mere ciphers, and must without quibbling obey the rulings of their betters – the chairmen of the various Councils.

'Privileges' for the Proletariat

Food cards are issued and admission by special permit. The Proletariat have the privilege of eating a hasty meal of beans, sitting at long deal tables in the Ritz. When they finish they must at one vacate. They have had the satisfaction of eating where once their betters are – if that is any satisfaction.

Their present masters do not eat in the common mess hall in the Ritz. They dine de-lux in decent restaurants where good food, good wine, music, and really good obsequious service is obtainable.

There is much to be seen and analysed in Barcelona, and the attitude of its huge population towards the present conflict. One thing seems certain. No matter who wins in Spain there will be a stern Catalonian problem to be dealt with. This province (the richest) is determined to cut adrift, and the future will see interesting and sanguinary developments.

Off For the Frontier
Barcelona has been overrun by writers and Drawing Room Reds eager to get 'copy' at a safe distance from the firing line. But they are all within a short walk from the French, British and American Consulates, whose good services they are not loath to take advantage of when dropped by their sceptical Spanish 'comrades'.[16]

Armed with additional papers, issued by the Catalonian Military Control, we set off for the frontier station of Port Bou, en route La Belle France. At the French frontier town of Cerberes the two French Legionnaires were allowed to enter France on producing cards of identity. The Hungarian and myself, minus these, must perforce return- and were escorted over the Pyrenees by relays of French Gendarmes, walking, climbing, and slipping all the way.

On sighting the Spanish frontier post they stopped and watched as we safely negotiated the No-Man's Land between France and Spain. It was raining when we left Cerberes. As we had climbed the mountain goat tracks, the rain changed to sleet and finished in a blizzard of blinding snow.

My Hungarian friend was a nervous wreck. Luckily, I have a wonderful store of optimism and a tough constitution, besides, I have the most implicit faith in St. Anthony, who has protected me though a not unadventurous life.[17]

Back in Barcelona, jaded and dispirited, I repaired to the British Consulate to obtain an emergency passport to prove nationality. The Consul General and his Staff (one of whom was a good Irishman) treated me with the utmost kindness and consideration. They begged of me to accept the hospitality of and a passage to Marseilles on a destroyer.

But I decided to leave Spain as an adventurer, not as a helpless refugee. I didn't like hauling down my flag as token of surrender to adversity.

A Dream That Was Shattered
I took the Pass and again set off for the mountains. Going through Figueras, in North Catalonia, I saw a small church picturesquely situated

at the foot of a vine-covered hill. I looked at the building with a feeling of gladness that up here Hate had possibly stayed her hand and the Spanish people were as they were but a few short months ago.

My dream was soon shattered. The door opened, two men walked out, followed by a truck loaded with petrol drums. I was denied even one pleasant memory to dwell on.

Close to Port Bou the Chief of police gave me a mule and a guide wherewith to cross the mountains. I reached Perpignan in due course and later took the train to Paris.

It was like returning to a new life to mingle with well-dressed and courteous human beings. But it was in Paris itself I appreciated the change most of all, and realised the vast difference between Christian and non-Christian principles.

At the Irish Free State Legation I was welcomed with open arms.[18] Art O'Brien, a courteous and worthy representative of Ireland, did all in his power to help a fellow soldier of the Anglo-Irish war days. There I met Commandant O'Byrne, and my passing through Paris will forever remain a pleasant memory.

In concluding these articles, I wish to state that the present Government of Madrid is 100% Red and violently opposed to the Catholic Church. Any Irishman preparing to fight for or defend vicariously this regime is defending the enemy of his faith. I learned these facts by bitter experience. If they will open the eyes of my misinformed or misguided countrymen, I shall have done a great service for Ireland.

The Independent articles – obviously written for quick cash – reek of O'Duffy (*see* his book *Crusade in Spain*, Dublin 1938).

Notes.

1. *Irish Independent*, January 4, 1937.
2. Bill Scott was a Dublin bricklayer whose father had fought with James Connolly's Citizen Army. He went to Spain to fight under Enrique Lister in defence of Madrid with the famous fifth regiment, fighting alongside the likes of English poet John Cornford. Scott survived.
3. Patton, who gave his life in the defence of Madrid was the first Irishman to die in the late winter 1936. There is a monument erected to him by his comrades on his native Achill.
4. *Irish Independent*, January 6, 1937.
5. McGarry, Fearghal: *Irish Politics and the Spanish Civil War*. Cork University Press 1999, p. 52. *See* also: PRO FO W16991/9549/41 and NAI D/Taois S12860.
6. Make that three.
7. No he wasn't.
8. No it wasn't.
9. In which he did not participate.
10. Make that three.
11. After a perusal of Spanish Civil War archives this appears to be a complete fabrication.
12. Such modesty – and grossly inaccurate.
13. Hmm! Death at the hands of 'depravees'.
14. Doubtless there was some prurient slaverings over these by the faithful Blueshirts and 'good thinking' Catholics. Nomad probably cleaned up with this early 'religious pornography'.
15. Reminiscent of the 'Anarchists are all freemasons' nonsense of Edward Cahill's *Freemasonry and the anti-Christian Movement* (Dublin 1929).
16. *see*, too, McGarry, op. cit.
17. First and only time we hear of this holy protector.
18. *see* note 5. And the odd bit of bootlicking never hurt when you're broke and far from home in war torn Europe.

NOTE ON IRISH VOLUNTEERS IN SPAIN:

Let us not forget some real Irish Republican heroes – like 21 year old Charlie Donnelly, the poet from Tyrone who died at Jarama, Frank Ryan, of the Republican Congress, captured and eventually killed by the Fascists, and Peter O'Connor of Waterford, who had the unique record of fighting in and coming through unscathed every battle that the Irish Brigade fought in. He brought out the body of Charlie Donnelly who died at his side, in extremely dangerous circumstances. He was the only survivor of his entire Irish group. He lived on into the 1990s.

Sources:
Michael O'Riordan in his book *Connolly Column* (New Books, Dublin 1979) listed 145 people; this list now exceeds 240.
 (According to Ciaran Crossey. Ciaran has produced an excellent Spanish Civil War site with Irish emphasis. He can be contacted at: cpcrossey@hotmail.com. The website is
 http://members.tripod.co.uk/spanishcivilwar/index. htm.)

Robert A. Stradling compiled a list for his book *The Irish and the Spanish Civil War 1936-1939*, published 1999 by Mandolin, an imprint of Manchester University Press.

Additional people have been added. Check the list of Feargal McGarry, in *Irish Politics and the Spanish Civil War*, Cork University Press, 1999, as well as the other references noted.

Nor should we forget the men of the North-West who did fight against fascism, as opposed to Nomad.
 Here is as complete a list of **Derry** and **Donegal** men who fought for the Republic in Spain as we can get.

The survivors: Phil Boyle, Paddy Roe McLaughlin, Patrick O'Daire, H. O'Donnell, Vincent O'Donnell (Donegal).
Died: Hugh Bonar, P. Glacken (Donegal).
Died: Eamonn McGrotty, George Gorman (Derry).

[We have been asked why we have not listed the Derry and Donegal men who served with O'Duffy and the Blueshirts in Spain. We are glad to say that of O'Duffy's 'XV Bandera' very few were from

Republican Derry and Donegal. Four men did serve, but, out of feelings for their descendants we omit their names. O'Duffy's Blueshirts, the men who sang 'The Peeler and the Goat' mainly came from the rural far west. They only served about four months in Spain, being involved in two minor skirmishes and a serious own goal when they shot their allies, the gallant Moors. Six of them died (out of more than 700). Many more returned home quietly to Ireland with assorted anti-social diseases, it was widely rumoured.

O'Duffy was a hopeless, pompous gay drunk, rarely seen without a bottle of whiskey in his hand. Franco sacked him and the 'XV Bandera' in April 1937 (they hadn't got to Spain until December 1936) and sent them back to dig sheughs after five months. Their welcome home in Tralee on June 21st was muted. The Catholic church soon turned to other more effective Fascist allies.

O'Duffy's death was rather sad. He ended up hanging out at the Abbey Theatre with his new friends Michael MacLiammóir and Hilton Edwards and died of the drink in December 1944. Despite his exemplary recruiting services for the holy mother church, at his funeral at Glasnevin not a single member of the Catholic Hierarchy bothered to show. Present however was the Taoiseach Eamonn De Valera, O'Duffy's old nemesis. As they said in Dublin at the time 't'was either a mark of respect or, ever the prudent man, he was making sure the old bastard was really dead.']

Chapter 11
Nomad And The German Spies

On January 12th, 1939, Lord Edward Frederick Lindley Wood Halifax, Neville Chamberlain's foreign secretary, received an ultimatum of war from the IRA. He binned it, assuming it was a crank letter. On Monday 16th of January 1939 small bombs started going off in England – two in London, one in Birmingham, one in Alnwick and one in Manchester. The targets were electrical installations but no one was hurt and not much damage done. This was the start of Jim 'Fingers' O'Donovan, Director of Chemicals of the IRA's 'S' (for Sabotage) Plan. That afternoon the German News Agency announced that 'proclamations were appearing in Ireland wherein the IRA demanded the immediate withdrawal of English forces from Northern Ireland'.

The proclamation bore the signatures of the then leading members of the IRA Army council – Stephen Hayes, soon to be denounced as a traitor and spy by his former comrades from Belfast,[1] Peadar O'Flaherty, Laurence Grogan, Patrick Fleming, George Plunkett and Seán Russell.

But it was to be hard times for Irish Republicans under the stern eye of their former political leader Eamonn De Valera. Within weeks of the English bombing campaign De Valera introduced both a Treason Bill and an Offences Against the State Act, paving the way for the military courts which came into existence on August 24th, 1939. The Special Branch were strengthened, Arbour Hill prepared and communications opened with the English hangman Pierrepoint. Two Republicans, Tony D'Arcy and Sean McNeela were allowed to die on hunger strike (April 16th and 19th, 1940).

The military were instructed to start setting up internment camps on the Curragh of Kildare. In June the IRA was again banned. The Bodenstown ceremonies for Wolfe Tone, the 'father of Republicanism' were banned.

The members of the military court numbered five, three of whom constituted a tribunal – they were Col. Francis Bennett, Col. Daniel McKenna, Major John Joyce, Major Cornelius Whelan and Major

Patrick Tuite. McKenna retired from the court in February 1940 and was replaced by Major Felix Devlin. Between them these men would sentence to death more than ten Republicans. [Go Mbéidh A N-Anamacha Meallaithe, Go Mbéidh Siad Deanta Eascainí, Agus Go Mbéidh Siad Faoi Chrann Smola Lena Shaolta!]

Meanwhile, in Berlin, the German Abwehr, under Admiral Canaris, knew very little about the Irish signatories, De Valera and his military courts or the state of the IRA in Ireland. After the start of the IRA bombing campaign in England the *Frankfurter Zeitung*, apparently in an aberration, praised the Irish as:

> "This red-haired and tough race, which has fought on all battlefields across the world and today provides both England and the USA's best policemen, has a temperament which differs from the British. They are not so even-tempered and imperturbable and are less patient; they are easily stirred up, and are livelier and more impetuous. An innate wildness which has been toughened by repression which frequently overcame ties of blood in the course of fratricidal strife, quickly breaks out. This reminds one of the *saeva indignatio* or rebel's anger which Jonathan Swift, an Irishman despite his English parents, immortalized in his epitaph. There is also a colourful saying that 'bomb throwing is the Irish form of original sin' and Bernard Shaw's claim that 'a Loyal Irishman must be a fearsome phenomenon because it could only be an unnatural creation.'"[2]

This may sound racist or stereotypical but it does seem to sum up some of the aspects of Charles 'Nomad' McGuinness. The Germans had had dealings with him in the past. They were shortly to have yet more encounters with the Nomad.

But, until February 1939 when Oscar Pfaus, an adventurer, dedicated Nazi and former co-ordinator of a nazi newspaper in America, arrived in Ireland at the behest of the Abwehr, the German secret service had virtually no contact with the IRA. Ironically, Pfaus' only contact was the aging and senile old Blueshirt 'führer' General O'Duffy, back from his Spanish Civil War fiasco where his 'Rosary Brigade' hardly earned too many medals, whom he asked to put him in touch with the IRA. O'Duffy was a broken man and was allegedly horrified, since the current IRA were his bitter enemies, but, nonetheless, through one of O'Duffy's aides, an introduction was arranged. (In 1943 O'Duffy even suggested to the German embassy that he might be flown to Berlin to organize an Irish Volunteer Legion for the Russian Front to save Europe from Bolshevism. Hardly surprisingly, the Germans did not treat his 'plans' seriously.) Pfaus did eventually get taken out on a blindfold ride to Clontarf to meet the IRA.

There links were set up and Jim O'Donovan became the 'Abwehr Liaison Agent' for Ireland. O'Donovan made three trips to Germany before the outbreak of the war on September 3rd, 1939. On the last of these he brought his wife 'Monty' who was forced to the indignity of a strip search when six packets of Sweet Afton cigarettes were found on her by an overly officious minor German customs official. O'Donovan was incensed. Was not his wife Monty the sister of the Irish martyr Kevin Barry!

It took much soft soaping by the Abwehr before O'Donovan was sufficiently mollified, enough to set up a code network so that the Germans could contact the IRA through various couriers who ranged (or deranged) from Bretons to Dutch. In a letter from Agent Bryan to the Minister of Defence, dated 21st December, 1945, O'Donovan is described as someone who fancied himself the future Irish Quisling or Führer but it should be noted that, although O'Donovan was briefly interned in the Curragh, because of his good cover he was released in September 1943, an indication that Irish Intelligence Services were not as aware as they should have been that the old Director of Chemicals was back in business. [One of O'Donovan's 'plans' which he presented to the Abwehr entailed a German fleet landing in Derry. Clearly a job for McGuinness! Needless to say the Abwehr ignored this ludicrous scheme.][3]

But the Germans thought they could now put their spies in and forge an alliance. Help undermine England from the soon to be neutral Republic of Ireland, then ruled by the Machiavellian De Valera.

That, at least, was the game plan of a small section of the Abwehr, but they were only a very small faction and they were soon to be disappointed.

In the meantime, the Brits were planning for World War II as well. They too would have their spies in Ireland, and, for them it was much easier. For a start, there were many Anglo-Irish in high places whose allegiance was always towards London rather than Dublin – particularly with that peculiar De Valera in power.

Brit Spies tended to be genteel, rather bumbling and part of the old boy (and old girl) network and consequently were undisturbed by DeV. No Brit spies were executed – most were released straight away or warned off. Captured airmen had a easy life in a camp on the Curragh and were at times allowed to 'escape' to cross the border into Northern Ireland. In contrast, the Republicans in De Valera's internment camp which adjoined that of the English and the Germans were subjected to harsh and brutal conditions and guarded by their former 'comrades' of 'the old IRA'.

One of the most incompetent Brit spies was the poet John Betjeman who was in Ireland from 1940-45. The IRA discovered his rather pathetic espionage efforts in 1942 and considered shooting him. He was reprieved because one member of the IRA HQ had read a book of his poems and declared that they could not execute the man who had written (in 1937) such a wonderful poem as *Slough*.

> "Come, friendly bombs, and fall on Slough,
> It isn't fit for humans now.
> There isn't grass to graze a cow
> – Swarm over, Death!
>
> Come, friendly bombs, and fall on Slough
> To get it ready for the plough."

Betjeman, who was knighted in 1969, became Poet Laureate in 1972 and died in 1984, never learning of his lucky escape.

By the time war was officially declared on September 3rd, 1939, O'Donovan's S Plan was in shreds. On July 24th Sir Samuel Hoare, the British Home Secretary, had introduced the Prevention of Violence Bill (1939). He stated that '127 terrorist outrages had been perpetrated since January, 57 in London and 70 in the provinces. One person had been killed and 55 injured. 66 Irishmen and women had been convicted of terrorist offenses.' On 28th July, after another IRA bomb the act was rushed through. Effectively the IRA 'bomb Britain campaign' was at an end, although more civilians in Coventry would die and many more Irish volunteers be jailed, tortured, interned and executed as in the cases of Barnes and McCormick.

Meanwhile, back in Ireland the German spies turned out to be stunningly incompetent. The principal ones were Dr. Hermann Goertz and Sergeant Gunther Schuetz, of whom more later, but the stories of the various would-be German agents who parachuted into Ireland are risible.

Walter Simon had been imprisoned for amateurish spying for Germany in Britain before the war, but Simon's Abwehr controller thought him 'the perfect classical Secret Agent' who 'had carried out all his assignments with discretion, élan, and pluck' although the farcical nature of his detection and arrest, after taking 'good deal of drink' and 'talking indiscreetly to detectives whom he met on the train from Killarney' scarcely bespeaks great mastery of tradecraft.

The majority of the German agents were not at liberty for long (the key exception being Goertz). Willie Preetz, who had lived in Ireland before the war, spent a good deal of time 'in dissipation' at the Abwehr's expense in Dublin, and managed to transmit a few enciphered reports on weather conditions (which were intercepted by both the Irish and the British), before being tacked down and arrested by the Garda. His radio and enciphering materials were seized, together with the text of the messages he had transmitted.[4]

Henry Obed, 'a Mohammedan, born in Lucknow' and his German South African companions Dieter Gaertner and Herbert Tributh stuck out a mile in Cork and, not surprisingly, were soon captured. Werner Uhland was picked up after documents incriminating him were found on the foolish Schuetz *(see infra)*.

More interesting was 'Atlas the Strong'. Ernst Weber-Drohl reported to the Garda after carrying out a courier mission to the IRA. When charged with illegal entry he explained that while touring Ireland as 'Atlas the Strong' in 1907 he had fathered two sons whom he hoped to track down.[5]

The last three agents to arrive were all Irishmen who had fallen into German hands while in the Channel islands in 1940. Joseph Lenihan, the black sheep of a prominent Athlone family – his nephew Brian Lenihan was to hold many ministerial posts including those of Justice and of Foreign Affairs between the 1960s and 1990s, was briefed and equipped to transmit weather reports from Sligo.

Instead, he went to Northern Ireland and surrendered. He gave information about the Abwehr in France and the Netherlands, and MI5 considered using him as part of the double-cross system, the intricate counter-intelligence and deception operation which had developed from the more straightforward practice of 'playing back' false reports by captured agents. However it was eventually concluded that he could not be so used, as his weather reporting mission was one in which any sustained deception would quickly become apparent. Furthermore, it was a cardinal rule of 'double-cross' that nobody could be used whose capture was known outside a very small circle of British security officials, lest the realization that one apparently active agent had been 'turned' lead the Germans to suspect that others had suffered the same fate.

John O'Reilly and John Kenny, both dropped by parachute in Clare in 1943, had been recruited for espionage in much the same fashion as Lenihan. Kenny was injured on landing and gave no further trouble, but despite surrendering himself to the Garda, O'Reilly proved a truculent and 'devious prisoner'. He set out to mislead his inquisitors, and as an unusually skilled cryptographer he made elaborate false statements about his ciphers which it took, despite British help, months to correct; although the investigations ultimately yielded 'important results', at least according to his interrogators.[6]

These were the kind of agents that Charles 'Nomad' McGuinness, sailor of fortune and now extremely broke, decided to tie up with. Presumably after the money from the *Irish Independent* ran out, according to Pax Ó Faoláin[7] he tied up with a Wexford man, Tom Donoghue, dodging U-boats and bringing in supplies. But McGuinness had more than one string to his bow.

From wireless intercepts the Irish security services found out that McGuinness was offering to the Germans information on English shipping movements and sailing conditions as early as 1941.[8]

And now enters Sergeant (but, to be fair, he survived and ended up Lieutenant) Gunther Schuetz. The meeting between him and Nomad McGuinness was to prove disastrous for both of them.

"It was 6.45 in the evening of 12th March, 1941, when a black two-engined Heinkel He III took off from Schipol Airport, Amsterdam, and disappeared into the darkness on a course set for England. At the controls was Flying-Officer Edmund Eduard Gartenfeld, the same pilot who had flown Captain Goertz to Ireland ten months previously. Goertz was still at large in Ireland. In the bomb bay a solitary man sat crouched. Under his flying suit he wore a uniform tunic and beneath that a civilian suit from good quality English material. A waterproof raincoat was strapped around his small case which contained wireless set, aerial, bundles of English and American money, a bottle of cognac and a salami sausage. A powerful microscope, packed to resist shock, was in the corner of the case.

The man, who was barely 29 years old, was sent on this mission by the Economic Section of "Ast" Hamburg. In the breast pocket of his civilian suit he had a South African passport in the name of Hans Marschner, but in his paybook, which he left behind in Hamburg, was the name Sergeant Gunther Schuetz."[9]

He was later to be regarded by the Irish press as 'the cleverest of all' according to author Enno Stephan – though that may have something to do with the fact that apart from Jim O'Donovan, Schuetz was about the only person who would talk to Stephan for his book. For the fact is that Schuetz was an incompetent bungler when it came to espionage.

He knew nothing about the geography of Ireland and was dropped near New Ross not Newbridge where he was supposed to land. Poor Schuetz had to set off to walk 75 miles to Dublin. He didn't get far. He'd barely eaten his salami when he was stopped by two Gardaí and asked what was in his suitcase. It burst open revealing the radio, bank notes and microscope. Schuetz was taken to the local pub, filled full of porter by the Gardaí and then driven to the Bridewell in Dublin for a leisurely interrogation. Next stop was Arbour Hill but not into a dank prison cell but into a comfortable officer's quarters. His money was returned to him and the prison governor played chess with him. It was hardly durance vile.

And after a brief few weeks in Athlone jail Schuetz ended up in Mountjoy in the hospital wing with the few other German spies. At first all went well. The Germans expected that the war would be over shortly and that they would be released. But after Pearl Harbour and the entry of the Americans into the conflict, the Germans began to suffer setbacks and morale in Mountjoy plummeted. By February 1942 de Valera's Government were executing IRA men like George Plant, acquitted in a court trial but then at once retried, sentenced by a military tribunal, and then hanged by the English executioner 'brought over from the sea'. DeV had already presided over the judicial murders of Republicans Tom Harte and Paddy McGrath in September 1940. Added to that Schuetz learned from a friendly guard that a friend and comrade of his, a fellow German spy from the Sudetenland who had been trained with him had been caught and executed just before Christmas in an English jail. Schuetz determined to escape.

And, perhaps amazingly, he did. Over the wall, and, dressed in a woman's fur coat and woman's shoes three sizes too small for him he struggled his way to the infamous O'Hanlon IRA house in Inishfallen Parade just near the jail. (There had been tunnels from the house into the jail in the old escape days.)

Now well and truly on the run Schuetz, who was still going under the name of Marschner, had to make more contacts – including Charles 'Nomad' McGuinness.

McGuinness had not been having a 'good war'. Permanently broke he felt thwarted that his seafaring skills were not sufficiently appreciated and he could not achieve a senior post in the new fledgling Maritime Marine – instead, he was just a chief petty officer. He needed money.

Back in September 1941 McGuinness had been put in contact with a would-be German spy, a steel worker from Haulbowline, Wilhelm Masgeik.[10] Nomad had indicated that he possessed material relevant to a German invasion and was prepared to pilot Masgeik in a motor boat to the French coast. Of course, as he told the German Ambassador Dr. Eduard Hempel, he would need money.

It seems that Hempel, like many others at the time were horrified by McGuinness. He was mercenary. He was a loose cannon. He couldn't keep his mouth shut. Hempel brusquely turned McGuinness down. He didn't think Masgeik was trustworthy either and what was he doing leaving a wife and two children in Dublin? Hempel wasn't having anything to do with the pair of them. But the danger had already been created.

Everyone who visited the German Embassy on Northumberland Road was of course put under surveillance, and McGuinness, who always insisted in swaggering around with his broad black brimmer was not noted for blending into the background.

Meanwhile Schuetz had to be moved around – first to Blackrock and an elderly couple called Cowman and then, almost inexorably to the infamous 'Ros na Riogh', the Brugha home at Temple Gardens in Rathmines, where, it seems, every right winger, IRA man or German spy on the run ended up.

Caitlin Brugha, the widow of the former Republican Minister of Defence Cathal, who died, guns blazing in the ruins of the Hammam Hotel in 1922,[11] shot down by former 'comrades', was a formidable lady. She knew everyone and they knew her. She had a successful business, Kingston Shirts of Dublin, which had several branches. She had five daughters. They were all 'mad Republicans'. But Caitlin believed that it would be an indelible stain on Ireland's honour if a fellow anti-British fighter were to be arrested in Ireland. Accordingly, her fashionable house in Rathmines became the most absurd refuge in Dublin for 'the boys on the run'. The only 'safety' being that the authorities believed for a time that no one would be as stupid as to allow themselves to be billeted in 'Ros na Riogh'.

After the war Schuetz told Enno Stephan that Mrs. Brugha had greeted him in a 'warm and motherly way' but she had run the 'mad household' on strict patriarchal lines. She broke it to Schuetz that Goertz had been arrested and that he was therefore more or less on his own. She carried out emergency drills when Schuetz had to hasten to a concealed trap door which led into the cellar while the Bean Mí Brugha timed him on the stopwatch.

"One evening a car arrived and Schuetz had to help stack up in the hiding place in the cellar some packets about the size of bricks which were done up in waxed paper. When he asked the contents of the packets, he was told "Explosives for Northern Ireland". The packets disappeared a few days later as secretly as they had come.

Noinin Brugha, the jolly philology student, also aroused his astonishment. Schuetz learnt that she was engaged to a man named Sean O'Brien, a teacher from Dingle Bay in County Kerry, who as an active I.R.A. member was now languishing in Mountjoy Prison. But Noinin had built up a secret intelligence service from Dublin to Northern Ireland. This intelligence service, though run on simple lines, functioned effectively. Secret little notes and messages by word of mouth were delivered by trustworthy people.

At the same time as Sergeant Schuetz was promoted in Germany to the rank of lieutenant for his successful escape from Mountjoy Prison, the I.R.A. leader in Northern Ireland received news that a German, who might be used for underground purposes, was in hiding at Mrs. Brugha's.

A few days afterwards three men appeared at the Brugha home in the late evening. [Sean McCaughey, Liam Burke and an unknown 'third man', probably Sean McCool, the then IRA O/C, since Pearse Kelly didn't take over until after McCaughey's arrest.] They gave Schuetz a friendly greeting. Two of them came from Northern Ireland, and one from Dublin: their spokesman was the I.R.A's new Chief of Staff. The men assured Schuetz that in Northern Ireland the I.R.A. were intact [a rather optimistic estimate] and its members a good lot, that its new generation was coming mainly from there, but that it lacked the wherewithal for a successful struggle against England. They urgently needed weapons, munitions, explosives, radio equipment, and money. Schuetz was, therefore, to be got to France with I.R.A. help in order to ask for German assistance.

A little while later there was a second meeting at the house of a family by the name of Bruton. The I.R.A. were in good spirits – everything seemed to be going according to plan. The Irishmen recounted that they had found a man who had already called at the

German Embassy and actually received there the £300 necessary for buying a boat for Schuetz's passage home. A crew for this seaworthy craft, which had a powerful Ford-Diesel engine, was already available and they would sail under the orders of an experienced naval officer. As soon as the weather permitted, and, at the latest in early May, they would take Schuetz to Brest."[12]

"The days at "Ros na Riogh" passed peacefully. Mrs. Brugha and her five daughters looked after the German fugitive as if he were a son and brother. Schuetz felt a little anxious when he thought about his impending trip. They would be under way for between 48 and 50 hours at least. British patrol boats and reconnaissance aircraft would have the route under continued observation, and storms threatened. His chances were not rosy.

Off and on he received short visits from an I.R.A. man. They discussed where German arms and materials for the I.R.A. should be landed. The I.R.A. wanted the landings made in the northwest of Eire, but near enough to the Northern Ireland border to facilitate onward transport into Ulster.

And then Schuetz was given a new task which for him was truly revealing and complicated."[13]

The IRA gave him a large bundle of manuscripts to translate – the so-called Hayes Confession. Diligently he worked on them and secreted them in his belongings which he hoped to take back to the homeland shortly.

April 30, 1942. A portentous day. Walpurgis Nacht, the evilest night of the year – eve of May Day. Three years later, to the day, Adolf Hitler was to kill himself, 33 years later, to the day, the Vietcong marched into Saigon and ended the Vietnam War. And on that very day, April 30th, 1942 Herr Schuetz was arrested at the Brugha's in Dublin. Nomad was arrested shortly thereafter but, as usual, mystery still surrounds the exact background to his arrest. Most sources cite 'somewhere in Dublin', but Pax Ó Faoláin claimed that "McGuinness and his three-man crew of local men were arrested before the Dingle fishing smack could set sail" from Co. Kerry. Ó Faoláin also adds that Nomad and his team may have been rumbled not by Noinin Brugha's train courier but because of a leak involving the purchase of the boat. Regardless of which, Nomad was arrested and sentenced to seven years.[14]

Back at 'Ros Na Riogh' the Brugha family were out. It was a lovely day and Schuetz was sitting outside on the veranda reading.

The Dublin Special Branch hit the place looking for Charles McGuinness and his crewmen. Schuetz, unconvincingly gave his name as 'Graves, from Sligo', but the easiest geographic question established that he had never been to the jewel of the West. "I'm the one you're looking for," he said. The SB looked baffled. "Yes, I'm Marschner." He was arrested.

> It was only after his recapture that [now] Lieutenant Schuetz learnt the identity of the "experienced officer" who was to be the leader of this dangerous expedition. One day at Arbour Hill Military Prison, to which he was first taken, he found a letter addressed to him under the lid of the lavatory seat. In this letter a certain Charles McGuinness told him that he had been detailed to take him to France. The boat had been all ready in Bray Bay, south of Dublin. Unfortunately the operation had been betrayed. [...]
>
> In the course of their daily walks at Arbour Hill Prison McGuinness gave Schuetz to understand that be had written the letter. In June 1942 he was brought to trial before a military tribunal. On the morning of the trial, Schuetz saw him dressed in naval uniform and in all the glory of his orders and medals. He gave McGuinness an encouraging nod. When he chanced to see him again in the late afternoon, Charles McGuinness was completely broken: the tribunal had sentenced him to seven years imprisonment."[15]

This seems extremely unlikely. Whatever his faults, Nomad was a hell of a lot tougher and more used to life's adversity than Schuetz. No one else has remarked on this, and it does not ring true.

However, as in the case of Stephen Carroll Held, McGuinness was treated not as a criminal but as a political detainee. This is the reason why the vast majority of Irish Republicans of the 30s and 40s did not encounter McGuinness. Eddie Keenan, who had himself escaped from Crumlin Road jail in May 1941 and was promptly interned in the Curragh after a few weeks 'freedom' in the Republic explained that the Republican internees were bitter about the treatment meted out to the 'aliens and spies', within which category McGuinness fell.

> "Our guards had orders to shoot any would-be escapers, and murdered Barney Casey, theirs were told not to shoot. They had it cushy. They were allowed money and food and alcohol and got extra provisions even though the war was going on."[16]

At the end of the war McGuinness was released, having served over three years.

Effectively, McGuinness was out of action for the next two years. The next public sighting of him is at the Protestant Chapel in Deans Grange Cemetery, Dublin. 11 a.m. on a cold morning on 26th May, 1947, shortly after his release from Arbour Hill. The Reverend K.D.B. Dobbs conducted a funeral of a corpse, 'wearing a simple Luftwaffe jacket'. (There was also a swastika flag on the coffin and the mourners *(see infra)* gave Nazi salutes.) It was Germany's master spy in Ireland, Dr Hermann Goertz[17] who, as a soldier of the Reich, and, scared of being sent back to the war crimes tribunals in Nuremburg, acted like a German gentleman, and swallowed the potassium cyanide. Most writers have claimed that Goertz was Germany's most effective spy in Ireland, but the facts don't seem to bear this out. Harry White scathingly reports: "Goertz had already been in prison for espionage through his own stupidity, in England from November 1935 until the summer of 1939." His arrival at Stephen Held's house 'Konstanz' in Templeogue led to the arrest of Held and the seizure of all the funds Goertz had brought – £20,000. "Thereafter, until October 1942 [his capture], he lived underground in billets in Rathmines, Monkstown and Clontarf, serving no useful purpose to anyone."[18]

He had been on the run longer than any other German spy. Had been arrested in a house in Blackheath Park in Dublin on either November 27th or December 4th 1941 – the 'authorities' differ. He had survived on the run for 19 months, but had been allowed, in the early days of the war a fairly free rein by DeV and the Special Branch. He had been billeted in Blackheath Park (a suburb of Clontarf) allegedly just prior to having a secret interview with Cardinal MacRory, Archbishop of Armagh and Primate of Ireland.

However, he spent the rest of the war inside, despite several pathetic escape attempts, and ended up a bitter man, excoriating his fellow German prisoners as 'cowards' and 'traitors'. He especially hated Schuetz. For most of the three years the ten German spies were held in Athlone jail in a special German wing. Conditions, according to most of them, weren't too bad, but Goertz fulminated against them. He went on a 21 day hunger strike. He and the one Dutch 'spy', Van Loon, were forever trying to escape – to no avail.

As early as August and September 1945 about 200 German service personnel, who had been interned in the Curragh were transported back to Germany. The majority were sailors who had been picked up in the Bay of Biscay by the Irish freighter *Kerlogue* after a destroyer battle. The remainder were normally Luftwaffe pilots and navigators who had crash landed or run out of fuel over Ireland. All had a fairly pleasant 'war' and were able to return home – except for quite a few who chose to stay and marry local girls.

In September 1945 the ten Germans 'spies' were tentatively set free and most indicated that they wanted to stay, since they believed they could get political asylum. Goertz got out with the rest of them and ended up living with the 'mad' Farrell sisters, part of the Brugha clan. In early 1947 he even became Secretary of the 'Save the German Children Fund', an Irish relief organization for German child orphans. He gained a living by making table lamps, and, after borrowing some money he started a relatively successful business selling British war surplus – pontoon bridges which had been used at the Normandy landings. By the spring of 1947 he even had his own car and married a young Irish nurse, Una Mackey, in May 1947.

Meanwhile Schuetz was getting married to a colleen and becoming a successful businessman. Van Loon, Gaertner and Tributh were partners in a joinery business in Dublin. Willie Preetz was happy in Galway and Werner Unland and his wife were living in a not too shabby Merrion Square in Dublin. Captain Atlas – Weber-Drohl – was engaged in yet more marital misadventures and nobody cared about the poor 'Mohammedan' Henry Obed. Only Walter Simon wanted to risk it back in Germany, despite the qualms of his former comrades, but, in the event, he proved correct. He returned and after a few weeks was released.

But Goertz was paranoid and edgy. His old boss Erwin von Lahousen, former Chief of Abwehr II had turned Turk and was a witness for the Nuremberg War Trials and he was talking about 'a German plan to invade Ireland' run by Goertz.

And then, April 12th, 1947, the unexpected knock on the door. DeV, caving in to the English Allies announces 'A new Nazi Plot Discovered In Ireland'. The Germans were going to be handed over to British Intelligence.

Preetz, Atlas, Gaertner and Tributh were all flown out on an American plane (they all got back to Ireland shortly). Unland won in court, but Schuetz and Goertz were only released on appeal and were tailed and followed. On May 23rd, 1947, at the Registration Office in Dublin Castle, Goertz allegedly dropped the cyanide pill and committed suicide.[19]

Deans Grange cemetery. The Reverend Dobbs looks at the miniscule band of funeral mourners who have come to Dr Hermann's last rites. It is not recorded what he thought of the swastika draped coffin.

Dr. Eduard Hempel, the German former Ambassador, isn't present. Dublin Castle has told him it would not be politic. It takes a band of old hardcore comrades to show up. Unfortunately, it's often like that at political/paramilitary/Republican funerals. V-1 (Stephen Held), Jim O'Donovan. Goertz's radio operator Anthony Deery showed too, as did Werner Unland. And, of course, clearly visible at the graveside is Charles Nomad McGuinness. He's been out a couple of months. He's virtually penniless and imposing himself upon the O'Currys out in Sandycove. But, a funeral is a funeral, and Charlie pays his debts. He has only seven months to live?

Notes.

1. The jury is still out as to whether or not Stephen Hayes was a traitor. The author has interviewed numerous old Republicans over the years on this and it seems to be a fact that virtually all the Republicans in the Republic believe that although he was weak and ineffectual, he wasn't a traitor (Maire Comerford certainly believed that when interviewed by the author in the 1970s). However, every Northern Republican, particularly the Belfast men who arrested and interrogated him, died convinced that Hayes had been in the pay of the Dublin Special Branch. And, of course, Hayes is blamed, quite rightly, for the death of Sean McCaughey, a Belfastman (though some say he was born in Aughnacloy). He died May 11, 1946. He had been on hunger and strip strike for three years and went on thirst strike on 19th April, after having been arrested on evidence given by Hayes. The prison doctor Duanne admitted that 'you wouldn't treat a

dog like that'.) Additionally, it should be mentioned that the top German spy in Ireland during the war, Hermann Goertz was convinced that Hayes was a tout – but then, on the other hand it must be said that Goertz is on record as being a partisan of the Belfast leadership of the IRA – McCaughey. "Sean McCaughey was a real man – a son of the North. He had no time for the intrigue. He wanted to fight with me in the six Northern counties." (Hermann Goertz, quoted in Stephan, Enno: *Spies in Ireland*. Four Square Books, London 1965, op. cit. p. 198.) Incidentally, Jim O'Donovan was nicknamed 'Fingers' because he had lost two while experimenting with home made explosives.
2. *Frankfurter Zeitung*, Editorial, January 24, 1939.
3. Herman Goertz, *Irish Times*, August 27, 1947.
4. A virtually unknown and ludicrous episode in the 'war' between Irish Intelligence and the German embassy in Dublin under Herr Hempel was revealed years later by two former Army officers, Sean McMahon and B.J. Keaney, who admitted that an Irish army officer, armed and dressed in civilian clothes had cat burgled the German legation to ensure that all their electronic equipment had been surrendered. Unfortunately the would-be Seamus Bond was caught by the embarrassed Germans who let him go. No formal protest was made by either side. (*Sunday Tribune Magazine* 03.01.1982)
5. This picaresque story, which was evidently the inspiration for the background of a SMERSH assassin in Ian Fleming's *From Russia With Love*, was true in so far as it went, and after a week's internment in June 1940 'Atlas' was released and fined £3. He borrowed £12 from the IRA and set up a sideshow which consisted of a platform upon which 12 people would stand and Atlas would hold them up. However unlikely an agent he was, Drohl did have something in common with Agent 007. Despite the ravages of ill-health and age 'Atlas' quickly fixed himself up with another Irish 'wife' whose husband was overseas fighting the Jerries and impregnated her, presumably doing his bit for the Fatherland. He was re-interned in 1942. Spook reports from Naval Intelligence were prepared by Agent Godfrey. Ian Fleming was Godfrey's personal assistant. (Source: O'Halpin, Eunan: *Defending Ireland. The Irish State and its enemies since 1922*. Oxford University Press 1999, p. 242.) See also *Irish Echo*, October 20-26, 1993, p. 6.

6. John Francis O'Reilly was an interesting character. He came from Kerry and had been sacked from the Irish Civil Service for 'striking a superior'. He went to Germany and was only 28 when arrested. His father was a well known former RIC man who had arrested Roger Casement in 1916 just by the lonely Banna Strand when he arrived from Germany by U-Boat. At the beginning of the war O'Reilly had broadcast for the Germans from Brunswick and Berlin under the name 'Pat O'Brien' but was regarded as 'unreliable'. His fellow broadcaster, a Galway born former Black and Tan, was one William Joyce, better known as 'Lord Haw Haw'. Parachuted into Ireland O'Reilly was soon arrested, but in 1944 he managed to escape from Arbour Hill. His father, the ex-RIC man turned his son in for a £500 reward which he invested. When his son was released he set him up in 'The Parachute Bar' in Dublin. In 1952 O'Reilly published a series of articles in the *Sunday Dispatch* (July/August) entitled "I was a spy in Ireland". The historic value of this, what Stephan calls, 'fantastic account', is without any intrinsic merit.
7. Pax Ó Faoláin quoted in MacEoin, op. cit., pp. 142-143.
8. References are: INA 5 12860 and IMA G2/X/0581.
Further proof is to be found in Roth, Andreas: 'Francis Stuart's broadcasts from Germany, 1942-4'. In: *Irish Historical Studies*, Vol. XXXII, No. 127, May 2001, p. 408, footnote 1): "Charles McGuinness undertook to offer his services to the German legation during the emergency: 'Personally I am desirous of getting across (to the Continent) to aid in any manner in the war against Britain – even broadcasting.' (McGuinness to 'Peterson' (Karl-Heinz Petersen, press attaché of the German legation), n. d. (N.A.I., DFA, Secretary's Office, A8, misc., correspondence with Col. Archer and Col. Bryan, 4/1940-6/1942)".
See also: O'Halpin, op. cit., pp. 242-243.
9. Stephan, op. cit., p. 185.
10. Duggan, John P.: *Neutral Ireland and the Third Reich*. Lilliput Press, Dublin 1989.
11. The traditional version of guns blazing in defiance has entered the Republican pantheon thanks to Dorothy MacArdle and her epic *The Irish Republic* (Irish Press, Dublin 1951). One lone dissenting voice was that of John Pinkman, a Liverpool IRA

man who was serving with the Free Staters at the time of Brugha's death. He and a Lewis gunner were observing the back of the Hammam in Thomas's Lane from Findlater Place. Many years later he claimed that the 'cowardly irregulars got out by using false red crosses and that Brugha, the last out, was only shot once'. We prefer Dorothy McArdle's version since after reading Pinkman's book *In the Legion of the Vanguard* (edited by Francis E. Maguire, Mercier Press, Dublin/Cork 1998) one is inexorably left with the opinion that Pinkman was an obnoxious little self apologist who ended up a blue shirt.

12. Stephan, op. cit., p. 240.
Reports vary as to whether or not McGuinness was successful in conning £300 from the Germans. Certainly the IRA never saw it, the boat never sailed, and Nomad was arrested and served three and a half years.
13. ibid., p. 241.
14. Pax Ó Faoláin quoted in MacEoin, op. cit., p. 143. In fact the three IRA men arrested at Fenit were Jim Crofton, Sean Brosnan and Johnny O'Connor.
15. Stephan, op. cit., p. 241.
Here is one of the points where it begins to get annoying. After Stephan interviewed Schuetz, after the war, he wrote the following:

> "Charles McGuinness was not unknown in Ireland. Stories circulating about his life suggested a most adventurous background. It was said that he had been the first Port Commandant at **Leningrad** after the Soviet October Revolution, that he had at one time been **President of a Central American Republic**, that **he had fought on the side of Red Spain in the Spanish Civil War**, and also that he had taken part in **Captain Scott's** expedition to the South Pole. **What is undisputed is that this adventurous seafarer – who incidentally was a Reserve officer in the small Irish Navy – had made a name for himself as author of children's adventure books among which was one with the title *The Nomads*.**"

[There is another problem here. The items highlighted are plain wrong, but this is how Nomad 'stories' have spread – cross-contamination.]

16. Personal interview with Eddie Keenan, Derry 2000. *See*, also, McGuffin, John: *Internment*. Anvil Press, Tralee 1973 (out of print but available online at http://www.irishresistancebooks.com).
17. However, Francis Stuart, the elderly eminence grise and 'former' fascist of Irish literature, who broadcast from Berlin for the Nazis during the war told the author, in 1998, that Goertz was 'an idealist who was completely inefficient.' Of course, in 1940 while Francis Stuart was living in Berlin with his new girlfriend, his former student, Goertz was in Ireland, staying with Stuart's estranged wife Iseult (daughter of Maud Gonne MacBride), who apparently became enamoured of the Teutonic hero. According to Geoffrey Elborn in his biography of Francis Stuart "It seems that she fell in love with him in the short time they knew each other. They were perhaps drawn together by a common interest in literature and eastern philosophy, but nothing could come of her love, which was probably unrequited. After Goertz's capture Iseult noted of the spy, "No voice has ever caressed my ears like one which I may never hear again, no smile has so inveighled [sic] me.""" (Elborn, Geoffrey: *Francis Stuart. A Life*. Raven Arts Press, Dublin 1990, p. 130.) She fantasized about being married to Goertz in a Nuremberg Church which she knew and that her husband Francis and his lover were there. Also present at the 'dream wedding' are her mother Madame MacBride and all Iseult's dead pets. (Alas for poor Iseult. Shortly before he committed suicide Goertz married an Irish nurse, Una Mackey.)
18. *See* MacEoin, Uinseann: *Harry*. Argenta Publications, Dublin, 1985, p. 72. White is correct of course. Goertz was mentally unstable to say the least. When he parachuted in he missed his drop by 75 miles and set off to walk, asking for directions at police stations, wearing his full military Nazi uniform, which occasioned, it seems, little more than a few bemused stares as he strode the laneways from Meath to Wicklow.
19. Somewhat bizarrely, three months after Goertz's death the ultra conservative *Irish Times* published a series of six articles allegedly written by Goertz for them earlier. Why they had not published them previously is a mystery. They appeared between August 25th and September 8th and add very little to what was already known of Goertz and his 'mission'.

Chapter 12
It Was Sad When The Good Ship Went Down?

When Nomad McGuinness had arrived back in Ireland from Spain at the beginning of 1937 he had been optimistic that as an experienced seaman he would have little trouble getting a high profile job in the newly formed Irish Navy (then named the Irish Marine Service). This apparently cut little ice with the authorities who gave McGuinness what he regarded as the 'paltry job' of Chief Petty Officer.[1]

The early history of the Irish Marine Service was at best an example of shortsighted incompetence and at worst a calamitous blunder. In the years following 1922 Ireland, unlike the majority of the more recently independent nations, made no attempt to encourage the development of her own mercantile marine. The new leaders, formerly farmers, lawyers and businessmen seemingly turned their backs upon the sea and ignored the obvious fact that as an island Ireland was dependent on many imports for its very existence. The idea of Sinn Fein – Ourselves Alone – did not, it appeared, embrace the necessity of having an adequate number of Irish registered ships to carry trade.[2] Nomad would have concurred. In 1935 he wrote:

> "My attempt to start an Irish Mercantile Marine […] was the first and last effort made in Ireland to perform the hopeless task; for although the country is an island geographically situated in the direct line of communication between the outer world and northern Europe, we have developed no argonauts. It is inexplicable. Much smaller countries, with but a tithe of our sea advantages, have had colonies all over the globe: Denmark, Holland and Belgium for instance. The subject is a sore one with me, and has done a great deal to alienate my sympathy from our repeated wails for independence."[3]

"Each year the fleet declined: from 127 in 1923, until in September 1939 we [Ireland] had only fifty-six ships flying the

Irish flag, none ocean going, all designed for the short sea trades. Only the Wexford Steamship Company had a modern fleet: three diesel-driven dry cargo coasters, *Kerlogue*, *Edenvale* and *Menapia*, the last just ready for delivery from her builders in Rotterdam. The locust years had seen the disappearance from the register of the *Knockfierna* and *Kilcredane*, ocean-going tramp-ships owned by the Limerick Steamship Company which fell victim to the shipping depression of the 1930s.

A whaling fleet based in South Georgia, Antarctica, consisting of two factory ships and six catchers, the property of H. Salvesen of Leith, Scotland, used the Irish register to take up the quota of whales allowed by international agreement. They transferred to British registry at the outbreak of World War Two in 1939.

The tide seemed to be turning in 1938 when Inver Tankers Ltd was established to operate seven oil tankers to carry crude oil to a proposed oil refinery in Dublin. The tankers were handed over that year from their builders in Germany, each being 500 ft long and capable of carrying 9,000 tons. They were named after Irish rivers with the prefix Inver, i.e. *Inverliffey*, *Inverlee*, *Inversuir*, *Invershannon*, *Inveriane*, *Inverilen*, and *Inverdargie*. Two days after the outbreak of the War all were transferred to the British registry and all were sunk within three years. So the situation arose that every drop of oil and petrol used in this country during the war years was carried here in Allied tankers, for we had none ourselves.

Almost all the cross-channel passenger ships trading into Southern Ireland in 1939 were registered in Ireland, including those operated by rail-way companies. They had been thus registered pre-1921 and remained so thereafter. In almost all cases they flew the Red Ensign, the flag of the British Merchant Navy. On 7 September 1939 the government issued Emergency Power (No.2) Order which required all Irish-registered ships to fly the Irish flag. When the Tricolour was hoisted on the railway vessels in Holyhead, the crews went on strike and refused to sail under the Irish flag; a few days later the ships were transferred to the British register.

After this exodus only fifty-six ships remained to serve Ireland, and for a variety of reasons seven of these carried no cargo to this country. Three, *Alexandra*, *Isolda* and *Ierne* were tenders in the Lighthouse Service and had no cargo-carrying capacity. Their duties were to check the positional accuracy of buoys; the efficiency of lights and fog signals; the condition of beacons, leading lights and other navigational aids. They also carried relief crews, stores, water and oil to lighthouses and lightships. The schooner *Edith May* of Wexford and ketch *Ivy P* of Dublin were actually owned in England and remained there throughout the War. The schooner *Isallt* of Skibbereen was taken over by the Department of Defence as a training vessel for the Marine Service at Haulbowline, Co. Cork [*see infra*], and the passenger vessel *Munster* traded between Belfast and Liverpool until mined and sunk in February 1940. So Ireland declared her neutrality and stood alone with her Lilliputian fleet. The oldest was the schooner *Brooklands* of Cork, built in 1859; the most modern the *Menapia* of Wexford, fitting out at her builders in Holland."[4]

The *Isallt* was used as a training vessel and was approaching senility, having been built in 1909. The chief petty officer training the raw recruits was none other than Charles 'Nomad' McGuinness. Gerard Harrington who as a young rating was taught by Nomad recalled that McGuinness "treated his superiors with offhanded gruffness, which they accepted – even if reluctantly. But to us subordinates he was a pleasant fellow and the greatest of story-tellers when we adjourned to the public houses of Cobh". Harrington recounts how he and a few other Bearamen had a lucky escape, when one night, and with much drink taken Nomad tried to recruit the Bearamen for 'a wee trip'. "When we get out beyond Roche's Point I will tell you where." Harrington and his pals slept it off and dismissed the whole episode but were not too surprised that McGuinness was arrested only a few weeks later for 'communicating with a foreign power' and incarcerated in Arbour Hill.[5]

During the war further difficulties arose for the Irish Navy in early November 1939

> "when the United States, also neutral in the conflict, ordered its ships not to enter the war zone which was defined as the area east of a line from northern Spain to Iceland. Lisbon became the terminal port for American cargoes and transhipment into Allied Irish or neutral ships was necessary to get the goods to Ireland. This double handling resulted in very heavy expense. Under the Emergency regulations all cargo space was allocated by the Department of Supplies and it was forbidden for importers to charter ships themselves.
>
> Irish merchants faced further bureaucracy from 1 January 1941 when the British Embassy in Dublin announced that importers and exporters in Ireland must hold navicerts to ensure

shipment of their goods to and from certain countries. It went on to explain that the navicert was like a passport and would exempt shipments from examination and subsequent delay. However in reality it was a measure to control the use of neutral shipping and deny it to Germany. Without the navicert a ship could not pass through Allied patrols or receive fuel, water, stores, charts or repair facilities in Allied ports. In the case of Irish ships trading to Portugal and Spain, it required them to carry coal outwards to Lisbon and to call at Fishguard homewards for examination by the Royal Navy.

In addition to the navicert, the masters of all Irish ships were issued in British ports with Routing Instructions for their voyage. These laid down the courses to be steered, the distance to pass off various headlands and the procedure for signaling with Allied ships. Most important for Iberian traders was the designation of a prohibited area which included the Bay of Biscay out to 12° west. East of that line Allied ships and planes had orders to shoot on sight without warning.

In the Dáil on 20 February 1941, Eamonn de Valera, replying to a request from James Dillon that Irish ships be fitted with weapons to defend themselves, gave details of attacks on the fleet during 1940:

> "Of eight attacked, two of them twice, four were sunk, twenty lives lost and seven men injured. In addition to these four ships, three others were sunk by mines and the cause of the loss of two others has not been ascertained. Seven of the ten attacks were from the air. In all but one case the attackers were identified as German. It is right to say however that I have also received reports of cases in which German planes have circled and examined Irish ships without attacking them.
>
> The loss of Irish lives and the sinking of Irish ships have naturally occasioned feelings of deep resentment here, which we have not failed to voice through official channels to the German government; we have protested, lodged a claim for compensation and reserved all rights to which we are entitled by International Law.
>
> However let us be clear as to the position in this regard. On 17 August 1940 the German government declared a large area around Britain to be a scene of warlike operations and announced that ships in this area exposed themselves to damage. As regards defensive armaments, the Government is not satisfied that the advantage outweighs the disadvantages."

February 1941 also saw the publication of a *Notice to Mariners* from the Marine Branch, Department of Industry and Commerce, Dublin, which stated that mines were numerous off our south, south-east and north-west coasts and advising all ships in these areas to navigate in daylight only. The mines referred to were contact mines which exploded when a ship collided with them. Originally placed as a defensive barrage in various areas (Iceland to Scotland, St George's Channel) and secured to the sea bed by heavy chain moorings, they frequently broke adrift in stormy weather and became a hazard to friend and foe alike. A sharp lookout was the only defence against them.

The greatest menace in the early years of the War came from the magnetic mine which was dropped from an aircraft and lay on the sea bed until activated by the magnetic field of a ship passing above. Three B + I Line vessels lost in 1940 fell victim to magnetic mines. To neutralise this indiscriminate weapon, ships were degaussed, which involved fitting coils of cable horizontally inside them and passing current through them from the ships' own generators."[6]

While all this was going on of course McGuinness was lodged in Arbour Hill prison. On his release gainful employment was hard to come by. He cadged a billet at an old Republican family home in Sandycove, Dublin. He attended the tragic and rather pathetic funeral of Dr. Goertz at Deansgrange but the few other mourners apparently couldn't help.[7] He had to go back to what he knew best – freelance smuggling. And then fate raised a strange ghost from the past (if you believe in synchronicity).

Nomad tied up with an English 'entrepreneur', Anthony A. Harris of Sale, Manchester. He commissioned McGuinness to obtain a boat for 'a little venture'. Funds must have been in short supply. Nomad chartered the *Isallt*.

Isallt was perhaps not the most propitious name for a boat. Its predecessor *Isallt* had gone down with all hands in 1909. The 'new' *Isallt*, built in 1909 in Portmadoc, Wales, a 134 ton schooner with twin diesel engines was registered at Skibbereen but she had already had a chequered career. In 1934, en route to Skibbereen from Birkenhead, she had had to be abandoned since she had begun to leak badly. Later the crew were able to bring her home but she was soon sold off to the Ministry of Defence who owned her from 1940-1946.

Nearing the end of her days she had been used as a training ship by the Department of Defence at Haulbowline. The 'skipper' entrusted with training the young cadets in 1942 had of course been Charles 'Nomad' McGuinness. It must have come as somewhat embarrassing for the Ministry of Defence when McGuinness was arrested from the job and subsequently jailed for 7 years (served 3½) for his activities with the German spies.

The Ministry of Defence sold the *Isallt* in 1946 but on her first voyage for her new owners she was disabled in heavy seas off the Baily Lighthouse, Co. Dublin. She was towed into Dublin by the Dublin gas company's steamer *Glenbride* and lay further rusting in dry dock until Lloyd's finally settled the *Glenbride's* salvage claim and then they, amazingly, certified the gallant old tub as seaworthy.

And now Nomad was to be reunited with the *Isallt*. The mysterious English 'businessman' Mr. Harris appointed McGuinness in charge, who quickly hired a crew.

>The first line that McGuinness read,
>A loud laugh laughed he;
>The next line that McGuinness read,
>A tear blinded his e'e.
>
>'O who is this has done this deed,
>Has told this man of me,
>To send us out at this time of the year,
>To sail upon the sea?'
>
>'Make ready, make ready, my merry men all,
>Our good ship sails the morn.'
>'Now ever alack, my master dear
>I fear a deadly storm.'
>
>'I saw the new moon late yestreen
>With the auld moon in her arm
>And if we go to sea, master,
>I fear we'll come to harm.'[8]

On Tuesday December 2nd 1947 the crew were signed on. They consisted of John Kelly of Dublin who was the engineer, first mate Thomas Corkish (62) and two deckhands – Thomas' son John Corkish and a seventeen year old lad Joseph Whelan, who until two days previously had been a van delivery boy. It was his first voyage. Also on board were Charles McGuinness, and the charterer (who was, according to the *Derry Journal*, 'a ship broker') Mr. Harris who was accompanied by a mysterious lady referred to only as 'Miss Mary Young'. Ms. Young is described in the Wexford *Free Press* of the next week as 'a stewardess'. Given that the ancient *Isallt* had no need, or indeed, hardly room, for a stewardess it seems that this was a 1947 euphemism for a lady of loose morals. The *Free Press* adds the information that Mrs. Harris was in fact living in the YWCA while her husband and his stewardess friend were 'gallivanting' in Ireland.[9]

Two days later, on December 4th the *Isallt* left Dublin at 11.45 a.m. She was reported on the Ballymoney Rocks at 4.30 a.m. on the morning of December 5th. There were only two survivors listed.

The next day, in what seems to have been a masterly piece of research and investigation in such a short time and with the postwar printing exigencies, the *Irish Times* of December 6th 1947 led with the headline 'Five Lost When Schooner Is Wrecked In Gale'. Next to the headline is a photograph of the stricken *Isallt* which is still afloat off the Ballymoney Rocks. There's also a photograph (which strangely does not look like any other contemporary photos of him) and an obituary of Charles McGuinness (which repeats many of the inaccuracies hitherto published), a photograph of the two survivors, John Corkish and young Joseph Whelan in the hospital. There's quite a long interview with young Whelan (*see infra*). Two days later, on December 8th, the *Irish Times* confirmed that the body of Miss Young which had been reported as missing had washed up on Courtown strand, some four miles away. McGuinness and Corkish Snr., missing presumed drowned.[10]

It's front page news in the *Irish Times*. What happens next? Nothing. Very strange.

But first, here's what John Whelan, one of the survivors has to say in an interview that day:

> "They left Dublin at 11.45 a.m on Thursday. The passage from Dublin to Dublin Bay was very smooth but from then on it was rough. The schooner began to roll badly and the crew became sick.
>
> Between 10 and 11 p.m. the engineer told them to get their lifebelts on as the ship was sinking. He told them to get a boat over the side but it was difficult to lower a boat as the ropes were being fouled.
>
> "I put the plug into the boat", said Whelan, " but I saw it come out. The chief engineer put it back. Just as we were pulling away a wave came over the bow and swamped the boat. Another followed and capsized it. We were all thrown into the sea.

> I drifted towards the rocks. Near the rocks I saw a figure in front of me which I **thought** was that of the **skipper** [authors' emphasis]. I tried to catch him but a wave washed him away.
> I was thrown on the sand and lay there for ten minutes. I shouted for help but got no reply. I then climbed the rocks. I got a shout from Jack [sic] Corkish who was right below me. I told him to climb the rocks but he could not because his hands were too cold. I got down and helped him to the top of the rocks. We lay there for about two hours and then Corkish said he could not hang on any longer".[11]

Whelan then described how he had walked a mile and knocked up a Mr Moffatt of Kildermott who had helped him put Corkish to bed.

Corkish also said that 'young Whelan had saved his life'.

The *Irish Times* reporter's next paragraph however seems astonishing. Remember. The *Isallt* is shipwrecked early in the hours of Friday the 5th. Corkish and Whelan take hours to reach the safety of Moffat's house and presumably several hours at least to get to the hospital in Wicklow, yet, with two survivors, two bodies washed up and three missing, the North Wexford coroner, Dr. A. J. Cantwell has impanelled a jury of seven for an instant inquest where they record in accordance with the Medical Officer that "Kelly and Harris had multiple injuries, [...] as if they had been battered against the rocks. Death was due to multiple wounds and drowning." The other three are instantly presumed missing and drowned dead, after hearing solely from an obviously shattered young Whelan.

First off – the two bodies recovered were Kelly and Harris, John Corkish's father was missing and like McGuinness' is never found. Miss Young's body doesn't wash up until Saturday – next day, and the inquest jury have delivered a verdict within 12 hours of the two survivors being found.

Another interesting follow up to this front page story came two days later in the *Irish Times* of Monday the 8th of December.

> "Hope of recovering the bodies of Captain C. J. McGuinness, master, and of Thomas Corkish, mate, of the schooner *Isallt*, which was wrecked off the Wexford coast on Friday, is receding. [...] The body of Miss M. Young was found on Saturday morning at Courtown, about four miles from the scene.
> The ship is a complete loss and cannot be saved, but there is a chance that the cargo may be salvaged by the use of the breeches buoy or shallow-drafted vessels.

The agents, Messrs E. Betson, have received a report on the position of the ship and the cargo, and efforts at salvage will be made when the weather is suitable."[12]

They prepare this report on the very Saturday and rush it to the *Irish Times* before the print deadline on Sunday evening. Why?

The assiduous coroner Dr. Cantwell pronounced a verdict of death by asphyxiation on Miss Mary Young, whose address was given as 'Cranleigh Drive, Sale, Cheshire'. Same address as Mr. Harris, though they could not have asked either of them since they were dead and must have been relying on whatever papers came off the corpses.[13]

It would perhaps be interesting to ask the *Irish Times* reporter and the authorities a few questions, but alas this is not possible. Dead men rarely tell accurate tales. But let us pose some queries.

a. The vessel was supposed to be carrying anthracite from Dublin to Waterford. The ship's manifest is lost, along with the skipper. Does one really believe that Mr. Harris and Miss Young have come over from England to go out on a boat trip in a leaky schooner in bad weather in the Irish sea to ferry anthracite down the coast a few miles to Waterford? Even stranger: according to Lloyd's register the vessel was owned by the South of Ireland Shipping company and on charter to Harris. Her cargo was not anthracite, but manure!

Why did the *Isallt* have to put to sea in weather no other boat would sail in to deliver a cargo of MANURE a few miles down the coast to Waterford? One would have thought that the rich farming community of Waterford were scarcely so void of dung that they had to hurriedly bring down a consignment from Dublin. Something smells – worse than manure!

Buried away in the fine print of the *Irish Times* front page story is a reference to Nomad saying that he (and Mr Harris and Miss Mary Young) 'had plans to sail the *Isallt* to the West Indies and that he wanted to go on to Fiji[14] to get in touch with Mr Frank Launder, the film director who is making a film there.'[15] – More on Fiji *infra*.

b. Who were Mr Harris and Miss Young, the 'stewardess'? Why are no details given about them, in the original article or in the following days? All we learn is that Mr Harris wife, Gladys Elizabeth was living in Manchester (at the YWCA in Urmston it turns out) and was unaware what her husband was doing or that he was dead until late Friday evening. (Again, how does the prescient *Irish Times* put this in on Saturday morning? They're going to press in the early hours of the morning. How did they even know Mrs Harris' name let alone that she was living not at the family home but in the YWCA?) What were they trying to smuggle? How did they meet McGuinness? Why did they try to sail in such inclement conditions in such a 'rusty scupper'? No other boats apparently left Dublin port that day, according to the shipping lists. It is perhaps understandable why Mr Harris wished to keep Miss Young's presence a secret from his wife but did they need to go on the *Isallt*? There were perfectly good trains to take them to Waterford, if, indeed, that was the real destination. They had been travelling around Ireland for four months, why on earth bring a young 23 year old girl on such a perilous voyage?

c. Why such a rush on the inquest before all the bodies had even been washed up?

d. Why didn't the reporter ask young Whelan a few more questions about what happened McGuinness and Corkish – or Miss Young? What was the cargo, Anthracite or manure? Did he know anything about any plans to go to the West Indies? In an interesting aside, Corkish's widow said at the instant inquest that her husband had 'been a seaman all his life and had sailed ships in the West Indies for two years'. Was McGuinness in league with Corkish and planning some Caribbean adventure – such as his eternal quest for 'pirate treasure' (*see* Appendix I)? Additionally, the *Irish News* (8th Dec. 1947) gratuitously throws in that "Captain McGuinness took the place of an Arklow man as Captain of the *Isallt* at the last minute."

e. How sure was an exhausted and terrified Whelan that the body which floated away from him really was McGuinness? He only is reported by the reporter as having 'thought' it was 'the skipper'. Had he ever actually seen McGuinness before the schooner set sail?

f. Why was there not one single sympathy notice, combhrón or commemoration insertion in the paper for Captain McGuinness? Nothing from his old republican or German comrades? Nothing from his family – even in the *Derry Journal*.

g. Why no mention of McGuinness' wife and his baby daughter Anita (born 1946, *see* Afterword)? Or his first wife Claire/Klara and son Patrick in New York?

h. Why did Harris and McGuinness charter the *Isallt* in the first place? McGuinness clearly knew that it was a potential death trap which could never have made it to the West Indies, let alone Fiji. Was it to be part of an insurance scam? Salvage? False manifestoes? The Wexford *Free Press* says that the late 'Captain' Harris set out on a voyage to the West Indies more than a year previously on the 87 year old *Brooklands* but was forced to return through bad weather and that project had been abandoned. Capt. Harris? Did young Whelan think that the Englishman 'Captain' Harris was the actually captain whose body he saw in the water or was it 'skipper' McGuinness?

i. The *Irish Times* photo clearly shows the *Isallt* afloat and less than hundred yards off the Ballymoney Rocks. Why could the log, and manifesto not be recovered and the cargo inspected? Surely that would have helped the insurance claim? Did they really have to abandon the boat? Joseph Whelan and John Corkish were in the water for at least half an hour before stumbling onto the rocks yet the *Isallt* obviously beat them to it and did not sink. Contraband? Well, if it walks like a duck ...

j. Why was the story allowed to die/quashed so quickly? As far as could be established, apart from the *Irish Times* and *Irish News* items on the 6th and 8th and the *Derry Journal* on the 8th it is a week before even a brief item on the wreck appears in the local paper.

k. Why weren't the bodies recovered eventually? Lots of bodies are washed up in the Irish Sea, very few are not recovered because of the tidal nature of the water, and especially if the wreck is only hundred yards or so off the coast. Of course, a corpus delicti is not necessary to have someone declared dead, but within 12 hours?

l. Nomad was a strong swimmer. He had qualified as an underwater diver in the Antarctica on the Byrd expedition. He'd been in several shipwrecks before. The boat went down only 100 yards off the shore. Is it feasible that he drowned? Hadn't he survived over an hour in the freezing winter Atlantic off Rockaway Beach previously?

Interestingly enough, the *Derry Journal* in its report of the demise of one of Derry's sons[16] added some 'facts' which the *Irish Times* had ignored. According to the *Journal* coast guard watchers had reported seeing distress signals off Ballymoney at 4.30 a.m. The Arklow lifeboat was launched. She found the *Isallt's* stern under water (it's not in the photo taken a few hours later) and she was deserted. The lifeboat cruised round for an hour but found no sign of anyone.

This raises the issue of not only where were Corkish and Whelan, the survivors – presumably they had clambered ashore and were lying exhausted on the rocks – but as to the time all these events happened. How could, and indeed, to reiterate, why was an inquest mounted within hours of Whelan and Corkish being brought to the Wicklow hospital?

> They had not sailed a league, a league,
> A league but barely three,
> When the light grew dark, and the wind blew loud,
> And gurly grew the sea.
>
> The ladies wrang their fingers white,
> The maidens tore their heair,
> All for the sake of their true love,
> For him they'll see nae mair.
>
> O lang, lang may the maidens sit
> With their gold combs in their heair,
> All waiting for Charlie, their own dear love
> For him they'll see nae mair.

And now the ultimate question. Did Nomad die in the Irish Sea or did he do a 'B. Traven'[17] and vanish?

THE FIJI STORY

When the authors began to research this biography of Charles McGuinness we knew very little about his death. The last thing we were thinking off was a 'conspiracy'. The few, very few, remaining 'close' relatives recalled little or nothing about it – it was, after all, more than fifty years ago. We knew that the *Isallt* had supposedly perished along with Nomad in the Irish Sea. We knew the date. We had a brief report in the *Derry Journal*. And then one of the authors came across a strange story. He met one of Nomad's few remaining great nephews who spoke to him briefly about 'his uncle Nomad'. He had not particularly liked his uncle. In Derry in the 20s, 30s, 40s and 50s Nomad's somewhat cavalier attitude towards the sanctity of marriage and mercurial views on Catholicism, plus his lengthy absences meant that he had few close connections to his home city. He was also regarded, by some, as a 'bit of a braggart'. But the nephew came out with a remarkable statement, which he solemnly averred to be true. He claimed that in 1955, 8 years after McGuinness supposedly drowned, he had been in London and was going down the Tottenham Court Road underground escalator. And he swears coming up and passing him was 'Uncle Nomad' who smiled at him and just said 'you never saw me'. By the time the nephew had reached the bottom and chased up after the man he had disappeared. He also confirmed Nomad's infamous tattoos – a full master sailing ship on his chest and the Union Jack on the soles of his feet.

Nomad's son Patrick, little 'Paudeen', also claimed to have seen his father circa 1950, three years after his supposed demise.

This of course was grist to our conspiracy minded psyches, but the authors were 7,000 miles apart and both involved in other projects. The nephew died a few years ago and it wasn't until McGuffin arrived back in Derry that the book was resurrected. On one level the 'wasted' eight years are a loss – more people have died, memories have faded, dust has gathered on the archives, but, on the other hand it has proved to be a blessing because of the spread of the internet.

Within a week we were able to ascertain the names of Nomad's German wife (Klara/Claire) and small child (Patrick) who he left in New York when he went to the Pole. A week later and we were in contact with Dr. Tim McGuinness, Patrick's son and Nomad's grandson. What with Charles John having several wives and children and his eldest son Patrick having had at least seven wives the direct McGuinness clan is expanding exponentially.

From the beginning McGuffin and Tim McGuinness agreed to share information but to do so in such a way as to minimize the cross-contamination which comes from various 'sources' repeating the few hearsay stories about Nomad. Dr Tim recalled meeting his grandmother Claire once when she came out from New York, where she lived most of her life – she died in her late nineties – to California. As a young boy Dr. Tim recalls his grandmother, still bitter about her abandonment by Nomad, commenting 'of course that bastard never went down with the ship, he's just doing another disappearance'.

Dr. Tim's father, Patrick, apparently took after his father. He ran away, abandoned women, married more, fathered children all over the place, lost a leg fighting in the Second World War in Italy, and ended up in California where he mingled with such famous people as Walt Disney, Mayor Yorty and Admiral Byrd, whom he claimed had been a great friend of Nomad's. He also, when in his cups, hinted to young Tim that Nomad 'probably had faked his death and was in Fiji'. 'Byrd knows the secret,' he allegedly claimed.

Fiji. When mooting the possibility that McGuinness had 'done a runner' as they say in Derry, we had discussed where he might have disappeared to. It had to be somewhere far away. Europe was probably out. Nomad had surely had his fill of the colder climes. He had had enough of the Arctic and the Antarctic. Rereading his manuscript it seemed that the only place where he had been really happy, where he would have wanted to settle down once that 'damn wanderlust' ebbed was surely the South Seas. Romantic. Still relatively unspoiled and where McGuinness had been, and enjoyed himself before the First World War and then again, twice, on his way to and from the South Pole. He also loved Tahiti.

> "We had the good fortune to spend Easter Week in this earthly paradise [Papeete, Tahiti] and had there not been urgent reasons to the contrary I would, I frankly confess, have stayed there for good."[18]

And what about the mysterious Panama connection? Nomad is supposed to have fathered a child while passing through the Panama canal and the child, called Charles McGuinness meets another of the McGuinnesses years later in Panama. And then there's Captain Thompson's pirate treasure which Nomad for years, like most other sea dogs had endlessly talked about. No, that way leads to madness, to say nothing of unsound methodology.

Let us concentrate on whether, if, and it's a big if, McGuinness did survive, did he go to the South Seas? And this is research for another day. *The Man Who Never Died*? Good title for a sequel? Only time will tell and will therefore suffer the usual punishment accorded informers.

At the end of the day, we find it hard to believe that Charles 'Nomad' McGuinness died for a shipload of manure! But, as yet, we can't prove it. Any information gratefully received via the publishers IRB.

Notes.

1. Harrington, Gerard: *The Adverntures of C.P.O. Charlie McGuinness*. In: *Cork Holly Bough*, 1992, p. 32.
2. For a basic history of the early Irish Merchant Marine, *see* Forde, Frank: *The Long Watch: The History of the Irish Mercantile Marine in WWII*. Gill & Macmillan, Dublin 1981.
3. McGuinness, *Nomad*, op. cit., p. 184.
4. Forde, op. cit., pp. 1-2.
5. Harrington, op. cit., p. 32.
6. Forde, op. cit., pp. 2-3.
7. The mourners were McGuinness, Stephen Held, Anthony Deery, Goertz's radio operator, and Werner Unland.
8. The Poem is a parody of 'Sir Patrick Spens', anon, 17th century.
9. Surprisingly the *Irish News*, the other paper to record the shipwreck, was more prurient than usual in those days and in its December 6th issue – which slavishly copies the *Irish Times* for details of the wreck – did add a 'salacious' tidbit. Apparently Mr Anthony Harris, variously described as 'Captain' and 'ship broker' had filed for divorce from Gladys Elizabeth, who was now reduced to the YWCA while Harris travelled around Ireland with Ms. Young.
10. *Irish Times* 08.12.1947.
11. *Irish Times* 06.12.1947.
12. *Irish Times* 08.12.1947.
13. *The Free Press*, Wexford, December 13th, 1947.
14. At this time the film director Frank Launder and his partner Sidney Giliat were in Fiji – scouting locations for 'The Blue Lagoon' which appeared in 1949, starring Jean Simmons and Donald Houston. It was a decided flop, despite splendid Fijian locations.
15. *Irish Times*, 08.12.1947.
16. *Derry Journal*, 08.12.1947.
17. B. Traven. Pen names – Ret Marut and Hal Groves (born February 23, 1882 in Schwiebus, Germany, died Mexico City March 26, 1969). Some have alleged (principally W. Wyatt) that his real name was Otto Feige (coward) born in Zwiebodzin, Poland. Also rumoured to have been born Benick Traven Torsvan. As Ret Marut he was an actor in Germany from 1907, published an anarchist journal *Der Ziegelbrenner* (Brick Burner), and was then involved in the Munich uprising in 1919.

Escaped and lived the rest of his life as a man of mystery in the jungles of Mexico. Highlighted the destruction of the indigenous Mexicans. Finally became popular, albeit anonymously as author of *Treasure of the Sierra Madre* filmed by John Ford. To 'do a B Traven' means to disappear under a slew of false names.
18. McGuinness, *Nomad*, op. cit., p. 245.

APPENDIX I
TREASURE HUNTING AND CAPTAIN THOMPSON

Charlie McGuinness had run away to sea. As a mere teenager he had been round the Horn several times, visited Latin America, the United States, Australia and Polynesia. He had brawled his way though a dozen ports. He had survived shipwrecks, hung out with pirates, cutthroats, thieves, murderers, deserters, desperados – his kind of people. To a young person growing up in boring Derry with its poverty, unemployment, discrimination and tedious existence, the adventure stories of far off exploits around the British Empire as served up in the comics and by a whole breed of writers of patriotic ripping yarns provided an escape for their imaginations. Nomad McGuinness, himself a local man, was a wonderful rarity on his occasional visits home.

In the cramped, atrocious and dangerous conditions in the foc'sle, on the long boring voyages in schooners, coal boats and troop ships, McGuinness would have listened avidly as the older men bragged and told their yarns and tall tales, when they spilled out their sorrows, their lost dreams, their dashed hopes.

They talked of fights and wars, of dusky maidens and women in every port. Some may have waxed melancholy at the thought of a wife or a girlfriend back home, thousands of miles away.

And of course it was a tough life – not for nothing did the noble Royal Navy describe seafaring as 'rum, sodomy and the lash'. And hindsight can romanticize it, but for the runaway sailors in search of adventure, only one in a hundred, if that, made their fortune, struck gold, found the elephant's graveyard and El Dorado, the buried treasure.

Is it any wonder that Nomad's life seemed to follow the philosophy of a fellow adventurer, Bret Harte:

> "Of all the words of tongue and pen,
> The saddest are: 'it might have been.'"[1]

But Nomad could tell treasure stories 'if he wanted to'.

> "In omitting a hunt for buried treasure or the rescue of a beautiful maiden in distress who turns out to be an heiress or a princess, I may be unorthodox. In the former case the treasure I know of still remains to be salved, but nothing could tempt me to cut through malaria-infested jungles for the sake of gold. And as to the latter and romantic omission, I must truthfully state that any distressful maiden who crossed my path attributed to the writer a goodly portion of the distress."[2]

In 1935 he makes another 'treasure' reference.

> "When the ripples of the Byrd expedition had died out of New York Harbour I endeavoured to promote an excursion into South America. My objective was to search for Inca treasure dumped in a sacrificial lake in the hinterland of Venezuela."[3]

Whenever he talked to children he told tales of pirates and buried treasure, like so many other 'old sea dogs'.

When he was on the run in Germany he used the alias 'Captain Thompson' (he also used 'Hennessey' which is a corruption of McGuinness) and it is perhaps not too farfetched – well, at least no more farfetched than some of Nomad's stories – that he told:

THE STORY OF CAPTAIN THOMPSON'S TREASURE – OR HOW THE ORAL TRADITION SPREADS

> "Queenscliff is a seaside holiday resort situated near the head of Port Phillip Bay, Victoria, Australia. One of the attractions it offers the public is the lure of Pirate treasure. According to local legend, the pirate Benito Bonito, entered Port Phillip Bay sometime in 1821 and concealed in a cave a treasure known as the 'Lost Loot of Lima'. After doing so, he ventured out of to sea to continue his evil trade.
>
> Waiting for him outside was a British Man-O-War, which gave chase and eventually stormed Bonito's ship. Following a Drum Head court martial, Bonito was allegedly hanged at sea. The only crew member to escape was a cabin boy who had a map tattooed on his arm. Such is the attraction of this treasure, many expeditions and syndicates have sought the treasure spending

thousands of dollars in the process, without recovering a single Spanish piece of eight.

The 'Loot of Lima' is one of the most sought after treasures and probably one of the most documented. Researchers, Historians, and authors all agree on one point that the so-called treasure is buried on a tiny island in the Pacific known as Coco's Island. Coco's Island lies in Latitude 5 32' 57" North, Longitude 87 2' 10" West, about 550 miles due west of Panama City. It is sometimes confused with Coco's Keeling Islands.

It became the perfect hideout and haunt of pirates during the 17th, 18th and early 19th centuries. Off the main shipping lanes, but still close enough to the rich Spanish colonies situated along the Coastline, it was strategically well situated to the pirates' needs. Coco's offered safe anchorage and a plentiful supply of fresh water and coconuts from which the pirates brewed alcoholic beverages. Deposits of loot on Coco's are associated with notorious names such as William Dampier, Edward Davis, Benito Bonito, Captain Thompson and some stories have it that even Captain Kidd buried his loot there too.

During a Trans Atlantic voyage a man named William Thompson, became friendly with another seaman John Keeting. One night, Thompson confided to Keeting and told the following story. In 1890, he had been at anchor in the British Brig *Mary Dear* in the Port of Callao. Chile and Peru were at war; the Chilean army was about to attack the City of Lima.

The Spanish has accumulated great wealth and riches at Lima. The largest collection being held in the Cathedral of Lima. Amongst the collection of gold and silver artefacts, mostly encrusted with precious stones, was a life-size effigy of the Virgin Mary holding the divine child, reputedly made of solid gold and encrusted with jewels.

The Spanish had gathered their riches together and transported them to Callao only to find the only ship in the harbour was the *Mary Dear*. Thompson was trusted by the Spanish because of prior dealing with them in the past. He was commissioned to cruise off the coast for several weeks.

Should Lima survive, he was to return the treasure to the Spanish Authorities in Panama. The treasure was loaded onto the *Mary Dear* together with six soldiers and two priests to guard it during the coming voyage. Thompson and his crew were overwhelmed at the value of the cargo they had stored in the holds of their ship and this immense fortune proved to be too great a temptation for him. Once they left port for the open sea, they waited until the guards and priest were asleep, then seized the opportunity to murder them all and dispose of their bodies over the side of the ship.

Thompson then set sail for Coco's Island and anchored in Chatham Bay. Two Bays, Chatham and Wafer Bay offer safe anchorage in the North of the island and both offer fresh water springs. There is also a smaller inlet in the South of the island called Bay of Hope where a landing could have easily been made.

Thompson unloaded the *Mary Dear* and his treasure in a cave in Chatham Bay goes one story, but in another he made an inventory which reads as follows.

"We have buried at a depth of four feet in the red earth: altar trimmings of cloth of gold with baldachin, monstrances, chalices, comprising 1,244 stones; 1 chest; two reliquaries weighing 120 pounds, with 624 topazes, carnelians and emeralds, 12 diamonds; 1 chest; 3 reliquaries of cast metal weighing 160 pounds, with 860 rubies and various stones, 19 diamonds; 1 chest; 4,000 doubloons of Spain marked 8, 5,000 crowns of Mexico, 124 swords, 64 dirks, 120 shoulder belts, 28 rondaches (small shields); 1 chest; 8 caskets of cedar wood and silver with 3,840 cut stones, rings, platens and 4,265 uncut stones; 28 feet to the north-east at a depth of eight feet in the yellow sand; 7 chests with 22 candelabra in gold and silver, weighing 250 pounds, and 164 rubies, 12 armspans west; at a depth of 12 feet in the red earth.

The seven foot Virgin of gold with the child of Jesus and her crown and pectoral of 780 pounds, rolled in her gold chasuble on which are 1,684 jewels. Three of these are four-inch emeralds on the pectoral and six are six-inch topazes on the crown. The seven crosses are of diamonds."

Having hidden his treasures and shared out several chests of gold with his crew, he left the island and was sighted by the Spanish Frigate *Espsigle* which engaged and captured them. The Spanish on finding some of the 'Loot of Lima' on board hanged the crew sparing only Thompson and another man on condition they disclose the hiding place.

Returning to the island they were able to break away from the Spanish guards and took cover in the dense overgrowth. After they spent a week searching for them, the Spaniards finally gave up and sailed away. Some time later a passing whaling ship called into the island for water and found Thompson and the other man who died shortly after from a fever. Thompson's mate's name in some reports was Benito Bonito, in others it was a man named Chapelle.

After his rescue from Coco's island, Thompson returned to the sea as a seaman, where he met Keating. Keating claimed Thompson gave him documents, maps and other information to recover the treasure concealed on the island. Since 1860 Coco's Island has been known chiefly as a treasure-hunting site.

It appears that the 'Loot of Lima' as it is called lies not in Queenscliff as claimed by local residents, but on an island many miles away. Sir Captain John Williams who salvaged the Niagra became involved in Benito's treasure when he was commissioned to dive at the scene in hope of recovering the virgin's effigy. Williams stated the individuals involved were a weird bunch. He agreed to accept the deal on condition he was paid in advance.

He was told that there was an underwater cave with a ledge inside with the statue of the Virgin Mary resting there. Everything was as it was described to his diver's except there was no Virgin to be found. After which he was accused of cheating the syndicate he had done the work for.

Historians believe the shadowy figure of a man known as Benito Bonito did exist, although they believe this name was used to disguise his real identity. It is agreed that the true identity of Benito Bonito was Captain Bennett Grahame, a British naval officer who had served with none other than Lord Nelson. In 1818 Grahame was sent to the Pacific in command of *H.M.S. Devonshire* to survey the coast between Cape Horn and Panama.

Grahame soon tired of his mundane task and instead turned to piracy, his crew was given the option to join him or be put ashore in Panama. Those that would not join him were instead taken to Coco's island where after being put ashore were slaughtered by Grahame and his crew. Thus he became know as Benito Bonito of the Bloody Sword. Treasure hunters, searching for the treasure years later uncovered a number of skeletons; these remains are believed to be members of Grahame's crew.

Apart from plundering richly laden Spanish vessels carrying cargoes of gold and silver Bonito also came ashore at a spot near Acapulco, Mexico where he seized a rich cargo of gold. According to reports he took it to Coco's island and buried it in Wafer Bay. One story tells of an occasion when Bonito spotted five Spanish ships, 3 of them being men-o-war and the other galleons laden with gold and silver. Bonito successfully engaged the Spanish in a running duel capturing the Latin ships. During the battle, the *Devonshire* was extensively damaged and Bonito decided to load his treasure on a Spanish ship, *Relampago*, which he sailed to Coco's and buried his treasure in a tunnel some 35 feet long.

Bonito's activities were common knowledge and complaints had been made to the British Admiralty, which despatched a warship to deal with him. However Bonito engaged the man-o-war and defeated it. Eventually he was cornered in the Bay of Buena Ventura after his ship had been sunk. Bonito and his crew were taken to England where they were tried convicted and hanged.

Several crew members were transported to Tasmania for life. Amongst them, a young girl named Mary Welch or Welsh told a dramatic story. She claimed Bonito's real name was Grahame who had picked her up in Panama several years earlier. It was Mary who started the Queenscliff version of the treasure tale.

She claimed the pirates came ashore at Queenscliff, buried the treasure in a cave and dynamited the entrance. Shortly after passing through the heads, they were spotted by a warship, which gave chase. After a running battle they were captured but Bonito blew his brains out on the deck rather than face the gallows.

The amazing part of her story is that after she married and secured her release instead of hunting for the treasure in the Queenscliff area, she sailed off to San Francisco where she raised an expedition to go to Coco's Island. The maps and documents she had in her possession proved worthless, many historians believe her tale to be nothing more than a fabrication of the imagination. Kenneth W. Byron wrote a book entitled, *Lost treasures in Australia and New Zealand*. In it he describes investigations made by Harry Riesberg, who visited the Cathedral at Lima.

He found that at no time was there a war between Chile and Peru. He was astounded when a priest pointed to a life-size effigy of the Virgin Mary, and also discovered that at no time had the Cathedral been plundered. The British Admiralty has no records regarding the capture of Benito Bonito, his trial, execution or even the transportation of prisoners to Tasmania. Treasure and the thought of instant wealth and riches are sufficient excuse for wealthy individuals to indulge themselves in making a quick profit, especially if the story, documentation and maps appear to be authentic and credible."[4]

Con games are as old as time – and people as gullible.

We admitted at the start that this Appendix was highly speculative. Had McGuinness told tales of Captain Thompson and the Cocos buried treasure? But there was no proof – until, as told in the chapter on *Behind the Red Curtain*, just before finishing the book we found the missing books. When we say 'found' we mean discovered proof of their existence. They are not listed in the National Library of Ireland and two of them are clearly short vanity press extended pamphlets, probably for children. The other is entitled *African Adventures* and has the publisher's name, Morris & Co as opposed to Pillar Press. Extensive searches of antiquarian book catalogues have so far proven fruitless, but, one never knows. Perhaps there's some kind reader out there who can help (for to paraphrase Blanche Dubois, 'we can surely always rely on the kindness of strangers?') Bad pennies, old books and Nomad McGuinnesses have a habit of turning up in the most unexpected places.

As you can see the books were rushed out in 1946 and 1947 from Dublin, which lends further weight to a 1946-47 publishing date for *Behind the Red Curtain* since Nomad was in Derry in 1946 with the new wife Anita and the baby Anita, to whom he dedicated *Behind the Red Curtain*. Recall also that Winston Churchill did not coin the phrase 'Iron Curtain' until 1946.

Anyway, here they are – the long lost works of Charles Nomad McGuinness, and we're sorry for doubting you, Nomad.

Damon, Peter: (pseud.): *African Adventure, etc.* Morris & Co., Dublin, 1947.
Damon, Peter: (pseud.): *Cocos. Island of blood and treasure.* Pillar Publishing Co., Dublin, 1946.
Damon, Peter: (pseud.): *The Curse on Cocos Gold.* Pillar Publishing Co., Dublin, 1946.

NOTES.

1. Harte, Bret: *Mrs Judge Jenkins*. In: "Argonaut Edition" of the Works of Bret Harte, Vol. 8, P. F. Collier & Son, New York 1882.
2. McGuinness, *Nomad*, op. cit., p. vii.
3. McGuinness, *Nomad*, op. cit., p. 250.
4. Hassell, Alan: The lure of pirate treasure. *See* http://www.geocities.com/TheTropics/Paradise/2951/benito.html

APPENDIX II
PIRATES OF THE INDIAN OCEAN

The Indian Ocean had had its infamous heroes like Captain Avery who captured the Moghul King's royal galley and made off with a huge prize. And there was Captain North and his crew, who also had a base in Madagascar, but the arrival of Captain Mission, on the run from the Mediterranean signalled the onset of the golden age of communitarian pirate colonies with the founding of Libertalia or Libertatia, as it was sometimes called.

Libertatia. Located near the NE tip of Madagascar was the home of the 'anarchist pirates', a place Nomad visited on several occasions during his voyages in the Indian Ocean. The pirate colony was, according to Daniel Defoe (who wrote the history of it under the pseudonym of Captain Charles Johnson)[1] founded in the early 1700s by Captain Mission, the youngest son of a Provençal family. Like Nomad he would run away from home at 15 and served on a French man of war in the Mediterranean. Captured by pirates he 'converted to atheism'. When the pirate ship's captain was killed Mission's 'mentor', a former Dominican priest called Caraccioli who was now 'a major blasphemer', persuaded Mission to try his powers of oratory upon the disorganized crew. Mission, according to Defoe, exhorted them with stirring words about 'Peoples' rights' and 'shaking the yoak [sic] of tyranny and throwing off their misery and oppression'. 'Pirates are men who often lead lives of no principle and lead dissolute lives, but our lives are to be brave, just and innocent.' Off the Dutch coast they captured a slave ship and freed the slaves. Those who wished were free to join them, the rest were put ashore. At first they settled on the island of Johanna, but soon moved to found Libertatia when more and more pirates flocked to join them. Life was remarkably libertarian for the times – or at least according to Defoe. Lord Byron described Captain Mission as 'the mildest manner'd man that never scuttled a ship or cut a throat.'

The English pirate Capt. Thomas Tew was elected – for the pirates had full and free elections of their 'officers' who could be removed at any time by a popular vote – and the other most famous pirate Captain associated with the Libertatians was a Captain Thompson, who acquired a huge reputation, not only in the Indian Ocean but also in the Caribbean where the rumours of buried treasure permeated the maritime annals.[2]

As a want to be swashbuckler it was natural for a free spirit and 'sailor of fortune' like Charles McGuinness to adopt 'Captain Thompson' as one of his principal noms-de-plume. (For other aliases and their origins, *see* Afterword.)

Whether McGuinness would have approved of the 'Liberi's' custom of putting all loot in the public treasury 'because money being of no use anywhere was common currency', is a moot point.

NOTES.

1. *See* Johnson, Captain Charles (pseud. of Daniel Defoe): *A General History of the Robberies and Murders of the Most Notorious Pyrates*. London, 1724.
2. The Indian Ocean and the Caribbean were not the only hotbeds for piracy. The Barbary coast, and, in particular the port of Salé in North Africa had been an egalitarian crypto-anarchist pirate colony for over a hundred years in the 17th century. Their corsairs had ranged as far as Iceland and they had sacked the Irish port of Baltimore. *See* Wilson, Peter Lamborn: *Pirate Utopias. Moorish Corsairs & European Renegadoes*. Autonomedia. New York 1995.

Afterword

Some questions (and a few answers) regarding Charles John 'Nomad' McGuinness.

A Skeely Skipper?

> The boss sits in old Dublin town,
> Drinking the blude-red wine;
> 'O where shall I get a skeely skipper
> To sail this ship of mine?'
>
> Then up and spake an eldren knight,
> Sat at the boss' right knee:
> 'Charlie McGuinness is the best sailor
> That ever sailed the sea.'

From his mid-life McGuinness always referred to himself as 'Captain'. He put himself forward, and, indeed was promoted as such by the Press – particularly the American Press, to some of whom he was excellent copy – as the almost legendary 'sailor of fortune', the swashbuckling, romantic, experienced and tough Irish skipper. But was Nomad ever a Captain, let along a 'skeely skipper'?

He certainly circumnavigated the globe on more than one occasion as a young man. He rounded the Horn. He sailed the Pacific and Indian oceans and the China sea. He was shipwrecked numerous times. But Captain? Master Mariner?

He ran away from Derry in 1908, aged 15. He signed up for the British Navy in 1914, aged 21. He certainly travelled widely but not (hardly surprisingly given his youth) as an officer let alone a Captain. He was a casual hand who signed on, often for very little pay and with the promise of atrocious conditions in order to travel to foreign climes by delivering coal (or, when in Antofagasto, hauling a load of bat guano) across the Atlantic and Pacific oceans. However, maritime coalman's helper is not the most glamourous occupation with which to regale one's avid readers.

According to Nomad he experienced a few weeks in the winter of 1914 shelling 'gallant little Belgium' and then was shipped to Africa. His war time service was varied and dangerous, but it was all on terra firma.

On all his hair raising shipwrecks, including the *Magellan* where he is the sole survivor, he is not even second mate. It is only during the mysterious period when he is in Chinese waters in 1919 that the lowly deckhand is allegedly promoted to Captain of a pirate junk by 'Whisky Brown'. His story is, shall we be charitable, quixotry at best.

July 1920 does see McGuinness back in his native Derry. He leads the Southern Donegal Flying Column, he participates in the War of Independence both in Tirconnell and in Derry. He helps rescue Frank Carty, is shot himself and escapes with derring-do. In June 1921 he is summoned to Dublin where Michael Collins ("He was my friend and a brainy fighter who made a fool out of the men in Dublin Castle. But he was out of his depths when he pitted his strength against the whirlpools of political trickery."[1]) whom he had previously never met, relied on the word of Liam Mellows, himself no sailor,[2] and delegated the German gun running to McGuinness. On those perilous voyages McGuinness is undoubtedly the captain (war time promotion)[3] and he is quite justified in claiming this as his life's crowning martial/maritime achievement, but the lack of paper qualifications apparently rankled with McGuinness.

On leaving Ireland before the Civil War broke out McGuinness' only claims to maritime activities before he became a failed contractor in New York was an offer to captain Chiang Kai Schek's new 'navy' in 1924. According to Nomad 'Chiang went Commie' and so McGuinness backed out (but he alleges this happened in 1926-7, as well Chiang 'went Commie' in 1923-4).

And so the next voyage is in 1928 with 'Commodore' Byrd.

McGuinness (whom no one yet calls Nomad) tells a preposterous story about bearding Byrd in the Biltmore Hotel. After a brief interview Byrd (who Nomad claims to have been 'half-Irish') decides McGuinness is the man for him (out of 50,000 applicants according, again, to Nomad).

> "My rating was chief officer and I was the first to be picked. Not being an American (in truth I had no nationality)[4] Commander Byrd regretted that he could not give me command. But the public

would not have tolerated a foreigner in command of a ship sailing under the 'stars and stripes' on a mission of national importance. For myself, I would have sailed as bos'n and been glad of the opportunity!"[5]

And *see* also Nomad's tale of how Byrd 'cheated' him in Chapter 9.

Nomad was to get his wish. He sailed as 'bos'n acting mate' on yet another coal delivery boat, under 'Captain Melville' with whom he did not get on.[6] This is not intended in any way to denigrate the bravery of the crews of the *City of New York*. It took incredible courage and toughness to sail and survive the Antarctic seas, but Nomad had no need to introduce absurd bombast about how he had been selected as the party's underwater diver – in the Antarctic Ocean! – because of his expert swimming skills – which must have improved since watching the pearl fishers.

Another legend about McGuinness, widely believed in his native Derry by older people is that he was the first Irishman to get to the South Pole. This is nonsense.[7]

Be that as it may, when he returned to America McGuinness did finally get back into the 'skippering business' on the rum runs and this raises another question.

So How Skeely Was 'Captain' McGuinness?

By his own admission he totally mis-navigated his gun running trips from Germany to Ireland. When it came to the rum running, he wrecked boats. He lost cargo. He nearly drowned. He confused Longitude with Latitude and managed to get the bark stuck amid the coastguard fleet, he botched up an escape in the inlets and lost the boat and the entire cargo.

He quits the 'rum running racket' and decides to try his luck, inexplicably, given his lack of politics, in Soviet Russia.

In Russia he skippers no boats. He does make a couple of trips out into the Gulf of Finland on the ice breakers the *Krassin*[8] and the *Yermak*, but he wasn't allowed near any controls. He was soon disillusioned with the conditions in 'the new Soviet' but it didn't stop him trying to get papers from them declaring him a captain. The authorities refused to do this 'unless I would become a Russian citizen which I would not do'. He had also failed to get navigational certificates as a ship's mate when in Hong Kong[9] – a port where most things were available for a price.

After turning his coat in Spain he arrived back home but again the authorities were not too impressed by his nautical skills. The best he could get was a job as a trainer on the *Isallt*.

Was Nomad secretly jealous of his father and dead brother and their maritime qualifications and that is why he doesn't mention them?[10] We shall never know.

And finally there is the death of the 'skeely skipper and expert diver and swimmer' fifty yards off the rocks (*see* Chapter 12). Either Nomad faked his death or he was most unadvised to set to sea in such conditions and in such a vessel. Most unskeely behaviour, unless, of course, he and Corkish didn't go down? (*see*, again, Chapter 12. *See* also the exploits of Orr in Joseph Heller's masterpiece *Catch 22*, although it is true to say that poor Sir Patrick Spens went down to a watery doom.)

FAMILY MAN?

> "But while McGuinness, in his craving for adventure expresses the dauntless spirit of man, at his home in Brooklyn for the next two years while the expedition is away a woman will sit with a child in her arms, exemplifying a different type of courage, which is perhaps more valorous and valiant."[11]

It is doubtful that Nomad shared this romantic vision. While one could truthfully call him a family man – he had enough of them – his attitude towards women was not something he chose to put on paper. Certainly throughout his two books there are no references to 'white' women. On the other hand he expresses approval of 'dusky Polynesian maidens' and 'exotic Chinese ladies' like Isobel and Inez. He praises their open attitude to sex and excoriates the missionaries for destroying these beautiful people. Yet, in a surprisingly prudish aside he castigates the Belgians he encountered in Africa.

> "Cohabiting with the native women is an open practice in the Belgian Congo – an unsavoury alliance for white officers, as these dusky courtesans share their favours without distinction of colour."[12]

At this stage we'll try to answer the mystery of how many wives Nomad actually had, for we have heard an amazing range of estimates.

The first wife was Klara Zuckerkandel whom McGuinness met and married in Berlin in 1922/3. Klara was Jewish and was born in the Polish town of Olesko, which at times was part of the Ukraine. She visited Derry with Nomad in the early 1920s and they stayed with Nomad's sister Daisie (Rose) with whom he normally billeted when making his short trips back.

They had a son Patrick (Paudeen) – the small boy who is seen seeing Papa off on the *City of New York* en route to the South Pole.

Wife no. 2 – Panama Anita? It's a rumour. According to Nomad's grandson there is a story that he had met a man in Panama who went by the name McGuinness and claimed his mother was Anita McGuinness, wife of an Irish adventurer. He claimed to have been born in 1947 which might rule him out, but hadn't a birth certificate and so remains a remote possibility. However attractive the idea seemed, there appears little or no evidence for the 'Panamanian Anita' – unless he did survive and met and bed her in 1948 in Panama on his way to the Pacific Ocean.

There definitely was another Anita – this one Irish. She arrived with Nomad and a baby daughter, also called Anita, in Derry in 1947. This is the baby Anita to whom Nomad dedicated *Behind the Red Curtain*. Anita was much younger than Nomad but was introduced as 'Mrs. McGuinness' and nobody asked too many questions about when and where they had been married. There is no evidence of any divorce he may have had from Klara, but, as previously noted, she later married a Mr. Eigen. The little Anita grew up to marry an Irishman called Coleman from Dublin and is still alive and well, last heard of in England.

Then we were led to believe that he was married to an Irish woman named Maureen. No one in Derry has heard of her and we seriously doubt her existence as a McGuinness wife.

And then of course there is speculation about later 'wives' in Fiji or Tahiti if he survived the *Isallt* wreck. Genealogists are working on this as we speak. But, in the meantime we feel that Nomad has been maligned as a 'serial womanizer'. Although, of course, as Sean MacBride said: "McGuinness: never behind the door where women are concerned. He probably now has a Russian wife."[13]

We prefer to think of McGuinness as a 'lovable rogue' when it came to the fairer sex, although not even his most devout fan could claim that he was 'a good family man'.

NOMAD – WELTANSCHAUUNG

Did Nomad have any real 'politics'?

Firstly, in his writing and apparently conversation he could be described as racist. Words like 'chink', 'nigger', 'kike' are used quite casually. It should be stressed that this occurred three quarters of a century ago – when 'political correctness' was but a gleam in some sociologist's eye.

It is unlikely that Nomad would have thought of himself as racist. He would point to the 'charitable' remarks he made about various 'poor blacks' whom he had helped along the road; one 'Chink' whom he met convinced him that 'a strange thing, but I learned, a true one – a 'Chink' pirate's word is his bond. A white streak, shall I say, among the yellow."[14]

Anti-semitism was another strand that wove its way through his psyche, apparently. When he was in Germany with the Jewish Briscoe, the latter felt that Nomad was a true friend of 'the chosen people'. He relates how Nomad beat up an Irishman who had insulted a Jewish friend of his. Later however Nomad was to blame many of the woes in Russia on 'those damned Russian Jews'. When he wrote of Spain and 'the evil Jewish Bolsheviks' he sneers at them as 'Hebrew legionnaires' and 'swinish Jew boys'. Jewish women fared little better: Is it coincidental that his first wife Claire was Jewish?

> "Occasionally, women came with the various drafts from France – Hungarians, Poles, Romanians, and Germans. Mostly all were Jewesses; they looked absurd trotting around in uniforms with Sam Brown belts and revolvers. As with many of the effeminate males, quite a few wore bracelets of revolver cartridges."[15]

So he didn't have much time for gays either, it appears.

For a time he poses as a communist of some sort, but not after Russia. And the anarchists of the FAI, the most gallant fighters in Spain, are nothing but 'freemason and blasphemers'. (The 'anarchists are freemasons' nonsense bears a startling similarity to *Freemasonry and the anti-Christian Movement* by Edward Cahill (Dublin, 1929), a best selling Catholic church potboiler). In short, not a very consistent let alone a left wing political analysis. As for the British communists he related how in the train in Spain he had told them that he was "not a Communist. Even worse, I suppose, as far as you Drawing Room Reds are concerned, I am an Irishman, and none too fond of Britishers of your type."[16]

And the Catholic church, in which faith he was raised? In his early years he is clearly anti-clerical. He denigrates the missionaries in Africa and the Pacific Islands and blames them of virtual genocide, the destruction of the native habitat, simplicity and predilection for promiscuity. He masqueraded as a priest when engaged on his own 'missions', travelling around Ireland. He doesn't refer to any Catholic clerics during his New York days and they do not rate favourable mention until just before he is leaving Russia when we have a little paean to 'the God of St. Isaac's, of St. Basil's, of all the Russias'.

Yet when he returns to Dublin after a few months in Spain he proceeds to spew out a rant that would do justice to O'Duffy's thickest Blueshirt. The only excuse that anyone has been able to come up with was that he desperately needed money and at that time would sell his soul (which, you may recall Robert Briscoe had saved on Mick Collins' behalf fifteen years previously) 'for the sake of Blueshirt pelf' as an old Republican put it.

Did he help the German spies for anti-British sentiments, or because he was pro-Nazi? Almost certainly not. He had no real interest in the war, he seemingly just wanted to survive and the only old Republican acquaintances were 'the mad old ladies' and men like Jim O'Donovan.

After the war, and several years in Arbour Hill, he was intent on getting back into smuggling apparently – or in chasing some elusive dream of buried treasure. Politics did not interest him.

Of course, there will always be those like Pax Ó Faoláin who believed that Charlie would show up again, somewhere, some when.

IN SUM

We are at the end of our story.

All we can do is guess about those things which are not revealed and recall those that are, and wish *envoi* to Charles John 'Nomad' McGuinness.

NOTES.

1. McGuinness, *Nomad*, op. cit., p. 121.
2. According to Greaves, op. cit., Collins was not known to have visited Derry or Donegal in 1920-21 and McGuinness was in the North-West. Collins, as Chief of Intelligence would obviously have heard of him as a Flying Column officer and for the escape of Carty, but he cannot have known him personally. According to McGuinness Collins greets him by the name 'Mac', which no one else seems to have used, let alone 'Nomad'.
Mellows himself only got back to Ireland in 1921 from America where he had been working with John Devoy on the *Gaelic American* so he barely knew McGuinness either, but after the arrest of Joe Vize, the Director of Importations, Mellows took over the job, which he held until the truce. As Director of Importations his word would obviously have had extra weight and, in the event, with the success of Nomad's importations, his choice was obviously vindicated.
3. McGuinness' two trips were of course fraught with misadventure. The Wexford IRA sailors may scoff at the Derryman's navigational skills or lack thereof, but it cannot be gainsaid that McGuinness, virtually single handed, delivered 90% of the weapons that the movement got in by gun running. When the various histories of the War of Independence were written, the murdered Erskine Childers and the *Asgard* rightly rated great credit, but the man who brought the real gear in was Charles 'Nomad' McGuinness and future generations of 'revolutionary historians' should not forget it.
4. Interestingly since McGuinness' father, Charles John McGuinness had been born in Brooklyn in 1855 Nomad might well have been able to claim American citizenship.
5. McGuinness, *Nomad*, op. cit., p. 213.
6. ibid., p. 215.
7. Years before McGuinness sailed with Byrd, an unassuming Kerryman from Annascaul, Tom Crean, went three times in all to the Antarctic in 1912 with Captain Scott and later in 1922 with Ernest Shackleton, amongst other trips. He retired to his birthplace, opened a small pub and lived another twenty years. He rarely told people of his epic 800 mile journey with Shackleton in a tiny boat across some of the stormiest seas in

the world – still regarded as the greatest feat of open boat navigation – before they crossed the unmapped frozen mountains of South Georgia in a 36 hour non stop climb to get help. He was a modest man (unlike Nomad). "He put his medals and his sword in a box in the wardrobe and that was that," said his daughter Mary.
8. The world famous icebreaker – *see* Footnote 11 Chapter 7.
9. McGuinness, *Nomad*, op. cit., p. 109.
10. Nomad makes no mention of this piece of information whatsoever, which is rather strange, but, according to the records he had an older brother, Denis Patrick (born 1890 in Moville), who was a sailor who drowned off Havana and is buried in Cuba.
11. *Detroit News*, Sunday October 7, 1928.
12. McGuinness, *Nomad*, op. cit., p. 83.
13. McEoin, *Survivors*, op. cit., p. 142.
14. McGuinness, *Nomad*, op. cit., p. 111.
15. *Irish Independent*, January 5, 1937.
16. ibid., January 4, 1937.

Envoi

Joy be with us, and honour close the tale:
Now do we dip the prow, and shake the sail,
And take the wind, and bid adieu to rest.
With glad endeavour we begin the quest
That destiny commands, though where we go,
Uncharted is our course, our hearts are tried,
And we may weary ere we take the tide,
Or make fair haven from the moaning sea.
Be ye propitious, winds of destiny,
On us at first blow not too boisterous bold;
All Ireland hath is packed into the hold.
Her hope flies at the peak. Now it is dawn.
And we away. Be with us Manannaun.'

James Stephens (1882-1950)

BIBLIOGRAPHY

Augusteijn, Joost: *From Public Defiance to Guerrilla Warfare.* Irish Academic Press, Dublin 1996.

Augusteijn, Joost: 'Radical Nationalist Activities in County Derry, 1900-1921'. In: O'Brien, Gerard (ed.): *Derry & Londonderry: History & Society. Interdisciplinary essays on the History on an Irish County.* Geography Publications, Dublin 1999.

Balzac, Honoré de: *Illusions Perdues.* Garnier-Flammarion, Paris 1966.

Basily, Nicolas de: *Russia under Soviet rule.* Allen and Unwin, 1938.

Bell, J. Bowyer: *The Secret Army. The IRA 1916-1979.* The Academy Press, Dublin 1979.

Betjeman, John: *Continual dew. A little book of bourgeois verse.* J. Murray, London 1977.

Briscoe, Robert (with Hatch, Alden): *For the Life of Me.* Longmans, Green and Co Ltd, London 1959.

Byron, Kenneth W.: *Lost Treasures in Australia & New Zealand.* Angus & Robertson, London/Sidney, 1965.

Cahill, Edward: *Freemasonry & the anti-Christian Movement.* Dublin 1929.

Carter, Carolle J: *The Shamrock and the Swastika.* Pacific Books, Palo Alto 1977.

Coogan, Tim Pat: *The IRA.* Fontana Books, London 1980 (updated edition).

Cordingly, David: *Under the Black Flag.* Random House, New York 1995.

Cronin, Mike: *The Blueshirts and Irish Politics.* Four Courts Press, Dublin 1997.

Cronin, Seán: *Frank Ryan: The Search for the Republic.* Repsol, Dublin 1980.

Cronin, Seán: *The McGarrity Papers.* Anvil, Tralee 1972.

Damon, Peter (pseud.): *African Adventure, etc.* Morris & Co., Dublin 1947.

Damon, Peter (pseud.): *Cocos. Island of blood and treasure.* Pillar Publishing Co., Dublin, 1946.

Damon, Peter (pseud.): *The Curse on Cocos Gold*. Pillar Publishing Co., Dublin, 1946.
Defoe, Daniel: *A General History of the Pyrates*. London, 1972.
Deschamps, Hubert: *Les Pirates á Madagascar aux XVIIe et XVIIIe siècle*. Paris 1949.
Duggan, John P.: *Neutral Ireland and the Third Reich*. Lilliput Press, Dublin 1989.
Elborn, Geoffrey: *Francis Stuart. A Life*. Raven Arts Press, Dublin 1990.
Fisk, Robert: *In Time of War*. Paladin, London 1985.
Fleming, Ian Lancaster: *From Russia, with Love*. Jonathan Cape, London 1957.
Forde, Frank: *The Long Watch: The History of the Irish Mercantile Marine in WWII*. Gill & Macmillan, Dublin 1981.
Goldman, Emma: *My Disillusionment in Russia*. Heinemann, London 1923.
Greaves, Desmond: *Liam Mellowes and the Irish Revolution*. Lawrence & Wishart, London 1971.
Griffith, Kenneth/ O'Grady, Timothy E.: *Curious Journey. An Oral History of Ireland's Unfinished Revolution*. Hutchinson, London 1982.
Heller, Joseph: *Catch 22*. Jonathan Cape, London 1968.
Hoyt, Edwin P.: *Guerrilla – Colonel von Lettow-Vorbeck and Germany's East African Empire*. MacMillan, London 1981.
Hudson, Geoffrey Francis: *Fifty Years of Communism. Theory and practice 1917-1967*. Penguin, London 1971.
Johnson, Captain Charles (pseud. of Daniel Defoe): *A General History of the Robberies and Murders of the Most Notorious Pyrates*. London, 1724.
Kelly, Bill (et.al.): *Sworn to be Free. The complete Book of IRA Jailbreaks 1918-1921*. Anvil Books, Tralee 1971
Kleinrichert, Denise: *The Argenta*. Irish Academic Press, Dublin 2001.
Lettow-Vorbeck, Paul von: *Meine Erinnerungen aus Ostafrika*. Koehler, Leipzig 1920.
Lilius, Aleko Eugene: *I sailed with Chinese Pirates*. Arrowsmith, London 1930.
MacArdle, Dorothy: *The Irish Republic*. Irish Press, Dublin 1951.
MacEoin, Uinseann: *The IRA in the Twilight Years (1923-1948)*. Argenta Press, Dublin 1997.
MacEoin, Uinseann: *Harry*. Argenta Press, Dublin 1985.

MacEoin, Uinseann: *Survivors*. Argenta Press Dublin 1980.
MacUileagóid, Mícheál: *From Fetters to Freedom. The Inside Story of Irish Jailbreaks*. Sásta, Belfast 1996.
Manning, Maurice: *The Blueshirts*. Gill & Macmillan, Dublin 1970.
McDermott, Jim: *Northern Division. The old IRA and the Belfast Pogroms 1920-22*. Beyond the Pale, Belfast 2001.
McGarry, Fearghal: *Irish Politics and the Spanish Civil War*. Cork University Press 1999.
McGuffin, John: *Internment*. Anvil Press. Tralee 1973. (Out of print but available online at http://www.irishresistancebooks.com)
McGuinness, Charles John: *Nomad*. Methuen, London 1934.
McGuinness, Charles John: *Sailor of Fortune*. Burt, New York, Chicago 1935.
McGuinness, Charles John: *Behind The Red Curtain*. Grafton Publications, Dublin 1947(?).
McInerney, M.: *Peadar O'Donnell. Irish Social Rebel*. O'Brien Press, Dublin 1974.
McKenna, G.B. (Thomas Donaldson ed.): *Facts & Figures. The Belfast Pogroms 1920-22*. Donaldson Archives, Belfast 1997
Mitchell, Arthur: *Revolutionary Government in Ireland. Dáil Éireann 1919-22*. Gill & Mcmillan, Dublin 1993.
Murphy, Brian P.: *John Chartres. Mystery Man of the Treaty*. Irish Academic Press, Dublin 1995.
Newman, Bernard: *German Spy*. London 1936.
O'Brien, Gerard (ed.): *Derry & Londonderry: History & Society. Interdisciplinary essays on the History on an Irish County*. Geography Publications, Dublin 1999.
O'Callaghan, Sean: *The Jackboot in Ireland*. London 1958.
O'Duffy, Eoin: *Crusade in Spain*. Browne and Nolan, Dublin 1938.
O'Halpin, Eunan: *Defending Ireland. The Irish State and its enemies since 1922*. Oxford University Press, 1999.
O'Riordan, Michael: *Connolly Column. The story of the Irishmen who fought for the Spanish Republic 1936-1939*. New Books, Dublin 1979.
Pinkman, John A.: *In the Legion of the Vanguard* (edited by Francis E. Maguire). Mercier Press, Cork/Dublin 1998.
Quiller-Couch, Arthur Thomas: *The Oxford book of English verse, 1250-1900*. Clarendon, Oxford 1919.
Quinn, Raymond J.: *A Rebel Voice. A History of Belfast Republicanism 1925-72*. Cultural and Local History Group, Belfast 1998.

Rumpf, Erhard: *Nationalismus und Sozialismus in Irland. Historisch-soziologischer Versuch über die irische Revolution seit 1918.* Hain, Meisenheim am Glan 1959.
Ryan, Meda: *The Real Chief: The Story of Liam Lynch.* Mercier Press, Cork/Dublin 1986.
Roth, Andreas: 'Francis Stuart's broadcasts from Germany, 1942-4.' In: *Irish Historical Studies*, Vol. XXXII, No. 127, May 2001.
Schapiro, Leonard: *The Communist Party of the Soviet Union.* Eyre & Spottiswoode, London 1960.
Stephan, Enno: *Spies in Ireland.* Four Square Books, London 1965.
Stradling, Robert: *The Irish and the Spanish Civil War 1936-39.* Mandolin, London 1999.
Taylor, Rex: *Assassination. The death of Sir Henry Wilson and the tragedy of Ireland.* Hutchinson, London 1961.
Thomas, Lowell: *Adventures of the Sea Devil.* Doubleday, New York 1932.
Tisa, J.: *Remembering the Good Fight. An Autobiography of the Spanish Civil War.* Bergin and Garvey, Mass. 1985.
Townsend, Charles: *The British Campaign in Ireland 1919-21.* Oxford, 1975.
Wexler, Alice: *Emma Goldman in Exile.* Beacon Press, Boston 1989.
Wilson, Peter Lamborn: *Pirate Utopias. Moorish Corsairs & European Renegadoes.* Autonomedia, New York 1995.

DOCUMENTS

Papers of Ernie O'Malley, 1916-1956, University College of Dublin Collections, IE UCDAD P17a/4
British Library
National Library of Ireland

NEWSPAPERS

Brooklyn Times
Cork Holly Bough
Derry Journal
Detroit News
Frankfurter Zeitung
The Free Press, Waterford
Irish Echo
Irish Independent
Irish News
Irish Times
New York Evening Graphic
New York Times
Sunday Independent
Sunday Tribune

INDEX

Abwehr 186-189, 197
Albacete 155-157, 163, 166-168, 170, 172
Andrievna, Xenia 144, 147-148
Anita 78-81, 83, 87
Annette 19, 21
Annie M. Reed 41
Antofagusta, Chile 14
Arbour Hill jail 138, 185, 191, 195-196, 200, 205, 207, 234
Ardara 47-48, 55, 57
Athlone jail 191, 196
Aud 85
Balchen, Bernt 108
Ballymoney Rocks 209, 213-214
bank robberies 47, 57, 156
Barrett, Dick 52, 94-95
Bay of Whales 106, 114
Beaumont, Billy 86
Beaumont, Séan 86
Belgium 25, 98, 203, 229
Bennett, Floyd 102, 108-109
Berkman, Alexander 141
Berlin 71-72, 83, 97-98, 101, 127, 144, 149, 186-187, 200, 202, 232
Betjeman, John 188
Blythe, Ernie 95
Bonar, Hugh 183
Bonito, Benito 220-221, 223-224
Boyle, Phil 183
Bremen 78, 93
Brett, Sergeant 56
Briscoe, Robert 70, 71-73, 78, 80, 82-83, 85-86, 93, 149-150, 233-234

Brooklands 205, 213
Brooklyn 11, 102-103, 110, 140, 231, 235
Brookshire 21
Brophy, Richard Gale 107-108, 112-113
Brosnan, Sean 201
Brown, 'Whisky' 37-38, 229
Brugha, Caitlin 192-194, 197
Brugha, Cathal 72, 94-95, 97, 192, 201
Brugha, Noinin 193-194
Bryce, Patrica (née Doherty) 137, 152
Buford 141
Burke, Liam 193
Byrd, Commodore Robert Evelyn 97-98, 100- 114, 122, 140, 159, 213, 216, 220, 229-230, 235
Byron, Kenneth W. 224
Byron, Lord 226
Cahill, Edward 182, 233
Callan, Owen 'Ginger' 47, 56-58
Cameroons campaign 26-28
Canaris, Admiral Wilhelm 186
cannibalism 112, 146, 149
Cantwell, Dr A. J. 210-211
Carricklee 43, 53, 55
Carty, Frank 49-56, 61, 65, 67, 101, 229, 235
Casement, Sir Roger 92, 99, 200
Catalonia 155, 167, 178-180
Cedarbrook 13-14
Chamberlain, Neville 185
Chelsea 104, 112

Chiang Kai Shek 98-99, 229
Childers, Erskine 235
Coco's Islands 221-225
Collins, Captain ('ancient
    mariner') 91-92, 96
Collins, Michael 47-49, 55, 61,
    63, 69-71, 73, 88, 95, 229,
    234-235
Comerford, Maire 94, 198
Congressional Medal 102, 110,
    139
Connolly, Roddy 86
Corbett, James 'Gentleman Jim'
    109
Corkish, John 208-210, 213-214
Corkish, Thomas 208-210, 212,
    231
Cornford, John 182
Crean, Tom 235
Crofton, Jim 201
Cuidad de Barcelona 155, 162
D'Arcy, Tony 185
Daly, Charlie 58
Damon, Peter (pen name of
    Charles McGuinness) 137,
    225
de Milhau, Ralph 114
de Valera, Eamonn 83, 95, 109,
    184-188, 191, 196-197, 206
De Wet, Christiaan (Rudolf) 28
Deery 198, 217
Defoe, Daniel 226-227
Delagoa Bay 34-35
Derry jail 49-50, 62
Derry Journal 62-64, 68, 208,
    212-214, 217
Devonshire 223
Devoy, John 235
Doherty, 'Dom' 43, 47, 52
Donegal 11-12, 18, 43, 45, 47-50,
    55-56, 61, 103, 140, 156, 159,
    183-184, 235
Donnelly, Charlie 183

Douala, Cameroons 27
Dowling, John 71-75, 85
Drumboe, Castle of 58
Dublin 13, 18, 28, 47-48, 55-56,
    61-62, 64, 69, 71, 87-88,
    '90-92, 137, 150, 154, 159,
    182, 184, 187, 189, 191-200,
    204-205, 207-209, 211-212,
    225, 228-229, 232, 234
Dungarvan 94-95
Dunkirk 25
Dunne, Reggie 70-71
Ebrington barracks 58, 61
Edwards, Hilton 184
Enright, Daniel 58
FAI 155-156, 233
Farrell, 'mad sisters' 197
Five-year Plan 141-142
Fleming, Ian 199
Fleming, Patrick 185
Four Courts 94, 97
Fox, Johnnie 43, 62
Franco, General Francisco 184
Freemasons 17, 125-127, 169,
    173, 182, 233
Frieda 83, 87-91
Gaertner, Dieter 189, 197
Gartenfeld, Flight Officer
    Edmund Eduard 190
Giliat, Sidney 217
Gillespie, Neil 43, 54, 64
Goertz, Dr Hermann 188-190,
    193, 196-199, 202, 207, 217
Goldman, Emma 141
Gorman, George 183
Grahame, Capt. Bennett 223-224
Grogan, Laurence 185
Halifax, Lord Edward 185
Hannah 87, 93-94, 96
Harding Street 50-52
Harrington, Gerard 205, 217
Harris, Anthony A. 207-213, 217
Harte, Tom 191

Hayes, Stephen 185, 194, 198-199
Hegarty, Patrick 43
Held, Stephen 195-196, 198, 217
Helvick Head 84, 88-90
Hempel, Dr Eduard 192, 198-199
Hennessey, Captain (pseudonym of Charles McGuinness) 28, 30, 32-33, 35, 53, 55-56, 58, 80, 83-84, 117, 220
Higgins, Sgt. 53-54
Hitler, Adolf 126-127, 194
Hoare, Sir Samuel 188
Hong Kong 36-37, 39, 230
Hoover, Edgar J. 141
Humphries, Sheila 91
Inna 126
International Brigades 151, 155-156, 161, 163-164, 167-168, 172, 178
Iquique, Chile 13-14, 36
Irish Independent 86, 155-158, 160, 177, 182, 190, 236
Irish News 212-213, 217
Irish Republican Army 43-46, 48-49, 52-56, 59-60, 62, 64-65, 68, 70-74, 81, 83, 85, 87-89, 91-92, 94-96, 111, 117, 159, 185-189, 191-194, 199-201, 235
Irish Republican Brotherhood 88
Irish Times 199, 202, 209-214, 217
Isallt 205, 207-214, 231-232
IWW (Industrial Workers of the World) 70
Jarama 183
Joyce, William 200
Kearns, Linda 62
Keenan, Eddie 195, 202
Kelly, 'Yellowback' 58, 67
Kelly, John 208, 210
Kelly, Pearse 193
Kennedy, Johnny 'Lip' 43, 47

Kenny, Dick 73-75
Kenny, John 190
Kilindini 28
Krebs, Danny 118
Kronprinz 125
Lahousen, Erwin von 197
Lansbury, George 149
Larkin, Sean 58
Launder, Frank 211, 217
Lenihan, Brian 189
Lenihan, Joseph 189-190
Leningrad 138-140, 143-145, 148, 150, 201
Lettow-Vorbeck, Colonel Paul von 28-29, 33
Liberador 35
Libertatia 226
Lichter, Hans 83-84, 90
Lister, Enrique 182
Lola 20, 21
Loot of Lima 220-223
Luciano, Lucky 115, 128
Luckner, Count Felix von 109, 125-127
Lynch, Liam 88, 95
Lynx 119-121
MacBride, Iseult 202
MacBride, Maud Gonne 202
MacBride, Sean 70, 83, 85, 150, 153, 232
Mackey, Una 197, 202
MacLiammóir, Michael 184
Madden, Owney 115, 117, 127-128
Madrid 154-156, 161, 163-164, 166, 172-178, 181-182
Magellan 34-35, 84, 229
Maguire, Sam 70-71
Martin, Hughie 47, 57-58, 61, 67, 69
Marty, Andre 168, 178
Mary Dear 221-222
Maureen 123

Mawhinney, Charles 56, 62
McCallion, George 43
McCool, Sean 193
McDermott, Donal 43
McGarrity, Joe 85-86, 96
McGrath, Paddy 191
McGrotty, Eamonn 183
McGuinness, Anita (daughter)
    111, 213, 225, 232
McGuinness, Anita (wife) 213,
    225, 232
McGuinness, Bridget Mary
    'Maisie' (sister) 11
McGuinness, Charles John
    (father) 11-12, 235
McGuinness, Claire (née
    Zuckerkandel, Klara) (wife)
    98, 101, 110, 114, 139-140,
    213, 215, 232-233
McGuinness, Denis Patrick
    (brother) 11, 13, 236
McGuinness, Hugh (brother)
    12-13, 29, 99, 103, 110, 113,
    138, 140-141, 152
McGuinness, Jack (brother) 11
McGuinness, Margaret (née
    Hernan) (mother) 11-12
McGuinness, Mary Ann (née
    Coyle) (step mother) 12
McGuinness, Patrick 'Paudeen'
    (son) 98, 110, 114, 137, 139,
    140, 213, 215-216, 232
McGuinness, Rose 'Daisy'
    (sister) 11, 232
McGuinness, Tim (grandson) 111,
    113, 215-216
McKelvey, Joe 52, 95
McLaughlin, John and Lizzie 52,
    64
McLaughlin, Paddy Roe 183
McMahon massacre 43, 62-63
McNeela, Sean 185
McRory, Father 55-56

Medway 35-37
Mellows, Liam 48-49, 70-72,
    75-78, 83, 85, 88, 90-91,
    94-95, 97, 149, 229, 235
Melville, Captain 102, 104-106,
    108, 112, 230
Mission, Captain 226
Moore, Pat 43, 47, 52
Mopelia 114, 127
Morocco 154
Moscow 86, 138-139, 140, 142,
    144-146, 150
Mulcahy, Dick 90, 94-95
Murmansk 137, 146-150, 153-154
Nem Wah 40-41
New Zealand 19, 104, 106-108,
    112, 224
Nighthawk 117, 139, 159
Nixon, District Inspector J.W.
    (RIC/RUC) 62, 63
Nobile, Umberto 103, 111-112
Norby, Oscar 43, 55
Nukuhiva Island 20
Ó Faoláin, Pax 84, 86, 88-90,
    92-95, 99, 111, 150, 190, 194,
    200-201, 234
O'Connor, Johnny 201
O'Connor, Peter 183
O'Connor, Rory 94-95, 97
O'Daire, Patrick 183
O'Donnell, H. 183
O'Donnell, Peadar 45, 47
O'Donnell, Vincent 183
O'Donovan, Jim 'Fingers' 72,
    185, 187-188, 191, 198-199,
    234
O'Duffy, General Eoin 181,
    183-184, 186, 234
O'Flaherty, Peadar 185
O'Higgins, Kevin 95
O'Malley, Ernie 110
O'Reilly, John Francis 190, 200
O'Sullivan, Joe 70-71

O'Sullivan, Tim 58
Obed, Henry 189, 197
Paris 19, 71, 98, 152, 155-156, 160-163, 166, 181
Patton, Tom 155, 167, 182
Perks, Dick 106
Pfaus, Oscar 186, 187
Pilgrim 14-16, 19
Pilkington, William 49
Pinkman, John 200-201
Pirates 34, 37-39, 41-42, 219, 220-221, 224, 226-227, 229, 233
Plunkett, George 185
Poisoned Glen 47, 48
Poitín 47
POUM 155, 169
Preetz, Willie 189, 197
Price, Albert 70
Prohibition 115, 124
Ransome, Sir Arthur 42
Reilly, Paddy 59-60, 68
Relampago 224
Rockaway Beach 110, 114, 119, 123, 127, 213
Rockefeller, John D. 102, 107, 109
Rolph, 'Sunny Jim' 41
Ros na Riogh 192, 194
Roth, Benny 107
Royal Irish Constabulary (RIC) 43-45, 49, 53-54, 58, 61, 63, 200
Russell, Seán 72, 96, 185
Ryan, Frank 183
Salé 227
Sao, Cheng I 39
Scapa Flow 24
Schuetz, Sgt. Guenther ('Marschner') 188, 189, 190, 191, 192, 193, 194, 195, 196, 197, 201

Schultz, 'Dutch' (Arthur Flegenheimer) 128
Scott, Bill 155, 163, 167, 182
Scott, Captain 100, 103, 106, 108, 109, 201, 235
Seeadler 126
Semiramis 119, 120, 122
Sherness 24
Shiels, Patrick 44, 52, 56, 64
Soloviki 149
South African Expeditionary Force 28
South Sea Islands 18, 216
Soviet Russia 17, 124, 138, 159, 161, 230
SS City of Dortmund 91-92
SS City of New York 99, 102, 103, 104, 105, 106, 107, 108, 109, 112, 230, 232
SS Dorelian 110
SS Eleanor Bolling 103, 104, 105, 106, 107, 108, 109, 112
SS Larsen 102, 103, 104, 105, 106
SS Saguache 140
SS Samson 99, 102, 105
SS Sir James Clark Ross 103, 105
SS Sirius 24, 25, 27, 28
SS Sverdlov 151, 152
St. Pierre et Miquelon 116
Stakhanov, Alexey Grigorievich 149, 153
Stalin, Joseph 142, 144, 153, 173
Stephan, Enno 191-192, 199-201
Stuart, Francis 200, 202
Swanson, Tom 117-118, 120
Sydney, Australia 14-15, 67
Tahiti 16-17, 105, 126-127, 216, 232
Tew, Capt. Thomas 226
The Warrior 96
Thompson Machine Gun 92, 96, 121

Thompson, Capt. William 216, 219-224, 227
Thompson, Captain (pseudonym of Charles McGuinness) 80-81, 83-84, 93, 117, 220, 227
Traven, B. (aka Ret Marut et. al.) 112, 214, 217-218
Tributh, Herbert 189, 197
Trotsky, Leon ('Bronstein') 42, 167, 169, 173, 178-179
Twaddell, Billy MP 68
Uhland, Werner 189
Upnor 92, 96
Valencia, Spain 156, 168, 177, 179
Vancouver 41
Vasco Da Gama 84
Venice, Italy 13, 22
Villa, Pancho 96
Vixen 13
Vize, Joe 94-95, 235
Voltaire 117-118, 121-123
Waddel, Walter 'Bimbo' 117
Walker, James 'Johnnie' 109, 159
Waterford 84, 87-90, 95, 183, 211-212
Weber-Drohl, Ernst ('Atlas') 189, 197, 199
Welch (Welsh), Mary 224
Wexford 56, 88, 94, 190, 204-205, 209-210, 213, 217, 235
Whelan, Joseph 208-210, 212-214
Wilson, Sir Henry (assassination of) 71
Winchell, Walter 115
Wyse, Joe 87, 94-95
Young, Mary 209-212, 217

The Authors:

Joseph Mulheron: Born 1947 in Belfast. Singer, Songwriter, Publican and founder of the 'Men Of No Property'. This is his first book publication.

John McGuffin: Born 1942 in Belfast. Civil Rights Activist, Lecturer, Lumberjack, Criminal Defence Attorney, Writer and Anarchist. Sadly John did not live to see this book in print. He died two weeks after its completion in Derry in April 2002.

Other Books by John McGuffin:

Internment, Anvil Books, Tralee 1973

The Guineapigs, Penguin, London 1974

In Praise of Poitín, Appletree Press, Belfast 1978, 1988, 1999

Tales from the Barricades, McNally&Loftin, Santa Barbara 1990

Der Hund, Edition Nautilus, Hamburg 1990

Der Mann, der mit Chuck Berry getanzt hat, Edition Nautilus, Hamburg 1992

Der Fette Bastard, Edition Nautilus, Hamburg 1996

Last Orders, Please!, Irish Resistance Books, Derry 2000

Irish Resistance Books

Irish Resistance Books will publish the books that the straight publishers won't. We intend to publish books on Irish history, primarily from a Republican and Socialist standpoint. In addition we hope to publish books on local history, prison memoirs, new Irish fiction, subversive texts, rants, the Irish Diaspora, and whatever is progressive and can't find a 'commercial' publisher. Immodestly we see ourselves as one of the very few groups out there who are attempting to write and assemble a true people's history of 'the troubles'. We won't publish any politicians' ghost written memoirs. We will record the working class' history, warts and all, and we will continue to name and shame the enemies of freedom.

We also want to produce and sell CDs of 'alternative' music – songs which have been censored for years, artists who aren't 'acceptable' to the main stream. Additionally, we hope to publish art work, murals, cartoons, video documentaries and posters. We unashamedly nail our colours to the mast.

That shameless old lexicographer Dr. Johnson castigated 'patrons' as 'wretches who support with insolence and are paid with flattery' (that didn't stop the old hypocrite from accepting a healthy pension from mad old King George III for 20 years). We however are not recipients of monarchical, governmental or indeed any largesse and welcome esteemed patrons such as perhaps your good selves. And if you have a book which you think we might be interested in and no one else will publish, contact us.

We take our philosophy from the 'Father of All Historians' the great Herodotus. In the 5th century BC he succinctly laid down the historian's function.

> *'Very few things happen at the right time, and the rest do not happen at all; the conscientious historian will correct these defects.'*

And, it must be said – 'amnesia is the handmaiden of hypocrisy' – which is basically what George Santayana meant when he wrote: 'Progress, far from consisting in change, depends on retentiveness. Those who cannot remember the past are doomed to fulfil it.'

Irish Resistance Books concurs and will attempt to encapsulate these views.